Pluralistic Counselling and Psychotherapy

Mick Cooper and John McLeod

SAGE

Los Angeles | London | New Delhi
Singapore | Washington DC

First published 2011

SAGE Publications Ltd
1 Oliver's Yard
55 City Road
London EC1Y 1SP

SAGE Publications Inc.
2455 Teller Road
Thousand Oaks, California 91320

SAGE Publications India Pvt Ltd
B 1/I 1 Mohan Cooperative Industrial Area
Mathura Road
New Delhi 110 044

SAGE Publications Asia-Pacific Pte Ltd
33 Pekin Street #02-01
Far East Square
Singapore 048763

Library of Congress Control Number: 2010924852

British Library Cataloguing in Publication data

A catalogue record for this book is available from the British Library

ISBN 978-1-84787-344-6
ISBN 978-1-84787-345-3 (pbk)

Typeset by C&M Digitals (P) Ltd, Chennai, India
Printed and bound by CPI Group (UK) Ltd, Croydon, CR0 4YY

MIX
Paper | Supporting responsible forestry
FSC® C013604
FSC
www.fsc.org

For Julia.
—JMcL

For Helen, whose openness, resourcefulness and capacity to love and embrace life so embodies a pluralistic way of being.
—MC

'Mick Cooper and John McLeod have produced a truly groundbreaking book in the field of counselling and psychotherapy which immediately ranks as one of the most significant in terms of influencing my own thinking and practice. The pluralistic approach is likely to resonate with many who have struggled to make sense of multiple approaches and practices which all seem potentially helpful, and the positioning of the collaborative relationship with the client at the centre of the approach fits very well with current thinking in mental health more widely. The book brings together a wealth of relevant theory and research, with illuminating examples. It is a valuable counter to the overly precious 'us and them' type thinking that can be so prevalent in the counselling and psychotherapy world, and gives us new and helpful ways of speaking our experiences of therapy.'
Meg Barker, Open University, co-author of 'Understanding Counselling and Psychotherapy

'Fifteen years of research amongst therapy users has shown me that most of them know and care little what therapy modality they receive. They want a therapy that works, that helps them meet their own goals, and that treats them respectfully and responsively as customers of a service. This book describes an approach which is groundbreaking in meeting these criteria. It is packed with interesting ideas and research, beautifully written and gripping to read.'
Nicky Forsythe, Mental Health Services Researcher

'Mick Cooper and John McLeod offer a book that skilfully distils a mass of literature and research to offer a clear conceptualisation of a pluralistic approach to counselling and psychotherapy.

The book comes at an opportune moment for practitioner training, practice and continuing professional development (CPD), in light of recent developments in the counselling and psychotherapy field, including statutory regulation, the publication of Skills for Health's National Occupational Standards and the development of a core curriculum for BACP-accredited training courses.

Cooper and McLeod facilitate the reader towards a deeper understanding of synthesis and coherence in therapy work and suggest a pluralistic framework that has relevance not only for practice but also for practitioner training where courses may be challenged by the concept of 'integrative' training. The text boxes and self-reflective activities are useful for self-directed CPD, as well as for use by trainers and practitioner educators as learning/teaching resources.

This book will be an invaluable source text for trainees and experienced practitioners seeking support in developing their understanding of and practice in, contemporary counselling and therapy.'
Dr Lynne Gabriel, Reader in Counselling and Relational Ethics and Chair, British Association for Counselling/Psychotherapy

'This book is necessary reading for all psychotherapists and counsellors who draw on a range of theoretical approaches when helping their clients. If you work, or want to work, pluralistically in this age of evidence, read this well-written book.'
Thomas Mackrill, Aarhus University, Denmark

'It is rare to read a new text book from cover to cover but this one is written in such an accessible style, it was easy to do just that. We have introduced this complex but practical reconceptualisation of therapy in all of our programmes. The key concepts of the pluralistic framework – understanding, collaboration, goals, tasks and methods – work well with a culture centred approach, which is vital in Aotearoa New Zealand.'
Jeannie Wright, Associate Professor Counselling, Massey University, Aotearoa New Zealand

Contents

Preface

We live in political times. A few days before drafting this Preface, for instance, we learnt that counselling and person-centred therapy have been dropped from the Scottish 'SIGN' guidelines for the treatment of depression (Scottish Intercollegiate Guidelines Network, 2010). Increasingly, counsellors and psychotherapists are concerned that we are moving towards a therapeutic 'monoculture', in which cognitive-behavioural therapy (CBT) dominates and in which other therapeutic orientations – such as psychodynamic, person-centred and integrative therapies – are marginalised and freely-available only for clients who actively decline CBT (National Institute for Health and Clinical Excellence, 2009), or in the private and voluntary sectors.

Aims

This book is about resisting such a drive towards a 'one size fits all' approach, in which any one practice is seen as being most suitable for all clients. It is about making the most of the vast body of methods and theories that exist in the counselling and psychotherapy world: looking at how we can draw on this near-infinite repository of knowledge to try to ensure that each client gets the therapy that is most suited to them. This book is about acknowledging and celebrating differences across the therapeutic spectrum, seeing the value in what each of us do. Most of all, though, this book is an attempt to draw together therapists from *all* orientations to begin to develop a new paradigm for our field: one that is based on mutual respect across the orientations, a commitment to collaborating with service users, and a desire to understand the many different ways in which clients can be helped.

Given this aim, our hope is that this book will be of interest to any student or practitioner of counselling, psychotherapy, counselling psychology or clinical psychology who is interested in moving beyond the 'schoolism' and 'dogma eat dogma' rivalries (Norcross, 2005: 3) of the psychological therapies world, towards an appreciation of what the many different therapies have to offer. The humanistic and progressive foundations of this book mean that we also think it may be of particular interest to any student or practitioner who is interested in developing – or consolidating – more collaborative, anti-oppressive ways of working with clients. A third group that we think this book might be of particular relevance to is students or practitioners who are interested in, or work in, integrative and eclectic ways. In fact, some integrative and eclectic practitioners may feel that they already think and practise in many of the ways mapped out in this book. However, we believe that this is the first systematic attempt to articulate such a way of working (see Chapter 1), and to map out a framework by which such a therapy can be helped to evolve.

For students or practitioners who want to work in 'pluralistic' ways, we hope that this book can provide a valuable starting point for practice. We map out the basic principles behind such a way of working, and a range of methods that practitioners can draw on (see Chapter 6) to support their work. As part of a basic training programme, however, we would encourage readers to supplement this book with one or more counselling or psychotherapy texts that can provide a more detailed introduction to specific therapeutic methods: for instance, John's *Introduction to Counselling* (McLeod, 2009b), Pete Sanders and colleagues' (2009) *Next Steps in Counselling Practice*, or one of the many excellent introduction to orientation-specific methods, such as Mearns and Thorne's (2007) *Person-centred Counselling in Action* or *An Introduction to Cognitive Behaviour Therapy: Skills and Applications* by Westbrook, Kennerley and Kirk (2007).

However, this book is not just for students or practitioners who want to work in a multi-orientation way. As will become apparent in Chapter 1, it is quite possible to embrace a pluralistic outlook and a range of pluralistic methods while still working within a single orientation. Pluralism, then, is a *sensibility* as well as a specific form of *practice* and, in this respect, we hope that this book will be very much of interest to trainees and practitioners who choose to work in 'specialised' ways, and who wish to locate this practice within an ethos of respect and valuing for clients and for other ways of working.

Beginnings

The origins of this book lie in a train journey that the two of us took together from Edinburgh to Sheffield in 2005. John had recently received funding to set up a counselling research clinic at the University of Abertay at Dundee, and we became increasingly involved in a dialogue about the kind of practice, research and ethos that we would like to see there, and in the counselling field more generally. By the end of our six hour journey to Sheffield and back, we had mapped out many of the key ideas within this book. John, with colleagues in the Scottish Consortium for Psychotherapy and Counselling Research, went on to develop the Tayside Counselling Clinic along pluralistic lines and, with colleagues at the University of Abertay, redesigned his Postgraduate Diploma in Counselling so that it trained students in pluralistic practice. Mick, meanwhile, worked with colleagues at Glasgow Caledonian University to develop the first Scottish Doctorate in counselling psychology, which was also underpinned by a pluralistic philosophical outlook. We first presented our ideas on a pluralistic approach at the BACP research conference in 2006, and published an initial article, 'A pluralistic framework for counselling and psychotherapy: Implications for practice,' in the British Association for Counselling and Psychotherapy (BACP) journal *Counselling and Psychotherapy Research* (Cooper & McLeod, 2007).

Of course, the personal and professional journeys that each of us took to reach this pluralistic worldview stretch back long before 2005. In the following paragraphs, we have both tried to map out some key factors that have led us towards this perspective, hoping that it will throw some further light on the background, rationale and trajectory for this approach.

John: I have a sense of always having existed in multiple worlds. A childhood split between a privileged lifestyle in India and traditional Scottish industrial working-class culture in Dundee. The first member of my family to go to university. Throughout all this, being exposed to a pragmatic belief in getting things done. These are some of the personal influences that I believe lead me in the direction of a 'pluralistic' approach to therapy. In my mid-30s, I trained in a purist form of Rogerian person-centred counselling. At the same time, I had read everything else – Freud, Jung, the behaviourists, all of it. For me, being a person-centred counsellor was both satisfying and frustrating. It was satisfying because I could see that it was effective some of the time, and the approach seemed intellectually coherent. It was frustrating because I felt as though I was excluding a vast range of possibilities, knowledge and resources, in the client and in myself, that might usefully be brought into the therapy room. Later in my career, I became disenchanted with what I regarded as school-based factional point-scoring within the counselling and psychotherapy professional community. As a textbook writer (McLeod, 2009b), I came to see that each school of therapy had its own unique contribution to make, but also that each approach, in itself, gives an incomplete account of what can be helpful for people. Over the past few years, I have found that working in a way which draws on a greater range of practices has had an impact on my work in two ways. First, it has allowed me to have a much clearer understanding with clients about what we are trying to achieve together, which has been energising. Second, it has a lot of meaning for me that I am now better able to see how the therapy that I do can make a contribution to creating a better society, in relation to three crucial values: respecting difference, working together, and treasuring the cultural and natural resources that make our lives possible.

Mick: I was born into a family that had radical, left-wing politics at its core (see Cooper, 2006b), and this has profoundly shaped my journey through the counselling and psychotherapy world. Right from my first days of my training, I was strongly drawn towards those therapeutic orientations, such as person-centred and existential therapy, that emphasised an egalitarian client–therapist relationship: client as 'agentic', intelligent being; and therapist as 'fellow traveller' and non-expert. Perhaps because of my radical background, however, I was also sensitised to some of the paradoxes and the closed-mindedness that could emerge in these radical worldviews. Just as my egalitarian-minded peers, for instance, could become decidedly 'unegalitarian' when it came to people who did not share their politics, so, it sometimes felt, some of my person-centred colleagues – myself included – could become very 'unperson-centred' (i.e., judgemental and unempathic) when it came to therapists from different therapeutic orientations, in particular CBT. What also became apparent to me, as I developed as a practitioner, was that many clients wanted a more directive and challenging approach than I was offering; such that following the client's wants, paradoxically, sometimes indicated a way of working that was less classically 'client-centred'. Consequently, over the years, my practice became less rigidly non-directive and more flexible – more attuned to what the client was specifically asking for – and, as it did so, so I found it more rewarding. I think this was mainly because it felt more genuine and real. That is, increasingly as a therapist, I was just me, Mick, using all the skills, strategies and methods I had to help the other person get what they wanted.

Structure

The book begins with an introduction to the pluralistic approach (Chapter 1), looking at how it has emerged as a means of moving beyond schoolism in the counselling and psychotherapy field. Chapter 2 then presents evidence and ideas from the domains of philosophy, psychology, psychotherapy research and policy that support, and help to develop, a pluralistic perspective. This chapter is particularly theory- and research-intensive, and readers may want to skip over it on a first reading of the book, perhaps coming back to it at a later point. Chapter 3 then introduces one of the most fundamental tenets of a pluralistic approach to therapy: a collaborative relationship between therapist and client. Here, we introduce the practices of negotiation and 'metacommunication': talking to clients about the process of therapy, what they want from it, and how they might get it.

The next three chapters are, in many respects, the heart of a pluralistic approach: 'goals', 'tasks' and 'methods.' Chapter 4 explains why clients' goals are the orientating point for pluralistic therapy and how clients can be helped to identify their goals; Chapter 5 looks at the different tasks that can be undertaken to achieve these goals; and Chapter 6 focuses on the specific, concrete methods through which these tasks can be fulfilled. In contrast to the rest of the book, these three chapters are particularly relevant to practitioners who want to work in a pluralistic, multi-orientation way. However, we hope that single-orientation, specialist therapists will also find practices and ideas here that they can draw into their own work.

In Chapter 7, we discuss the implications of the pluralistic approach and the pluralistic framework for counselling and psychotherapy research. We argue that it can help therapists to draw much more fully from the full range of empirical evidence, and we give examples of what pluralistically-informed research might look like. Chapter 8 then looks at the implications of a pluralistic approach for supervision, training, continuing professional development and service delivery. Finally, in Chapter 9, we summarise the book, answer some Frequently Asked Questions, and look at key challenges for the future.

To download the measures and protocols presented in our appendices, as well as other resources, please go to www.pluralistictherapy.com

Terminology

A few words about the language in this book.

First, we have tended to use the terms 'therapy' or 'counselling and psychotherapy' to cover all forms of psychological intervention, including those delivered by counsellors, psychotherapists, counselling psychologists and clinical psychologists. In fact, we do both have quite strong views on the debates around definitions of counselling and psychotherapy (see, for instance, Cooper, 2009; McLeod, 2009a), feeling that counselling and/or counselling psychology could, quite legitimately, be viewed as discrete professional activities, orientated around the facilitation of psychological well-being and client empowerment – much like the pluralistic approach outlined here. This is the subject, however, of a different text, and given the considerable degree of overlap among these practices, it seems sensible, for now, to stick to a unified term.

Second, we appreciate that some of the terms in this book, particularly 'goals', 'tasks' and 'methods', may appear somewhat technical, and may give the impression that we are advocating a highly structured, mechanistic and target-focused approach to therapy. In particular, the concept of 'goals' may suggest that we are primarily interested in specific achievements and outcomes, rather than the process by which people move towards their desired ends. It is important to emphasise, therefore, that we are using these terms in a relatively loose sense: to simply refer to the kinds of things that people want (goals), the paths that they can take to get there (tasks), and the specific things they can do to make this happen (methods). Furthermore, as we will discuss in Chapter 1, it is assumed that there is a great deal of overlap across these three domains, such that we would not want readers to get too caught up in trying to work out whether something is a 'goal', 'task' or 'method'. Rather, the key point we want to emphasise here is that therapy should start with what clients want and work back to how this can be achieved; and if readers find any of these terms unhelpful, or have better ways of conceptualising these components of therapy, then this should not, in any way, interfere with working or thinking pluralistically.

Third, although we sometimes write about 'the' pluralistic approach in this book, it is important to acknowledge that there may be a diversity of pluralistic approaches to therapy (see Samuels, 1993, 1997 for a particularly interesting alternative reading) and we are, by no means, the first psychological therapists to use this term (e.g., Hollanders, 2003; House & Totton, 1997; Lazarus, 1981; Norcross, 2005). Indeed, for some time, we did consider referring to our approach as '*collaborative* pluralism', but came to the conclusion that collaboration was so intrinsic to pluralism that it was not necessary to include this qualifier. Nevertheless, it is important to recognise that this framework merely represents *one* of the ways in which pluralism can inform counselling and psychotherapy practice. An inevitable implication of the concept of pluralism is that there will always be a plurality of pluralistic therapies. One of the aims of this book is to invite other colleagues within the field of counselling and psychotherapy to share their own ideas and insights about working in a pluralistic fashion.

Finally, for reasons of confidentiality, all of the details of clients presented in this book have been substantially altered, and in many instances we have amalgamated narratives or details from a range of clients to ensure that no one can be personally identified.

Acknowledgements

In developing the pluralistic approach to counselling and psychotherapy, we are enormously grateful to colleagues at the Universities of Abertay, Strathclyde, Aberdeen and Glasgow Caledonian University, who have helped us to develop, refine and articulate this framework: Joe Armstrong, Lorna Carrick, Robert Elliott, Ewan Gillon, Julia McLeod, Alison Shoemark, Mhairi Thurston and Dot Weaks. We are also very grateful to the therapists at the Tayside Centre for Counselling, who have worked with John to translate pluralistic theory into practice: Fiona Arnott, Bud Baxter, Elaine Craig, Alice Curteis, Kate Kaiser, Roddy Mackenzie, Lynsey McMillan and Kate Smith.

Thanks to Maria Bowens, David Johnston, Annette Lee, Angela McBeath and Krista Rajkarnikar, trainees on the Doctorate in Counselling Psychology at the University of Strathclyde and Glasgow Caledonian University, whose research has made a very valuable contribution to this book.

We are extremely grateful to the following individuals, who provided feedback on earlier drafts of the manuscript: Meg Barker, Art Bohart, Maria Bowen, Anne Chien, Sue Cooper, Helen Cruthers, Alison Cumming, Nicky Forsythe, Lynne Gabriel, Moira Ledingham, Noreen Lillie, Thomas Mackrill, Tasim Martin, Katherine McArthur, Sue McKenna, Carol Morgan, Andrew Reeves, Brian Rodgers, Alison Rouse and Paul Wilkins.

As always, we would like to express our appreciation for colleagues at Sage Publications for their support, guidance and encouragement throughout the writing of this book: Alice Oven, Susannah Trefgarne, Lucy Do, Imogen Roome and the many other people 'behind the scenes' who have made this book possible.

Finally, we would like to say a very big 'thank you' to all our clients over the years, without whom this work would not have been possible.

1 Introducing the Pluralistic Approach

This chapter discusses:

- The rationale for the development of a pluralistic approach to counselling and psychotherapy.
- The development of 'schoolism' in the counselling and psychotherapy field and its limitations.
- The development of integrative and eclectic approaches.
- The basic assumptions and framework underpinning the pluralistic approach.

From Schools to Schoolism

Since the first days of psychoanalysis, the psychotherapy and counselling world has been characterised by the emergence of divergent schools of thought and practice. 'Over the years', write Duncan, Miller, and Sparks (2004: 31), 'new schools of therapy arrived with the regularity of the Book-of-the-Month Club's main selection.' Today, it is estimated that there are more than 400 different types of therapy (Norcross, 2005), offering a vast array of practices, techniques, and understandings of mental distress.

Within the United Kingdom, most practitioners adhere to one or other of these schools, and single orientation approaches remain the predominant way of practising, commissioning and thinking about the therapeutic field. In the British Association for Counselling and Psychotherapy (BACP), for instance, less than 25% of therapists are trained in an integrative approach (Couchman, 2006, personal communication), and the UK Council for Psychotherapy (UKCP) has recently restructured along orientation-specific lines. An orientation-based conceptualisation of counselling and psychotherapy is also evident in recent moves – both within the UK and internationally – towards 'evidence-based practices', in which highly specific, manualised forms of therapeutic intervention are recommended for specific psychological 'disorders' (e.g., Department of Health, 2001). As a consequence of this, trainings for such initiatives as the Improving Access to Psychological Therapies programme in the UK are almost entirely orientation-based, with trainees schooled in very specific manualised treatments for specific psychological problems.

Exercise 1.1: Therapeutic attitudes

For each of the following therapies, write down a number from 1 to 7 in the box after it indicating how much you like or dislike it. Try to respond with your immediate gut feeling and try and to be as honest as you can – don't think too much about it. If you haven't heard of the orientation, just leave the box blank. Scoring is as follows:

1 = Strongly dislike, 2 = Moderately dislike, 3 = Slightly dislike, 4 = Neither like or dislike, 5 = Slightly like, 6 = Moderately like, 7 = Strongly like

Psychodynamic therapy ☐
Person-centred therapy ☐
Cognitive-behavioural therapy ☐
Gestalt therapy ☐
Integrative therapy ☐
Hypnotherapy ☐
Arts therapy ☐
Classical/Freudian psychoanalysis ☐
Pharmacological/drug therapies ☐

Please write down any other therapies that you have a gut feeling of like towards:

____
____
____
____
____

Please write down any other therapies that you have a gut feeling of dislike towards:

____
____
____
____
____

If there are any therapies that you have given a score of 3 or less to, or stated that you dislike, spend some time (maybe 10 minutes) thinking why you have come to feel that way towards them. Is it something to do, for instance, with your personal experiences of that therapy, the practitioners of that therapy you have met, or what you have come to associate that therapy with?

Now take some time (maybe 10 minutes) thinking about why you like the therapies that you do.

Finally, ask yourself the following questions (maybe 10 minutes):

- Can you think of ways in which the therapies that you *dislike* may be *helpful* to some people?
- Can you think of ways in which the therapies that you *like* may be *unhelpful* to some people?

Without doubt, the emergence of specific schools within the psychotherapy and counselling field has done much to foster growth and creativity within the field (see Samuels, 1997). We are now in a position where clients have a vast diversity of practices to choose from, and where forms of therapy are constantly developed and refined to be of as much benefit as possible to clients. And yet, there is also the danger that the existence of schools can tip over into an unproductive 'schoolism': 'characterized by binary thinking (i.e. "This", against "That"),' where, 'those immersed in schoolistic attitudes are likely to defend passionately the "truth" of their own school and attack with vigour the "error" of rival schools' (Hollanders, 2003: 277–278). In other words, rather than practitioners of different orientations respecting and valuing the others' work – as a heart surgeon might do to a paediatrician – a tribalism emerges that is more akin to rivalries between supporters of different football teams.

Such schoolism can be highly destructive, and this is for a number of reasons. First, such a 'battle of the brands' (Duncan et al., 2004: 31) makes it difficult for adherents of any one orientation to learn from, and develop their practice in response to, adherents of other orientations. Second, schoolism can degrade further into an 'ideological cold war', with 'Mutual antipathy and exchange of puerile insults between adherents of rival orientations' (Norcross, 2005: 3). This can then create a professional environment that is experienced as hostile, unsafe and unproductive by all. Third, and perhaps most importantly, schoolism can lead practitioners to be 'blind to alternative conceptualizations and potentially superior interventions' (Norcross, 2005: 3), such that they can end up imposing upon clients less helpful – or actively unhelpful – practices. Ultimately, then, it is clients who are most likely to lose out as a result of schoolism – people who, as the research shows, do not tend to be particularly interested in the therapist's 'brand' (Binder, Holgersen & Nielsen, 2009). As the philosopher William James writes (1996: 219), 'It is but an old story, of a useful practice first becoming a method, then a habit, and finally a tyranny that defeats the end it was used for.'

Box 1.1: Pathways to schoolism

Why is it that schools of therapy can, so easily, deteriorate into schoolisms? Interestingly, perhaps, many of the theories developed in these schools, themselves, can help us to understand this transition. For instance, in person-centred theory (Rogers, 1951, 1959), it is hypothesised that people tend to form, and then defend, fixed concepts of self (e.g., 'I am a person-centred therapist'), out of a desire to maintain self-consistency, and out of a fear of how they might be judged by themselves and those around them if they relinquished that identity. Similarly, at the core of CBT is the belief that people tend towards absolutist, black-or-white thinking (Beck, John, Shaw & Emery, 1979), in which all experiences are placed in one of two opposite categories – e.g., 'This therapy is effective', 'That therapy is ineffective' – rather than

(Continued)

acknowledging 'the complexity, variability and diversity of human experiences and behavior' (Beck et al., 1979: 15). This emphasis on the tendency to split between 'good' and 'bad' 'objects' is also evident in the psychodynamic theory of Klein (Cooper, 1996). Another way of thinking about the emergence of schoolism comes from an existential perspective, which holds that one of our most fundamental needs is to feel that our lives are of meaning (Frankl, 1986). From this stance, it might be argued that we need to feel that our approach is 'better' than others to give ourselves a sense of significance and purpose in the work that we do. To face the possibility that other therapists' work may actually be more valuable and helpful might be decidedly anxiety-evoking.

Social psychological theories can also be very valuable in helping us understand this shift from schools to schoolism. 'Social identity theory', for instance, highlights the way that we instinctively tend to favour our in-group because, by feeling positive about a group we are part of, we feel better about ourselves (Tajfel & Turner, 1979). Research around 'cognitive dissonance' (e.g., Festinger, 1957) has also highlighted the fact that, once we make a choice (for instance, to train in a particular orientation), we then tend to feel more positive towards that standpoint, as a means of justifying to ourselves why we made that choice in the first place.

What may also fuel schoolism is a desire – perhaps a basic human one – to have simple, neat, definitive answers to complex questions. In other words, it may be much more satisfying and reassuring for people to believe that the answer to the question: 'What is of help to people?' is 'X' rather than 'X and Y and a bit of Z… though for some people it is U and P and possibly Z… but we are not sure…' As William James (1996: 45) states, this latter, pluralistic worldview – the belief in a 'messy universe' – is by no means appealing: 'It is a turbid, muddled, gothic sort of affair, without a sweeping outline and with little pictorial nobility.'

In discussing this tendency towards schoolism, it is probably important to emphasise also that we are not just talking about cognitive processes here, but about deeply affective and emotional ones. 'When your faith is disturbed your being is rattled,' writes Connolly (2005: 93). 'You react bodily through the roiling [churning] of your gut, the hunching of your shoulders, the pursing of your lips, and the tightening of your skin.'

At the heart of many of these issues, however, may be the fact that the field of psychotherapy and counselling is, in essence, still in a 'pre-paradigmatic' state (Kuhn, 1970; Norcross, 2005). The philosopher Thomas Kuhn uses this term to refer to a period in the development of a scientific discipline in which a shared understanding has yet to be reached, and is characterised by 'competing schools of thought' that 'possess differing procedures, theories, even metaphysical presuppositions' (Bird, 2009). Here, in the absence of any agreed-upon evidence, dogmas are likely to flourish. Moreover, without such certainty, psychotherapists and counsellors may be more likely to experience anxiety and defensiveness in the face of alternative viewpoints and practices.

Integrative and Eclectic Approaches

Since the 1930s, psychotherapists and counsellors have attempted to overcome the problems associated with single orientation therapies by developing more integrative and eclectic approaches (Goldfried, Pachanakis, & Bell, 2005). Growth in this field has been particularly marked from the 1970s onwards (Nuttall, 2008), such that it can now be claimed that an integrative or eclectic stance is currently the most common theoretical orientation of English-speaking psychotherapists (Norcross, 2005), with around 25–50% of American clinicians identifying in this way (Norcross, 2005; Orlinsky & Rønnestad, 2005d). Furthermore, research indicates that many practitioners identified with specific orientations, in reality, tend to integrate into their practice methods from other orientations (see Box 6.1 on page 99). For instance, psychodynamic therapists, on average, have been found to strongly endorse the CBT practice of challenging maladaptive beliefs, while cognitive-behavioural therapists have been found to prioritise the person-centred stance of empathy (Thoma & Cecero, 2009).

Recommended reading

McLeod, J. (2009). *An Introduction to Counselling* (4th edn). Maidenhead: Open University Press (Chapter 13). An overview of current ideas about therapy integration.

Norcross, J. C., & Goldfried, M. R. (Eds.). (2005). *Handbook of Psychotherapy Integration.* New York: Oxford University Press. An invaluable, US-based compendium of chapters on all aspects of integrative and eclectic practice.

It is possible to distinguish between four contrasting modes of therapy integration. First, there is 'theoretical integration', in which aspects of two or more approaches are synthesised together into a new therapy, such as cognitive analytic therapy (Ryle, 1990). Second, there is 'assimilative integration', in which therapists gradually introduce new techniques and ideas into their pre-existing approach, over the course of their career (Messer, 1992). Third, there are common factors approaches, which involve attempts to identify active ingredients across a range of therapies (see, for instance, Hubble, Duncan, & Miller, 1999). Finally, there is technical eclecticism, such as Lazarus's multimodal therapy, in which the therapist makes an initial assessment of the client, and then draws on an extensive range of methods from a variety of orientations (see, for instance, Palmer, 2000) to address the client's problems.

In contrast to a schoolist perspective, integrative and eclectic therapists tend to hold that no one school has all the answers (Lazarus, 2005; Pinsof, 2005), and that different methods may be of help to different clients. Arnold Lazarus, for instance, founder of multimodal therapy, writes that the multimodal therapist asks '*Who or what is best for this particular individual?*', and he describes his approach as both 'personalistic' and 'individualistic', flexibly tailoring the therapeutic method and style of relating to the individual client. However, as Downing (2004) points out, there can be a tendency for many of these attempts to transcend singular models of theory and practice to end up replicating something quite similar, albeit with elements synthesised from a variety of sources. Ryle's (1990) cognitive analytic therapy, for instance, outlines a very specific model of personality functioning, while Egan's (1994) problem management approach advocates a highly specified set of procedures for helping clients overcome their difficulties. Even multimodal therapy (Lazarus, 1981, 2005) locates itself within a specific theoretical framework, and has a highly specified form of assessment. Lazarus (2005: 107, italics added) writes, for instance, that 'the multimodal therapist *does not embrace divergent theories* but remains consistently within social-cognitive learning theory'. And he goes on to state that, 'The polar opposite of the multimodal approach is the Rogerian or Person-Centered orientation, which is entirely conversational'. While integrative and eclectic approaches, then, tend to be less tied down to specific methods and specific theories than their single orientation predecessors, there can still be a tendency to promote certain practices and understandings above others.

Pluralistic therapy is an integrative approach that seeks to build on the ideas of existing models of therapy integration (see McLeod, 2009b), while avoiding their tendency to end up with the privileging yet another single orientation school of practice. The pluralistic approach accomplishes this intention through the use of two key strategies. First, it is organised around a philosophical construct (pluralism) rather than psychological constructs, and so is not identified with any particular psychological model. Second, it commits the practitioner to sustained engagement with the client's view of what will be helpful for them. This commitment inevitably requires the therapist to accommodate ideas and practices that are outside their existing assumptions about therapeutic concepts and methods.

Introduction to a Pluralistic Approach

The aim of the present book is to develop a way of practising, researching and thinking about therapy which can embrace, as fully as possible, the whole range of therapeutic methods and concepts. This is an approach which starts from the assumption that different things are likely to help different people at different points in time, such that it is meaningless to argue over which is the 'best' way of practising therapy, *per se*. It can be summed up as a 'both/and' standpoint (Gergen, 2000) – that CBT can be helpful, *and* person-centred therapy can be helpful, *and* psychodynamic therapy can be helpful… – in contrast to an 'either/or' one (Castonguay & Beutler, 2006b). As a corollary of this, the approach introduced in this book also starts from the assumption that it is not just therapists who should decide on the focus and course of therapy. Rather, therapists should work closely with their clients to decide on how the work should proceed. The two basic principles underlying this approach, therefore, can be summarised as follows:

1. Lots of different things can be helpful to clients (see Box 1.2 on page 7).
2. If we want to know what is most likely to help clients, we should talk to them about it.

Box 1.2: Ashok: Many ways to health

Below are some of the things that Ashok, a young man experiencing depression and isolation, described as helpful in his 40 weeks of therapy:

- Just talking.
- Focusing on practical solutions to problems.
- Looking at each relationship with a man in the past and seeing what attracted me to him.
- Realising that I am loved.
- Deciding to look forward and turn a corner.
- Reading a letter from my father and getting the therapist's take on it.
- Just being allowed to go off tangent.

As can be seen here, for Ashok, as for many clients (see Chapter 2), there are many different things that were helpful, and these cannot be reduced down to one, orientation-specific 'super-factor.' Rather, both within one individual client, and across clients, there would seem to be 'many ways to health' (Lambert, Bergin, & Garfield, 2004: 809).

We have come to describe this approach to therapy as 'pluralistic', as the term seems to describe, very fittingly, these two core principles. 'Pluralism' is a word used in a variety of fields (see Chapter 2), and refers to the belief that 'any substantial question admits of a variety of plausible but mutually conflicting responses' (Rescher, 1993: 79). It is a viewpoint that has becoming increasingly prevalent in the field of philosophy (see, for instance, Berlin, 1958; Connolly, 2005), and which has had a major role in debates within political science and sociology as well as in psychology and psychotherapy (see Chapter 2). Pluralism can be contrasted with 'monism', the belief that every question has a single and definitive answer. In other words, a pluralist holds that there can be many 'right' answers to scientific, moral or psychological questions which are not reducible down to any one, single truth. Central to this standpoint is also the belief that there is no one, privileged perspective from which the 'truth' can be known. That is, neither scientists, philosophers, psychotherapists nor any other kinds of people can claim to have a better vantage point on reality. Each of us has our own quite special and unique understanding of what is there.

In developing this pluralistic approach to psychotherapy and counselling, we have come to find it useful to distinguish between pluralism as a *perspective* on psychotherapy and counselling and pluralism as a particular form of therapeutic *practice* (see Figure 1.1 on page 8).

A pluralistic 'perspective', 'viewpoint', or 'sensibility' refers simply to the *belief* that there is no, one best set of therapeutic methods. It can be defined as *the assumption that different clients are likely to benefit from different therapeutic methods at different points in time, and that therapists should work collaboratively with clients*

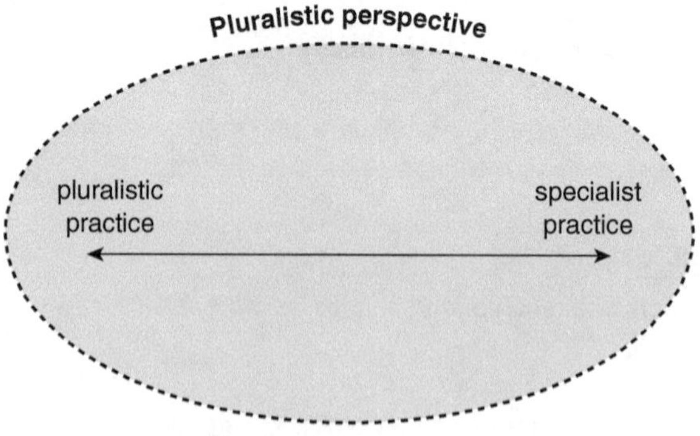

Figure 1.1: Pluralism as a perspective on therapy and as a particular practice

to help them identify what they want from therapy and how they might achieve it. This is a general definition, which does not make any specific recommendations about *how* a therapist might go about implementing a pluralistic perspective in their own practice.

By contrast, 'pluralistic practice' or 'pluralistic therapy' refers to a specific form of therapeutic *practice* which draws on methods from a range of orientation, and which is characterised by dialogue and negotiation over the goals, tasks and methods of therapy. Making this distinction is important because, although pluralistic practice is rooted in a pluralistic viewpoint, it is also quite possible for therapists to hold a pluralistic viewpoint while working in a non-pluralistic, single orientation way (see Box 1.3 below). It is also quite possible for single orientation therapists to draw on a range of pluralistic practices while remaining within a single therapeutic orientation. For example, '*working collaboratively with clients to help them identify what they want from therapy and how they might achieve it*' describes an approach to practice that is consistent with any therapeutic orientation, whether person-centred, psychodynamic or CBT. In addition, most well-established therapy orientations encompass a diversity of ideas and methods, which provide scope for therapist responsiveness and flexibility.

Box 1.3: Single orientation practices within a pluralistic framework: 'Schoolism' versus 'specialism'

While a pluralistic standpoint fundamentally challenges the assumption that any one form of therapy is superior ('schoolism'), it does not, in any way, question the value of single orientation therapeutic practices (which we describe here as 'specialisms'). From a pluralistic standpoint, different clients will want and need different things, such that specialists in approaches such as CBT, classical person-centred therapy or psychoanalysis are all essential resources within the therapeutic community. Moreover, the existence and development of specialisms in the counselling and psychotherapy fields ensures that the rich heritage and diversity of psychotherapeutic theory and practice is maintained and that a healthy flow of innovative new therapies continues to emerge. Ultimately, then, a pluralistic approach can be strengthened and enhanced through the development of specialised theories and practices.

Undoubtedly, there is considerable overlap between the pluralistic approach introduced here and much integrative and eclectic thought, practice and vision – particularly technical eclecticism (e.g., Lazarus, 2005). Indeed, when eclectic therapists are asked to define and explain their approach, the most common answer is in relation to fitting their practice to the individual client (Thoma & Cecero, 2009). In this respect, as John (McLeod, 2009b: 382) has written, 'collaborative pluralism can be regarded as an adaptation and elaboration of central themes found in other strategies for therapy integration'. Even within single orientation specialists, as we have seen above, there is a considerable degree of overlap in the actual methods used, with many (if not most) striving to flexibly tailor their practice to the individual client's needs (Thoma & Cecero, 2009). However, there are several elements of the pluralistic approach that, we think, give it a distinctive flavour, and distinguish it from much integrative and eclectic writing – if not practice. A lot of this flows from the fact that, in contrast to most (if not all) integrative and eclectic therapies, the present pluralistic approach is rooted in a particular set of humanistic, progressive values (see Chapter 2). These differences can be summarised as follows:

- The pluralistic approach is not just a form of therapeutic *practice* but, as indicated above, is also a particular outlook on, or sensibility towards, therapy as a whole (which means that non-integrative or non-eclectic specialisms can also be embraced within this perspective).
- A pluralistic perspective, and pluralistic practice, is not just confined to one particular combination of methods or theories (as many integrative and even eclectic therapies are) but has the potential to embrace an *infinite* variety of theories, practices and change mechanisms – including those in such domains as politics, physiology and economics.
- In contrast to many 'standardised' integrative therapies, the pluralistic approach puts particular emphasis on tailoring each episode of therapy to the individual client.
- In contrast to some integrative and eclectic therapies, the pluralistic approach puts particular emphasis on the formation and maintenance of a collaborative therapeutic alliance, emphasising dialogue around the goals, tasks and methods of therapy.
- In contrast to common factors approaches, the pluralistic approach does not hold that any one set of factors – whether the quality of the therapeutic alliance or instilling hope – are the key determinants of therapeutic change for *all* clients.
- In contrast to most eclectic and integrative therapies, the pluralistic approach puts particular emphasis on the client as an active agent of change.
- The pluralistic approach introduces a particular framework for thinking about, researching and practising therapy, introduced on the next page.

A Pluralistic Framework

If a pluralistic approach strives to embrace an infinite diversity of therapies, how does it avoid an anything goes 'syncretism': the haphazard, uncritical and unsystematic combination of theories and practices (Hollanders, 2003)? Clearly, there needs to be some kind of structure, some focal point for thinking about therapy and what might be effective. Coming from a pluralistic philosophical standpoint with its commitment to prioritising the perspective of the client (Cooper, 2007; Duncan, et al., 2004), what we will suggest in this book is that the focal point for therapy should be, ultimately, what the client *wants* from it (see Chapter 4). That is, not the client's diagnosis, their assessment, or the therapist's personal beliefs about what is effective in therapy, but the clients' own *goals* for the therapeutic process. This then sets the basis for what the client and therapist see as the *tasks* of therapy (i.e., the different foci, or strategy, of the therapeutic work) and, from this, the specific *methods* (i.e., the concrete activities that they will undertake). (Note that we have used the term 'tasks' in a slightly different way from how it is sometimes adopted in the therapeutic literature (see, in particular, Bordin, 1979). We use it to refer to more macro-level therapeutic strategies, while the term 'methods' defines the actual, concrete-level, moment-by-moment activities.)

Box 1.4: Therapy as a journey

A useful way of remembering the key ideas of the pluralistic framework, which was suggested to us by qualitative researcher Nicky Forsythe, is the metaphor of therapy as a journey that the client and therapist undertake together. From this perspective:

- the goal is the destination – where you're trying to get to;
- tasks are like routes – the roads you take to change – motorway or B road, winding or straight, scenic or boring, stages in the journey, etc.;
- methods are the vehicles that you use to travel on a particular route – bus, plane, walking, swimming, flying.

Taken together, all this constitutes a route map or road map to change that needs to be continually reviewed and renegotiated by client and therapist, in the light of climate conditions, energy levels, and other factors.

These overlapping domains of goals, tasks and methods (and sub-domains of life goals/therapy goals (see Chapter 4), and client activity/therapist activity (see Chapter 6)) can be mapped out as a basic framework for therapy (see Figure 1.2). What this

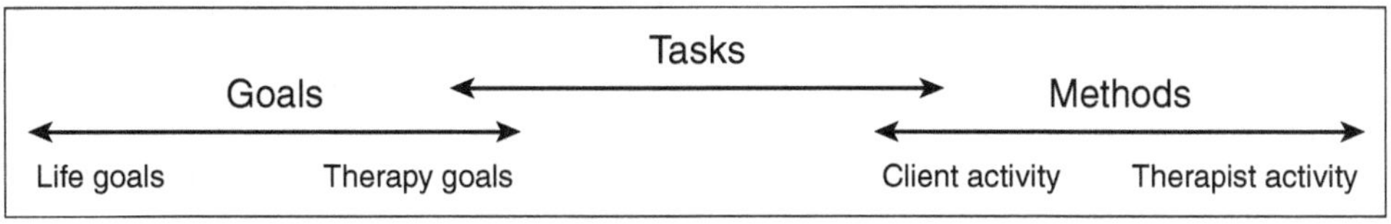

Figure 1.2: A pluralistic framework for conceptualising the therapeutic process

framework offers is a basis for collaborative dialogue around what will happen in therapy. Each key concept within the framework (goals, tasks, methods) provides a topic for discussion, reflection and collaborative choice-making by both client an therapist. For instance, Dave came to therapy with an overall desire to be happier in his life and less anxious ('life goal'). More specifically, he wanted to look at ways in which he could have better relationships with other people ('therapy goal'). In discussing this with his therapist, it became apparent that one thing that he might helpfully do is to look at ways of changing his behaviour ('task') so that he might make himself more available for close friendships. To achieve this, Dave and his therapist talked about the ways that Dave behaved in social situations and what he might do differently ('method'). Dave reflected on how he might come across to others ('client activity'), and his therapist gave him feedback on how he perceived him ('therapist activity').

For us, the value of this pluralistic framework lies in the fact that, while it provides some structure for thinking about, researching and practising therapy, it does not, in any way, circumscribe the particular goals, methods and tasks that may be conceptualised or endorsed, nor the relationships between them. So, for instance, the framework allows for the possibility that the same client may have a range of goals, or that different clients may have very different goals, or that the same goal may be reached in very different ways by different clients, or even by the same client. While Dave, for instance, might achieve his therapeutic goal of getting on better with people by focusing on changing his behaviour (a task associated with CBT), it might also be that he could achieve this goal by trying to make sense of his early relationships with his parents (a task associated with psychodynamic therapy, see Figure 1.3 on page 12). And while these might be the most helpful tasks for Dave to pursue, it might be that a different client finds it much more useful to focus on their here-and-now feelings of anxiety with their therapist (a more humanistically-orientated task). In this respect, then, the pluralistic framework provides a 'space' in which methods and theories from the whole pantheon of therapeutic orientations can be brought together and articulated. Like an 'open source' repository of information (cf. Lopez & Kerr, 2006) – for instance, Wikipedia or the operating software Linux – it does not try to define content (i.e., how people should practise), but a set of structures by which an infinite variety of pathways can be articulated.

In Chapters 4, 5 and 6, we will look much more specifically at these three domains of goals, tasks and methods, and how therapists can use them in practice. Chapter 7 then looks at how research might be used to populate this framework.

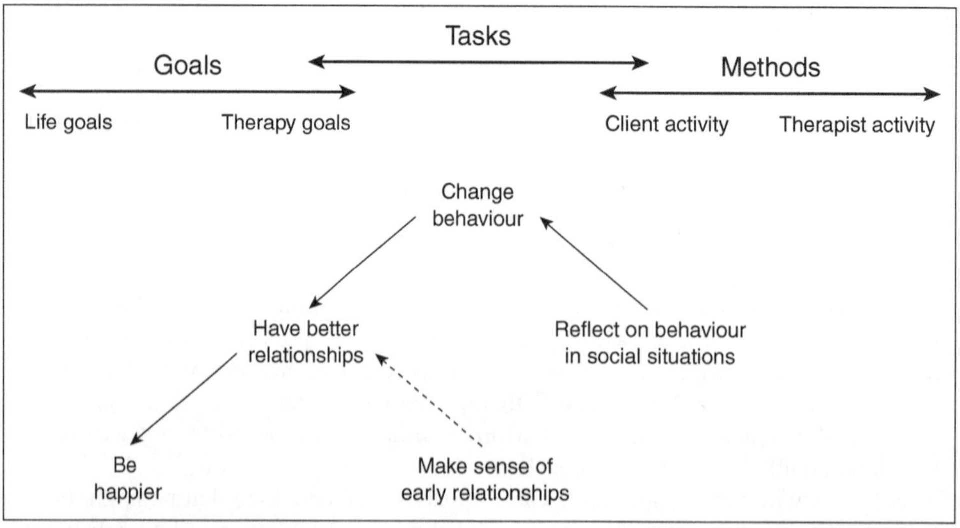

Figure 1.3: Dave's goals, tasks and methods

Box 1.5: Key terms

Pluralism: The standpoint that any substantial question admits a variety of plausible but mutually conflicting responses (Rescher, 1993).

Pluralistic perspective: The belief that different clients are likely to benefit from different things at different points in time, and that therapists should work closely with clients to help them identify what they want from therapy and how they might get it.

Pluralistic practice: A form of therapy, based on a pluralistic perspective, which draws on methods from a multiplicity of therapeutic orientations, and is characterised by dialogue and negotiation over the goals, tasks and methods of therapy.

Pluralistic framework: A conceptual structure for thinking about the therapeutic process, consisting of the three overlapping domains of goals, tasks and methods.

Goals: What clients want from life ('life goals') and from therapy ('therapeutic goals').

Tasks: The macro-level strategies by which clients can achieve their goals.

Methods: The specific, micro-level activities that clients ('client activities') and therapists ('therapist activities') can undertake to accomplish tasks and achieve their goals.

Summary

Single orientation schools of therapy have made enormous contributions to the field of psychotherapy and counselling. But there is always a danger that schools can lead to 'schoolisms', generating conflict and closed-mindedness within the field. In an attempt to overcome this, many counsellors and psychotherapists have moved towards integrative and eclectic perspectives. However, in some cases, these also tend to offer relatively limited prescriptions of how effective therapy can be conducted. In an attempt to offer a broader and more inclusive perspective, a 'pluralistic' approach to counselling and psychotherapy is introduced. The essence of this approach is the assumption that different clients may want different things from counselling and psychotherapy at different points in time, and that if we want to know what is best for clients, we should start by asking them. To provide a focal point for thinking about, researching and practising therapy, the pluralistic approach suggests a framework of three overlapping domains: goals, tasks and methods.

Questions for reflection and discussion

1. What is your initial 'gut' response to the pluralistic approach, as introduced in this chapter?
2. What do you consider are:

   (a) The advantages/strengths of a pluralistic approach over a schoolist approach?
   (b) The disadvantages/limitations of a pluralistic approach over a schoolist approach?

3. What would you consider are the principal differences, if any, between the pluralistic perspective outlined in this chapter and previous integrative/eclectic approaches?

2 Foundations for a Pluralistic Approach

This chapter discusses:

- Pluralism, as a *philosophical* concept, and its relationship to the pluralistic approach to therapy developed in this book.
- *Psychological* research and theory supporting a pluralistic perspective.
- *Psychotherapy* research evidence that supports a pluralistic perspective.
- Contemporary health and social policy developments that are closely aligned with a pluralistic approach.

The aim of this chapter is to present research, theory and policy from a range of fields which support the development of a pluralistic approach to therapy. As stated in the Preface, this chapter is more 'academic' than others in this book, and readers who are primarily interested in practical applications of pluralism may choose to skip over this material for now. However, we do encourage you to come back to it at some point: the pluralistic approach we are introducing is much more than a superficial, anything-goes eclecticism and, in this chapter, we hope to show how deep, strong and contemporary the foundations of a pluralistic approach are.

Philosophical Foundations

Unlike many therapies, the pluralistic approach developed in this book is, first and foremost, rooted in a particular philosophical perspective and set of guiding values. Most significantly, this is the pluralistic philosophy that has rapidly evolved over the course of the twentieth century.

Pluralistic philosophy

Pluralism refers to the belief that any significant question can be answered in a variety of legitimate ways (Rescher, 1993). It signals a preference for diversity over uniformity, multiplicity over unicity (McLellan, 1995), and pragmatism over idealism (James, 1996). It is a way of thinking that goes back to pre-Socratic philosophers (McLellan, 1995), who held that the diversity of nature could not be reduced to a single principle ('monism'). It is closely associated with postmodern and poststructuralist thinking (McLellan, 1995), which also challenges the idea that there are any single, definitive truths (e.g., Derrida, 1974), or that we can ever fully capture and articulate the totality of being (James, 1996; Levinas, 1969). For Rescher (1993), all understanding is dependent on experience and it is inevitable that, in a complex and imperfect world, human beings will have a range of experiences. Hence, he argues, the normal human condition is 'dissensus' rather than consensus. Similarly, for postmodern thinkers such as Derrida, the fact that all knowledge rests, ultimately, on language, means that we can never penetrate down to the 'true' essence of how things are. Rather, we will always be caught up within a world of perspectives, narratives and discourses.

Another way of thinking about pluralism is that it is the philosophy of a 'messy universe' (James, 1996). In contrast to a monistic perspective, which holds that everything can be reduced down to a definitive set of fundamental laws, it suggests that the universe is 'littered' with a range of laws, values and possibilities, many of which are irreducible to others. Connolly (2005: 73) writes: 'Our experience of the world is more comparable to the relation we have to our desks in the middle of a project than to the desk after the project has been completed.'

As with the pluralistic approach to therapy developed in this book, however, it is essential to recognise that the pluralistic philosophy discussed here is not, primarily, rooted in epistemology (i.e., theories of knowledge), but in ethics. For pluralist philosophers such as Isaiah Berlin (1958), the monist belief that all experiences, realities and values can be reduced down to a 'single formula' – that there is one 'final solution' – is responsible for some of the greatest inhumanities of man to man. He writes:

> For if one really believes that such a solution is possible, then surely no cost would be too high to obtain it: to make mankind just and happy and creative and harmonious for ever – what could be too high a price to pay for that? ... Since I know the only true path to the ultimate solution of the problems of society, I know which way to drive the human caravan; and since you are ignorant of what I know, you cannot be allowed to have liberty of choice even within the narrowest limits, if the goal is to be reached. You declare that a given policy will make you happier, or freer, or give you room to breathe; but I know that you are mistaken, I know what you need, what all men need; and if there is resistance based on ignorance or malevolence, then it must be broken and hundreds of thousands may have to perish to make millions happy for all time. What choice have we, who have the knowledge, but to be willing to sacrifice them all? (Berlin, 2003: 15)

Along similar lines, Emmanuel Levinas (1969, 2003) argues that the essence of an ethical relationship is to respect the 'otherness' of the Other, and not to try to squeeze them into our pre-existing constructs and beliefs. In the words of the American pragmatic philosopher William James (1996: 3), 'Individuality outruns all classification.' Recognition of this 'impossibility of conciliation to the same' (Levinas, 1969: 294) allows us to be open to the infinite diversity of others, and to honour and prize them in all their uniqueness.

For Berlin (1958), the assertion that different, mutually exclusive truths can exist is particularly emphasised at the level of values ('value pluralism'). By this, he means that different people will see different things as important and meaningful in life (for instance, being happy, living life to the full, making a contribution to society) and that we can neither reduce all these values down to one, universally agreed 'supervalue', nor reach an ultimate solution as to which is the right value to hold. *Nor*, for Berlin, should we be trying to: for him, the essence of a liberal, free-thinking society is its capacity to allow others to choose their goals and values for themselves.

Box 2.1: A multiplicity of values requires a multiplicity of therapies

Berlin's (1958) assertion that a plurality of legitimate values and goals exist has important implications for the provision of psychological therapies. Within a medical context, for instance, it might be quite appropriate for just one main treatment to be available for a specific condition – people's bodies and biological functions can be relatively similar. But if we accept that different people have different values, and that some therapies are more aligned to one set of values than another, then the standardisation of psychological treatments becomes much more problematic. What right do we have, for instance, to impose CBT values (that people should think in rational ways) on a client whose goal is to develop their intuitive, spiritual being? Or, similarly, to impose person-centred values (that people should act according to their inner felt-sense) on a client whose sense of meaning comes from being of service to others? And even if it can be shown, through empirical research, that clients, on average, get better in therapy X than in therapy Y, this cannot be taken as evidence that everyone should then be given therapy X. Indeed, to do so would be a bit like finding that, on average, people feel better after seeing an imam than a priest or a rabbi, and thereby concluding that anyone with any spiritual questions should consult an imam, whatever their religious faith. In this respect, an acceptance of value pluralism points towards the need for a diversity of therapeutic provisions; and it is interesting to note that recent moves in the UK towards the standardisation of mental health treatments – the Improving Access to Psychological Therapies programme, which has primarily focused on the development of CBT interventions – is closely associated with the assertion that there is one 'supervalue': happiness (Layard, 2006).

Recommended reading

Connolly, W. E. (2005). *Pluralism*. Durham, NC: Duke University Press. Contemporary, insightful and passionate exposition of a pluralistic politic, philosophy and theology. For a briefer introduction to the development, and scope, of pluralistic approaches in the social sciences, see McLellan's *Pluralism* (Buckingham: Open University Press, 1995).

Humanistic and existential philosophy

The pluralistic approach developed in this book, then, is rooted in a set of ethics. These can be described as pluralistic but, beneath that desire to acknowledge and celebrate diversity, lies a more fundamental 'humanistic/existential' commitment to 'conceptualizing, and engaging with people in a deeply valuing and respectful way' (Cooper, 2007: 11). This ethic is, perhaps, most eloquently articulated in the concept of the 'I-Thou' attitude, as developed by the existential and humanistic philosopher, Martin Buber (1958). Buber describes this stance as one in which we behold, accept and confirm the Other as a unique, unclassifiable and unanalysable totality: a freely-choosing flux of human experiencing. Buber contrasts this with the 'I-It' attitude, in which the Other is experienced as a thing-like, determined object: an entity that can be systematised, analysed and broken down into universal parts. This is very similar to Levinas's ethic of 'welcoming the Other' (1969: 215), in which the 'Thou' – 'the stranger, the widow, the orphan, to whom I am obligated' – is given precedence over the I. The pluralistic commitment to tailoring the therapeutic relationship and method to the individual client's wants and understandings, then, can be seen as an attempt to actualise this humanistic ethic of deeply valuing and respecting the client's individual way of being. Indeed, both James (1996) and McLellan (1995) suggest that pluralism may essentially be synonymous with humanism.

Here, it is important to note that we are not using the terms 'existential' or 'humanistic' to refer to specific forms of therapeutic practice (as these terms are generally used, see, for instance, Cain & Seeman, 2002; Cooper, 2003), but to a general *ethic* (Cooper, 2007) that has the capacity to underpin a very broad range of interventions. Person-centred, gestalt or existential therapy may be expressions of this ethic but, from this viewpoint, it is quite possible to practise CBT or psychodynamic methods from a humanistic philosophical base. Here, what makes a therapeutic practice humanistic is whether it is developed in collaboration with the client, is tailored to the client's particular wants and understandings, and engages with the client as a unique and unsystematisable being. In this respect, a humanistic intervention such as person-centred therapy has the potential to be quite a-humanistic, if it is utilised with a client irrespective of what that client might actually want or prefer.

Coming from a standpoint that wants to value and respect the role of clients, a key humanistic assumption behind the pluralistic framework is also that therapeutic change is not something that therapists do *to* clients, but something that clients actively work to bring about. This is very consistent with the 'client-directed' approach of Barry Duncan and colleagues (2004), which strives to see the client as the 'star of the therapeutic drama' (2004: 22), rather than as an extra or observer to their own change process. Our approach has also been inspired by Art Bohart and Karen Tallman's (1999) classic text, *How Clients Make Therapy Work*, which holds that the 'Client has a strong, proactive self-healing capacity, however emotionally distressed they are' (Bohart & Tallman, 1999: xii). From this standpoint, the therapist is less akin to a medical expert who heals their patients, and more akin to a home decorating consultant, who helps clients identify what they want and how they might go about getting it. A third approach to therapy which shares this emphasis on service user agency and privileging their perspective is contemporary family therapy which, like the pluralistic approach, is closely associated with a postmodern perspective (see Sundet, in press). Most importantly, however, this client-led standpoint is closely aligned with the views and wants of many health service users (Kaplan, Sheldon, & Ware, 1989). David Crepaz-Keay (2007), for instance, Head of Patient and Public Involvement at the UK Mental Health Foundation, states, 'there needs to be a slight move away from this attitude that we [service users] are passive recipients, eager to receive the wisdom and gifts that you [therapists] all have to offer us in helping us banish this depression that's dogged us for so long.'

Recommended reading

Bohart, A. C., & Tallman, K. (1999). *How Clients Make Therapy Work: The Process of Active Self-Healing.* Washington, DC: American Psychological Association. A brilliant basis for developing and understanding therapeutic practice, starting with the client's own capacity for self-healing and self-direction, and looking at how the therapeutic dialogue can facilitate this process.

Duncan, B. L., Miller, S. D., & Sparks, J. A. (2004). *The Heroic Client: A Revolutionary Way to Improve Effectiveness through Client-directed, Outcome-informed Therapy.* San Fransisco: Jossey-Bass. Wonderfully rhetorical, impassioned call for a client-directed approach to therapy.

For Bohart and Tallman (1999: 209), such a client-directed starting point is actually fairly rare in the counselling and psychotherapy world. They write:

> With very few exceptions ... the client as an active, generative thinker does not exist in current theories of psychotherapy. It is as if, in therapists' eyes, clients have become lobotomized when they enter therapy. A perusal of the indexes of most books on psychotherapy either have no references to client thinking at all or have references only to clients' dysfunctional thinking. Clients are not granted the ability to think the same active, generative way therapists do.

Even in person-centred therapy, with its specific emphasis on the client's self-healing capacity, the emphasis tends to be on the therapist as agent of growth. Rogers' (1957) hypothesis regarding the necessary and sufficient conditions of therapeutic personality change, for instance, focuses primarily on the therapist and what they communicate, requiring only that the client is in contact with the therapist, in a state of incongruence, and *receiving* the therapist's empathic understanding and unconditional positive regard to some degree. Here, no mention is made of a necessity for clients to be motivated to bring about change, wanting therapy, or involved in the therapeutic process.

This understanding of the client as an active agent of change, as well as the humanistic commitment to engage with clients in respectful and valuing ways, leads us to put a collaborative therapeutic alliance at the heart of a pluralistic approach to therapy (see Chapter 3). Like Duncan and colleagues (2004: 22), we have a 'revolutionary desire to overthrow mental health practices that do not promote a partnership with clients in all decisions that affect their wellbeing'. Hence, a pluralistic approach to therapy involves collaboration with clients over all aspects of therapy, including its goals, the tasks that can be undertaken to achieve those goals, and the specific methods that will be used by therapist and client.

Closely related to this concept of the active client and the commitment to deeply respecting service users, the pluralistic approach also draws from existential thinking the idea that people are meaning-seeking, purposeful beings. 'Man first of all,' writes the existential philosopher Jean-Paul Sartre, 'is the being who hurls himself towards a future and who is conscious of imagining himself as being in the future' (1996: 259). What Sartre means by this is that we are not, first and foremost, machine-like 'things' that are caused to act in particular ways by particular forces. Rather, we are future-orientated beings who set for ourselves particular goals and aims, and then find ways of working towards them. From this standpoint, people's actions are also understood as being 'intelligible'. That is, even the most deeply distressed person does things for a reason, and not out of sheer irrationality or pointlessness. This 'teleological' assumption is part of the reason why, as will become apparent in Chapter 4, the pluralistic approach puts the client's goals at the heart of the therapeutic process.

Finally, it should be said that the humanistic philosophy underpinning this approach leads us to adopt a relatively non-diagnostic approach towards clients. This is not to say that we see diagnoses and clinical categories as redundant – from a pluralistic standpoint, they are likely to be helpful for some clients some of the time – but the focal point for the approach is the clients' individual wants from therapy, rather than any generalised assessment or labelling of particular groups of clients.

Multicultural theory

Finally, pluralism in counselling and psychotherapy reflects the increasing degree of cultural diversity in clients and therapists, and the importance of developing therapeutic practice that embraces the multiplicity of beliefs that exist regarding healing and change (Pedersen, 1991). The main approaches to therapy that are most widely used at present, such as CBT, psychodynamic psychotherapy and the person-centred approach, embody assumptions about human nature that reflect Western cultural traditions, but which can be at odds with the worldviews of people from other cultural backgrounds. It seems clear, for example, the Western idea of an 'autonomous, bounded self' represents an individualist stance that may not match the experiences of people from more collectivist cultures (Sampson, 1988). In addition, there exist many indigenous healing practices, such as the use of shamens and other spiritual sources, that are highly meaningful to people from some cultural groups, but which are hard to reconcile with the scientific, rational basis of Western counselling and psychotherapy (Gielen, Fish & Draguns, 2004; Moodley & West, 2005).

As a result, there has been a movement in many counselling and psychotherapy professional associations in recent years to promote the adoption of flexible, culture-centred practices that acknowledge cultural difference. The pluralistic approach is informed by these developments, and has been designed as a way of doing therapy that is maximally sensitive to cultural preferences and the role of constructive dialogue between therapists and clients from different cultural communities. The pluralistic approach to therapy goes beyond merely seeking to develop specific services for clients from Asian, Hispanic,

Muslim or other ethnic or religious groups. Instead, a pluralistic approach acknowledges that different cultural traditions and identities may be represented within any individual person, and that effective culture-informed therapy needs to be able to take account of the multiplicity of cultural 'voices' that may be arise within the therapy process (Pedersen, Crethar & Carlson, 2008).

Psychological Foundations

Are people the product of their genes or their environment? In the 1970s, debates such as these raged. Today, however, few psychologists would argue that any one factor can be held responsible for the totality of human being. Rather, there is a widespread acceptance that human development, functioning and dysfunction is 'multifaceted, multidetermined, and multilayered' (Lazarus, 2005: 112), with a wide range of different factors – including cognitive, genetic, family, social, affective, neurological and volitional – contributing to an individual's psychological processes. Here, not only have psychologists acknowledged a multiplicity of factors, but also the way in which interactions between these factors can play a critical role (Rutter, 1987). For instance, a young girl may be born with a tendency towards extroversion, but the positive response she receives from her social environment for this behaviour may then reinforce this disposition. More broadly, many theorists and researchers now think about human functioning in terms of complex feedback loops between the various different elements of a person's being – 'circular', rather than 'linear', models of causality (Borrell-Carrio, Suchman & Epstein, 2004).

Box 2.2: The plasticity of human functioning

The idea that there exist *multiple* possible ways to achieve the same goal is one of the fundamental principles of a pluralistic approach to counselling and psychotherapy. In this respect, pluralistic therapy is consistent with key ideas in contemporary social and biological sciences. For example, the continuation of the human race requires that people join together in family structures in order to raise children. However, as social anthropologists have shown, there is no single model of family structure that has been adopted within all cultures; by contrast, there can be found a huge array of different living arrangements. In neuroscience, much recent research confirms the plasticity of the brain. In the past, it was believed that brain function was localised – the processing of visual information took place in one area, processing of auditory information in another areas, and so on. However, it has been shown that even if the visual processing system is destroyed (or has never functioned, as in people who are blind), it is possible to establish alternative brain pathways that allow this function to be re-created (Doidge, 2007). The lessons of cultural diversity, neural plasticity, and other examples, such as the resilience of ecological systems, serve as a guiding principle for pluralistic therapists: there are always different means to achieve the same outcome.

Exercise 2.1: Factors that influenced *your* development

Take 10 minutes or so to list all the factors that you think may have influenced your personality and development. For instance: relationship with parents/carers, genes, school environment, relationships with siblings, culture that you were born into, socio-economic environment, choices, birth order, traumatic experiences, physical health.

Spend some time (maybe 10 minutes) reflecting on, or discussing with a partner, whether you think all these factors can be boiled down to a single 'super-factor' and, if so, whether this super-factor is the same for other people. To what extent do your answers to these questions fit with, or challenge, a pluralistic viewpoint?

Such trends towards understanding human being as multidetermined can be seen as part of a wider move within the health field towards 'biopsychosocial' approaches to health and well-being (Engel, 1977). Here, clinicians are invited to consider the full range of biological, psychological and social factors that may lead individuals to experience the problems that they do, and not simply a narrow range of biomedical difficulties.

Along these lines, there are also few psychologists today who would hold that any one theory of personality or development can account for the full spectrum of human being and becoming. Larsen and Buss (2002: 610), for instance, authors of the textbook *Personality Psychology*, write:

> People have many facets, and these facets can be observed and studied from many perspectives. To say that people have evolved psychological mechanisms to solve social problems does not imply that the principles of psychoanalysis are wrong. Similarly, to say that a proportion of the variance in personality traits is due to genetics does not in any way imply that people do not develop or change their personalities in adulthood.

For many psychologists, then, different theories of human functioning and dysfunction can be seen as complementary rather than competing, helping to build up a more complex and multilayered understanding of human psychological distress. Comer (1998), author of the authoritative textbook *Abnormal Psychology*, for instance, gives the example of sexual dysfunctions, which may be caused by a variety of factors: internal conflicts in childhood (psychodynamic), learning incorrect sexual techniques (behavioural) and misconceptions about sex (cognitive). And, again, many of these factors may be understood to interact: for instance, Oedipal fears about intimacy with a woman may lead a young man to avoid sex education classes, which then leads to a lack of knowledge about sexual techniques, which then leads to misconceptions about what a woman may feel about sex, which may then reinforce fears about women.

Another example of a psychological difficulty that has been found to be irreducible to any one cause or understanding is obsessive-compulsive disorder (OCD). Over the last few decades, some cognitive theorists have argued that the core of all obsessional thinking in OCD is an over-inflated sense of responsibility for harm towards oneself or others (for instance, 'If I don't turn the lights off it might start a fire, and it will be all my fault') (Salkovskis, 1999). However, while there is very good evidence to suggest that this may be true in many cases, research also shows that 'the emphasis on inflated responsibility may not describe significant numbers of OCD sufferers' (Markarian, et al., 2010: 81). For instance, people with obsessive counting, ordering and arranging tendencies seem to do it to reduce feelings of discomfort, and not out of a fear of harm or shame. Summarising the research, Markarian and colleagues state that OCD is a 'symptomatically diverse condition' (2010: 79), and that 'several lines of genetic, neuroanatomical, neurochemical, and psychological research point to OCD as a complex neurobehavioral illness that has multiple etiological determinants' (2010: 79).

Against this background, where leading researchers and writers in the psychological field hold that development and psychological functioning is multifaceted and multi-determined – and still, to a great extent, unknown – therapists would be hard pushed to justify a firm allegiance to any one, orientation-specific understanding of psychological processes. Certainly, theories such as Rogers' (1959) model of self-alienation or Beck and colleagues' (1979) concept of faulty information processing may act as very useful hypotheses in helping to untangle the reasons why clients feel and behave in the way that they do. But to hold any of these theories as self-evident *truths*, and to assume that they will be relevant to each and every client – in the absence of confirmatory psychological evidence – borders on the unethical. This is not, of course, to suggest that it is unethical to practise in any single orientation way: we know from the research, as discussed below, that such practices have the potential to be extremely helpful. But what it does suggest is that we need to distinguish our specialist ability in any one form of practice from an allegiance to the psychological principles on which that practice might be founded.

Box 2.3: Psychological distress as 'problems in living'

Within many psychotherapeutic theories, the reasons that people seek therapy tend to be understood in terms of psychological distress – processes and dynamics that go on *within* the individual: for instance, incongruence between self-concept and actual experiences (person-centred), internal conflicts between id and superego (psychodynamic), or irrational thoughts (cognitive therapy). A pluralistic standpoint suggests that it may be valuable to adopt a wider perspective on reasons for seeking therapy. It is also important to consider factors that exist *outside* an individual, or *between* an individual and their social, cultural or political environment. The concept of 'problems in living', introduced by the psychoanalytic writer Thomas Szasz (1961), provides a useful way to think about this issue. 'Problems in living' refers to anything that may have happened to make a 'personal niche', or 'life space', unliveable in some way, and the assistance of a therapist is sought in order to resolve this crisis. The idea of 'problems in living' implies that the client is active and resourceful in creating a life for himself or herself, but is for the moment stuck in relation to making progress towards their life goals. Problems in living is a concept that is compatible with psychologically-oriented approaches to therapy, such as psychodynamic therapy and CBT, and also with more socially-oriented approaches, such as narrative therapy and family therapy. As a result, it is a way of thinking about client problems that invites and encourages a plurality of perspectives.

Psychotherapy Research Foundations

The ubiquitous dodo bird

The pluralistic approach is based on the assumption that there is no one, best, therapy. This is very consistent with one of the most commonly cited findings in the counselling and psychotherapy research field: that, overall, there appears to be very little difference in the effectiveness of different therapeutic orientations (see, for instance, Luborsky, et al., 2002; Wampold, 2001). In a study of the comparative effectiveness of different therapies in primary and secondary care, for instance, Stiles and colleagues (2006) found that CBT, person-centred therapy and psychodynamic therapy all brought about relatively similar reductions in levels of distress from pre- to post-therapy. Within the counselling and psychotherapy research literature, this finding of equivalence has come to be known as the 'dodo bird' verdict (Luborsky, Singer & Luborsky, 1975; Rosenzweig, 1936). This is after the dodo bird in *Alice in Wonderland*, who, after judging a race around a lake, declares that 'everyone has won and so all must have prizes' (see Cooper, 2008: Chapter 3, for a more extended discussion).

Not all researchers in the field agree with this interpretation of the data. Some, for instance (e.g., Hunsley & Di Giulio, 2002), argue that there *are* meaningful differences in effectiveness between different therapies (e.g., Reid, 1997), with CBT generally coming out on top (e.g., Shapiro & Shapiro, 1982). However, even if it is the case that one therapy, *on average*, is somewhat more effective than another, it still means that a large number of clients in the 'less effective' therapy will do better than the average client in the 'more effective' therapy (see Box 2.1 on page 16). Hence, the existence of small average differences in effectiveness between two therapies cannot be taken as evidence that *all* clients will do better with one particular approach than with another.

Aptitude by treatment interactions

In support of the argument that different clients need different things, psychotherapy research shows that 'patients with certain characteristics will do better in one treatment than another and that the reverse will be true for patients without those characteristics or with other contrasting characteristics' (Elkin, et al., 1999: 438). This is known as an 'aptitude by treatment interaction', and provides a growing body of support for a pluralistic standpoint. One of the best established of these interactions is that clients with high levels of resistance (i.e., who have a tendency to behave in oppositional ways) tend to benefit more from non-directive practices, whereas those who are judged to be non-defensive seem to benefit more from directive therapeutic procedures (Beutler, Blatt, Alimohamed, Levy & Angtuaco, 2006; Beutler, Engle, et al., 1991). Similarly, clients who have a predominantly 'externalising' coping style (i.e., who deal with new or problematic situations by behaving impulsively, actively and excessively), tend to do better with technique-oriented therapies than clients with an 'internalising' coping style (i.e., who deal with new or problematic situations by turning in on themselves and becoming self-critical or depressed), and vice versa (Beutler, Machado, Engle, & Mohr, 1993; Beutler, Mohr, Grawe, Engle & MacDonald, 1991).

Preferences and predilections

One special kind of aptitude by treatment interaction, of particular importance to the pluralistic approach, is that of the relationship between clients' preferences for different therapies and the effectiveness of those interventions. It is clear from the research that clients *do* have preferences for different types of therapy to varying degrees (see Box 2.4 below), but does this have any impact on the outcome of different orientations, or do clients improve irrespective of what they actually seem to prefer?

Box 2.4: What kind of therapies do clients want?

Do all clients want the same kind of therapy, or are there substantial differences in preferences? Given the emphasis on user choice within service provision frameworks (see, for instance, *Our Choices in Mental Health*, Care Service Improvement Partnership, 2009) such a question would seem to be of considerable importance, yet it is interesting to note that research in this area is only beginning to emerge. In one of the most relevant studies to date (King, et al., 2000), depressed patients in primary care were given the option of choosing between non-directive counselling and CBT. In non-directive counselling, patients were told that the therapist would give them the opportunity to talk about what was troubling them so that they could explore their thoughts and feelings about it. In CBT, patients were told that the therapist would identify thoughts, feelings and behaviours that affected their mood and help them develop a more positive approach to them. Of those patients who specifically opted to choose one of these two therapies, around 40% opted for non-directive counselling, while 60% chose CBT. Interestingly, however, a follow-up study by Lee (2009) with students found significant differences between males and females, with 74% of males expressing a preference for CBT, but 64% of females expressing a preference for non-directive counselling.

In another study (Bragesjo, Clinton & Sandell, 2004), a random sample of 500 Swedish individuals were asked which of three therapies – CBT, cognitive psychotherapy and psychodynamic therapy – they would choose if they needed psychological help. Again, CBT proved the most popular, with around 35% choosing this option, 27% for cognitive psychotherapy and 16% for psychodynamic therapy. However, Bragesjo and colleagues found that individuals who had had some experience of treatment for psychological distress showed an increased preference for psychodynamic therapy – a finding replicated in a subsequent study (Frovenholt, Bragesjo, Clinton & Sandell, 2007).

Studies such as these suggest that, on average, clients tend to see cognitive-behavioural therapies as slightly more credible than alternative approaches, but there is clearly a large number of individuals who are more drawn to a non-CBT therapy than a CBT one. Given the significant relationship between preferences and outcomes, this suggests that clients should have access to a range of therapeutic options, rather than being squeezed into a 'one size fits all' service provision. It should be noted, however, that none of these studies allowed participants the option of saying that what they would have preferred was a flexible approach that combined elements of different therapies. Instead, these studies reflect the pervasive influence of the idea that therapy needs to be delivered in accordance with the approaches specified by different 'schools' of practice.

In the most thorough review of the research to date, Swift and Callahan (2009) found that clients who received a preferred therapy *did* do significantly better than those who did not. On average, the effect on outcome was small but, in many instances, clients were only given minimal information about the different therapies (for instance, just a paragraph on each to read) on which to base their judgement. The effect was also larger when strongly liked therapies were compared against strongly disliked therapies, rather than being compared against therapies in which the clients had no strong preferences. As an example of the former type, and where clients had substantial information about the different therapies, Devine and Fernald (1973) showed people with snake phobia videotapes of four different therapists describing, and then illustrating, their particular ways of working. Clients were then asked to rate each of the four therapies, and were assigned to a therapeutic condition that they had either rated as strongly disliking or strongly liking. The results of this study showed that clients who had been allocated to their preferred form of treatment did significantly better than those allocated to their non-preferred form of treatment, and they also did significantly better than clients who had been randomly allocated to those therapies. In their review of the research, Swift and Callahan (2009: 376) also found that 'clients who received their preferred treatment were almost half as likely to drop-out compared with clients who did not receive their preferred treatment'. On the basis of such evidence, Swift and Callahan (2009: 378) recommend that treatment selection should be based on 'a collaboration where both parties share information and discuss options and preferences openly'.

Although it may be assumed that clients do better in a preferred therapy because it is more matched to their individual needs and wants, there is also evidence to suggest that they do better because it gives them a feeling of being more in control (Handelzalts & Keinan, 2010). That is, if a client states what kind of therapy they want, and then receives it, they may feel that they have a greater influence on their environment and the kind of provision available to them. This may then enhance feeling of self-efficacy and self-esteem, boosting – or even instigating – a positive feedback cycle of improving mental health.

Research has also examined the relationship between a client's 'predilection' – their beliefs about the origins of their distress and what they expect will be helpful to them (Elkin, et al., 1999) – and the effectiveness of different interventions, and here, too, it indicates that therapies are more effective when they are aligned with clients' beliefs and

Table 2.1: Dimensions of client preferences for therapy (source: Berg, Sandahl & Clinton, 2008)

Outward orientation
It is important to help me define concrete goals.
Good treatment would teach me to behave in a different way.
I would be helped by homework that focuses on applying practical problem-solving.
I need a therapist who can take the initiative and give me good advice when it is needed.
Inward orientation
I need to reflect on painful experiences from earlier in my life.
I want to understand my relationships with others better.
I want to be able to reflect on my dreams together with my therapist.
I want to have help putting my feelings into words.
Support
I need a therapist who can offer support.
I need help from someone who can encourage me.
A good therapist is warm and friendly.
The most important thing is that my therapist likes me.
Catharsis
I need help to become more spontaneous.
It is important for me to express strong feelings in treatment.
A basic requirement for successful treatment is being able to 'blow off steam'.
I need to express feelings that have been suppressed.

values. For instance, Addis and Jacobson (1996) found that the more clients understood their depression in relatively abstract (i.e., cognitive) terms, the better they did in cognitive therapy (which gave them an opportunity to examine their personal meanings), but the worse they did in behavioural therapy (which focused on more discrete behavioural changes). Furthermore, Addis and Jacobson found that the more clients understood their problems in relationship terms, the less well they did in cognitive therapy (with its intrapersonal orientation).

The studies mentioned so far have generally explored client preferences in relation to broad therapy approaches, such as CBT or psychodynamic. However, each of these approaches encompasses a wide range of specific therapeutic activities. A study by Berg, Sandahl & Clinton (2008) invited clients to indicate their preferences for particular therapeutic processes, using a questionnaire (see sample items in Table 2.1 above). These clients, all of whom were suffering from anxiety disorders, were then randomly allocated to two contrasting forms of therapy. At the end of treatment, they completed the questionnaire again, to report on the extent to which their initial preferences had been reflected in the therapy they had received. Berg and colleagues found that clients whose therapy matched their preferences were more likely to get better. In this study, even though one of the therapy approaches proved to be more effective than the other, preferences were a stronger predictor of outcome than was the actual type of therapy that was delivered. This study has important implications for pluralistic therapy. It suggests that being asked to indicate their preference for specific elements of therapy may be more meaningful for clients than preferences for therapy approaches as a whole, and more likely to be linked to good outcome.

A further source of evidence about client preferences for therapy comes from studies that have attempted to explore what happens when clients do not benefit from the therapy that they have been offered. In a study by Nilsson, Svensson, Sandell & Clinton (2007), clients who had completed either psychodynamic or cognitive-behavioural therapy were interviewed about their experiences. Those clients who had felt disappointed by the therapy they had received consistently reported that there had been 'something missing' in the therapy. They had appreciated the skill of their therapist, and what the therapist had done for them, but they stated that they had known that what their therapist had been doing had not been right for them. The disappointed clients who had received psychodynamic therapy stated that they had wished that their therapist had operated in a more structured manner, using homework assignments (i.e., more like a CBT therapist). The disappointed CBT clients, by contrast, stated that they had wished that their therapist would have been more interested in their feelings, and given them more time to tell their story (i.e., had been more like a psychodynamic therapist). This study suggests that it may not be therapist lack of competence or client lack of motivation that necessarily leads to poor outcomes (although these issues are clearly also relevant). Instead, the extent of client–therapist concordance around preferred ways of working together seems to be the key factor.

Pathways of change: one or many?

Do all clients, or all clients with the same difficulties, change in the same way? Currently, there is very little evidence to indicate that this is the case. Even with clients who participate in the same therapy, the evidence seems to indicate that multiple change processes have the potential to take place. Clarke and colleagues (2004), for instance, conducted interviews with five clients who had received a brief course of cognitive therapy for depression. Some clients, like 'Anna', talked about the value of having their thoughts challenged: '[The therapist] summarized what I had said and checked it back with me, and that would reveal something illogical or contradictory' (2004: 86). But others, like 'Dave', did not, and described instead the value of a 'safe, trusting environment' (2004: 85) as well as 'resistance to some of the techniques and tools' (2004: 84) and 'irritation with the American style' of the cognitive therapy (2004: 84). Similarly, an interview-based study of young people's experience of school-based counselling (Cooper, 2004; see Chapter 7, present volume) revealed that most young people found it very helpful being listened to and having a chance to get things off their chest. But others put particular emphasis on being asked questions by the therapist, or on being offered suggestions and advice. What is also evident in both of these studies is that diversity exists at the intra-individual level as well as the inter-individual one, with each client describing a range of different helpful factors. Such findings do not deny the possibility that many clients may change in similar ways, but they suggest that we should try to stay open to a range of possible change processes in our clients, rather than assuming that one 'super-process' is at work. Even if the latter does turn out to be the case, the empirical research suggests that we are still a very long way off from establishing what that super-process may be.

A collaborative stance

At the heart of a pluralistic approach is the belief that therapists should collaborate closely with their clients on the goals, tasks and methods of therapy. Such an assertion is particularly well-supported by the empirical evidence, with an abundance of research to indicate that 'goal consensus and collaboration' within the therapeutic dyad is a 'demonstrably effective' element in the therapeutic relationship (Tryon & Winograd, 2002). Indeed, in the largest ever review of research on the therapeutic relationship commissioned by the American Psychological Association (Norcross, 2002), goal consensus and collaboration was found to be more clearly linked to outcomes than many more familiar relational variables, including congruence, unconditional positive regard and transference interpretations. This association is also evident from qualitative, interview-based research. Maluccio (1979), for instance, found that client dissatisfaction was often related to a failure to discuss, or agree, concrete and specific goals between therapist and client. In one 'failure' case, for example, a therapist attempted to help a couple work through their desire to control their son's life, while the parents wanted the therapist to induce their son to return to school.

Recommended reading

Horvath, A. O., & Bedi, R. P. (2002). The alliance. In J. C. Norcross (Ed.), *Psychotherapy Relationships that Work: Therapist Contributions and Responsiveness to Patients* (pp. 37–69). New York: Oxford University Press.

Tryon, G. S., & Winograd, G. (2002). Goal consensus and collaboration. In J. C. Norcross (Ed.), *Psychotherapy Relationships that Work: Therapist Contributions and Responsiveness to Patients* (pp. 109–125). New York: Oxford University Press.

In addition, within the psychotherapy research literature, the one factor that has been shown to be more clearly related to outcomes than any other is that of the 'therapeutic alliance' (Horvath & Bedi, 2002; Martin, Garske & Davis, 2000). This is closely linked to goal consensus and collaboration, and can be defined as the 'quality and the strength of the collaborative relationship between client and therapist' (Horvath & Bedi, 2002: 41), particularly collaboration on the goals and tasks of therapy. For instance, the revised short form of the Working Alliance Inventory (Hatcher & Gillaspy, 2006), the most commonly used alliance measure (Martin, et al., 2000), asks clients to rate their therapists on statements like '[The therapist] and I are working towards shared goals', and '[The therapist] and I have established a good appreciation of the kind of changes that would be most helpful for me'. What the research indicates, then, is that clients who more strongly endorse these items also tend to do better in therapy.

Client as active agent of change

Closely related to the emphasis on collaboration, another core principle of the pluralistic approach is that 'clients, not therapists, make therapy work' (Duncan, et al., 2004: 12). That is, the pluralistic approach assumes that it is clients who bring about change in their lives, with therapists as catalysts, rather than creators, of these improvements. Such an assumption is, again, strongly backed by the empirical research. For instance, Michael Lambert (1992), one of the world's leading psychotherapy researchers, has estimated that around 40% of therapeutic improvement is due to 'client variables and extratherapeutic events'. This increases to 75% if it also includes the client's expectations for change and their contribution to the therapeutic relationship. Bruce Wampold (2001), on the other hand, using a more exact method of calculations, estimates that as much as 87% of change in therapy is down to the client and the events in the client's life.

The idea that 'clients make therapy work' is discussed in detail by Bohart and Tallman (1999), who suggest a number of lines of evidence to support the active client hypothesis. For example, clients can often make substantial gains without any therapy at all or only a minimal degree of therapist input: for instance, through using self-help material (den Boer, Wiersma, & van den Bosch, 2004). Drawing together research findings in the counselling and psychotherapy field, Mick (Cooper, 2008: 157) has written:

> [A]t the heart of most successful therapies is a client who is willing and able to become involved in making changes to her or his life. If that client then encounters a therapist who she or he trusts, likes and feels able to collaborate with, the client can make use of a wide range of techniques and practices to move closer towards her or his goals. For different clients, different kinds of therapist input may be more or less helpful; and there may be certain kinds of input that are particularly helpful for clients with specific psychological difficulties; but the evidence suggests that the key predictor of outcomes remains the extent to which the client is willing and able to make use of whatever the therapist provides.

Box 2.5: Therapist satisfaction and pluralistic practice

How rewarding is it for the therapist to be working in more integrative or eclectic ways? Although evidence on this question is limited, a survey of the experience of around 5000 therapists by the Collaborative Research Network of the Society for Psychotherapy Research (Orlinsky & Rønnestad, 2005d) found that 'therapeutic work is experienced most favourably by therapists who have a broad theoretical perspective' (Orlinsky & Rønnestad, 2005a: 79): that is, therapists who considered a greater number of theoretical orientations as being salient to their practice. The research also found that broad-spectrum, integrative-eclectic therapists experienced the highest levels of growth in their work (Orlinsky & Rønnestad, 2005b). Orlinsky & Rønnestad (2005c: 169–170) suggest that these associations may emerge because a breadth of perspective enables therapists 'to view patients from different angles, and in a multiplicity of conceptual contexts, rather than fitting all patients to a single theoretical template'. They go on to suggest that theoretical breadth 'enhances the therapists' adaptive flexibility in responding to the varying challenges that patients present and enriches the process of "continual professional reflection" ... through which therapists learn the lessons imparted by clinical experience'. Orlinsky & Rønnestad (2005a) conclude that therapists who are not experiencing much growth and are in stasis should consider seeking greater variety or diversification in their therapeutic work, with an active openness to different theoretical perspectives.

The effectiveness of integrative therapies

In relation to a pluralistic way of working, we can also ask the question as to whether integrative, eclectic or pluralistic practices have been shown to be any more effective than single orientation ways of working. Integrative practices are, in fact, widely believed by therapists to improve the effectiveness of their work (Schottenbauer, Glass, & Arnkoff, 2005), but research on this question is relatively limited and a specifically pluralistic approach to practice has yet to be tested against any other form of therapy.

Recently, some studies have found that an integrative approach is more effective than the single orientation practice on which it is based. For instance, Constantino and colleagues (2008) found that integrative cognitive therapy (assimilating humanistic and interpersonal elements) was more effective at treating depression than classical cognitive therapy; and Hayes and colleagues (2006) found similar indications for acceptance and commitment therapy (ACT). However, in the main, integrative or 'enhanced' therapies have tended to do about as well as the therapies from which they are derived (Ahn & Wampold, 2001), with a review of the research indicating that they can be effective for a range of psychological problems, but little evidence to suggest that they are superior to single orientation alternatives (Schottenbauer, et al., 2005). From a pluralistic standpoint, however, this finding is not particularly surprising: the application of a standardised integrative practice across all clients would not be expected to be any more effective than the application of a standardised single orientation protocol.

The effectiveness of flexible practice

Is there evidence that more flexible and individually-tailored practices leads to better outcomes? Unfortunately, there have been few studies in this area. This is mainly because most therapy research has tended to focus on the delivery of standardised therapy protocols, where therapist flexibility would be defined as lack of adherence to the protocol, and therefore as a source or error.

Of those studies that have been conducted, there is some evidence that flexibility leads to improved outcomes. Jacobson and colleagues (1989), for instance, found that a clinically flexible version of marital therapy led to better long-term outcomes than a structured approach; Chu and Kendell (2009) found that therapist flexibility led to greater engagement of child clients in certain circumstances; and Ghaderi (2006) found that clients with bulimia did better on some outcome indicators when CBT was delivered in an individualised, rather than standardised, fashion. On the whole, though, these studies have tended to find few differences in outcomes between individualised and standardised treatments, and there are other studies which have found that more standardised therapies have outperformed individualised ones (Schulte, Kunzel, Pepping & Schulte-Bahrenberg, 1992). A key problem with much of this research, however, is that the 'tailored' therapies tend to remain within a relatively narrow band of CBT practices, or are tailored according to specific CBT principles, such that the effect of a wider, cross-orientation tailoring is not clear.

The value of more flexible and tailored approaches to therapy can also be examined by comparing the effectiveness of 'manualised' therapies (i.e., those in which practitioners are required to follow an established set of practice guidelines) against non-manualised alternatives. Here, again, results are fairly mixed. On the one hand, some studies have indicated that competence in specific manualised therapy techniques predicts the outcome of psychotherapy (e.g., Shafran, et al., 2009; Shaw, et al., 1999), but others have found that use of particular manualised techniques are associated with poorer outcomes (Castonguay, Goldfried, Wiser, Raue & Hayes, 1996), or lead to therapists being experienced as less warm and friendly (Henry, Strupp, Butler, Schacht & Binder, 1993). This suggests that, while knowledge and skills in specific practices may lead to enhanced outcomes, rigidity and inflexibility of intervention does not.

Such a conclusion is supported by research into 'ruptures' in the therapeutic alliance, i.e., times of tension or breakdown in the collaborative therapist–client relationship (Safran & Muran, 2000). Here, research indicates that greater resolution is achieved when emerging ruptures are acknowledged and addressed, and also when therapists adopt a more accommodating stance (for instance, by apologising or by changing their behaviour) rather than being rigid in their behaviours. In support of such findings, Piper and colleagues (1999) have shown how drop-out in psychodynamic therapy is often linked to therapists' persistence in making transference interpretations, at times when clients are raising concerns or frustrations about the work.

Qualitative interviews with clients also suggest that, from a service user's perspective, flexibility is generally experienced as helpful and important to the relationship. For instance, in a recent study of factors that clients in primary care counselling felt had contributed towards long-term successful outcomes, the therapist's ability to adapt to individual need was seen as being a critical ingredient (Perren, Godfrey & Rowland, 2009). One respondent said: 'I felt that she bent … to me. I felt that she sort of moulded herself to me to the way I needed, what I needed, the style I needed. It may not work for everybody; it just fitted perfectly like a glove in a way' (Perren, et al., 2009: 243). In a second study, another client said: 'I do not believe in standardized ways of working, I think the therapist has to be a wise person, someone who has made his knowledge a part of himself, and who sees what needs to be done in the specific situation (Binder, et al., 2009: 253).

An interesting source of evidence around therapist flexibility can also be found within the literature on systematic case studies (McLeod, 2010). Cases that are written up in detail, using multiple sources of evidence, invariably show that the therapist has been innovative or flexible in some respects, even while working within a single orientation (see, for example, Hill, et al., 2008; Hougaard, et al., 2008; Karon, 2008; Kasper, Hill & Kivlighan, 2008; Kramer, 2009).

In summary, then, there is an emerging body of evidence that flexibility and the individual tailoring of therapies *can* lead to improved outcomes, but much more research is needed on the specific circumstances under which it does so – and also the specific circumstances in which it may, actually, lead to a worsening of outcomes. As Schulte (1996) points out, however, we do not need to see tailored and standardised therapies as mutually exclusive. Probably, with certain clients at certain points in time, it is important that practitioners avoid 'therapist drift' (Shafran, et al., 2009) and maintain a relatively consistent way of working; but with other clients at other times, flexibility and responsiveness may be the key. As we will emphasise throughout this book, therefore, a pluralistic approach needs to remain pluralistic about pluralism itself – it should never get to the point where it assumes that one way of working, even a pluralistic one, will be best for all clients at all times.

Policy Foundations: The Personalisation Agenda

As discussed in the Preface, recent shifts towards the commissioning and delivery of 'evidence-based' psychological therapies (such as the UK government's Improving Access to Psychological Therapies programme, Clark, Layard, Smithies, Richards, Suckling & Wright, 2009) may give the impression that public policy-makers are moving towards a more monist agenda. However, within the UK, the shift towards evidence-based practice is just one part of a broader revolution in health and social care policy, many aspects of which are not only consistent with, but at the leading edge of, pluralistic thinking and practice. In the final part of this chapter, we want to discuss some of these developments, showing how a pluralistic approach is aligned with many elements of a contemporary political zeitgeist.

Health and medical care

Consistent with a pluralistic approach, recent years have seen a 'growing trend in health care towards patient empowerment and greater patient choice' (Ford, Schofield & Hope, 2003: 590). This development is nowhere more evident than in the UK Department of Health's (2009) 'New Horizons' programme (www.dh.gov.uk/en/Healthcare/Mentalhealth/NewHorizons). This sets out a cross-party vision and a programme of action for improving the mental health and wellbeing of the population of England from 2010 onwards. The guiding values for New Horizons are almost synonymous with those underlying the pluralistic approach to therapy: equality, justice and human rights; helping people reach their full potential; helping people be in control of their lives; and valuing relationships.

Concomitant with this, one the key developments in the New Horizons vision is a move towards more *personalised*, individually-tailored mental health services. Louis Appleby, former National Clinical Director for Mental Health in England, writes that a key theme of New Horizons is ensuring that care is based on 'individuals' needs and wishes' (Appleby, 2009: 4); with service users 'able to make decisions about their care, treatment and goals for recovery, as well as to monitor their own condition' (Department of Health, 2009: 5). New Horizons, as with the pluralistic approach, also moves towards a greater emphasis on service users' strengths and resources, and away from defining users in terms of mental health problems or diagnoses. 'This is about more than preventing mental illness,' states former UK Prime Minister Gordon Brown, 'it is also about helping individuals and communities to bring the best out of themselves' (www.newhorizons.dh.gov.uk/index.aspx).

Such a shift of emphasis, from mental distress to mental wellbeing, is consistent with many other developments in political circles (see, for instance, the highly influential Foresight Mental Capital and Wellbeing Project, 2008), and with the increasing influence of the 'recovery' agenda (e.g., National Institute for Mental Health in England, 2005). Here, people who experience mental illnesses are seen as still having the capacity to enjoy mental wellbeing. Recovery is about 'building a meaningful and satisfying life, as defined by the person themselves, whether or not there are ongoing or recurring symptoms and problems' (Department of Health, 2009: 24).

Alongside these shifts in broad health care policy, recent years have also seen a growing interest in developing more collaborative, egalitarian and dialogical ways of working in the specific physician–patient encounter (Borrell-Carrio, et al., 2004; Makoul & Marla, 2006). Going under such titles as 'shared decision making', 'mutual participation', 'enhanced autonomy', 'evidence-based patient choice', 'client-centred care', 'meetings between experts' and 'relationship-centred care' (Borrell-Carrio, et al., 2004; Ford, et al., 2003; Makoul & Marla, 2006; Suchman, 2006), the emphasis here is on 'discussions between professional and patient that bring the knowledge, concerns, and perspective of each to the process of seeking agreement on a course of treatment' (Makoul & Marla, 2006: 304). As with the pluralistic approach, authors in this field have emphasised that such a collaborative approach does not involve making reluctant patients assume too much of a burden of knowledge about a decision, nor does it imply uncritical acceptance of whatever the patient believes or hypothesises (Borrell-Carrio, et al., 2004). '[B]ut neither does it allow for the uncritical negation of the patient's perspective, as so frequently occurs, for example, when patients complain of symptoms that physicians cannot explain' (Borrell-Carrio, et al., 2004: 578). The emphasis, then, is on a balanced, collaborative 'autonomy in relation', an informed choice supported by a caring relationship, in which the physician can move flexibly from a primarily doctor-led degree of sharing to a primarily patient-led one. Importantly, in support of this approach, evidence indicate that such collaborative activity within the medical encounter does, indeed, improve outcomes (Greenfield, Kaplan & Ware, 1985; Kaplan, et al., 1989).

Social care

In the UK, shifts in health care policy towards more individualised service provisions are mirrored by policy developments in the social care sector. *Putting People First* (HM Government, 2007: 2), the UK government's 'shared vision and commitment to the transformation of adult social care', states that the time has now come to replace 'paternalistic' systems of care with 'high quality personally tailored services'. It goes on to state, 'In the future, we want people to have maximum choice, control and power over the support services they receive.'

Within the social care field, this process of tailoring support to people's individual needs has come to be known as 'personalisation':

> Personalisation means starting with the individual as a person with strengths and preferences who may have a network of support and resources. ... Personalisation reinforces the idea that the individual is best placed to what they need and how those needs can be best met. It means that people can be responsible for themselves and can make their own decisions about what they require, but that they should also have information and support to enable them to do so. ... Personalisation is about giving people much more choice and control over their lives. (Carr, 2008: 3)

This shift towards personalisation is closely linked to other developments in the social care field, such as 'person-centred planning' for people with learning disabilities, in which the aim is to support them to live as independently as they can (Carr, 2008), and 'person-centred working,' in which people who use care services are helped to have 'as much control over their own lives as possible' (Carr, 2008: 19). Personalisation also links to the social model of disability (in which social factors, such as discrimination, are seen as the ultimate cause of disablement), the service user movement, and an increasing involvement of 'experts by experience' (Carr, 2008). As with the pluralistic approach, then, personalisation is closely linked to a user-empowerment agenda, and this is not just at the individual level, but at the level of collective organisations (for instance, MIND, Depression Alliance Scotland), which can represent more powerfully the voice of user experience.

Summary

The pluralistic approach to therapy is underpinned, and informed, by a pluralistic philosophical outlook. This holds that many key questions in the human and social sciences have a range of 'right' answers and that, at a moral and political level, it is essential that we can acknowledge and value this diversity and difference. Psychological research, too, supports a pluralistic perspective, by indicating that there are many different reasons why people are the way they are. Likewise, psychotherapy research provides good evidence for a pluralistic perspective by showing that there is no one, 'best' way of helping people; that different clients seem to need different things; and that working collaboratively, supporting client agency, and being flexible in practice are often closely associated with good outcomes. Finally, the pluralistic approach introduced in this book is closely aligned with key contemporary developments in health and social policy, most notably the Department of Health's (2009) *New Horizons* programme, which sets out a vision for addressing mental health difficulties in personalised, respectful and user-empowering ways.

Questions for reflection and discussion

1. To what extent do you agree or disagree with the pluralistic assertion that there are many 'right' answers to the same question?
2. Do you think it is true that personality and human development are influenced by a multiplicity of diverse factors? Are there one or two factors that you think are, universally, much more influential than others?
3. What is your reaction to the suggestion that as much as 87% of the change in therapy is due to the client and factors in the client's life? What implications does this have for how you think and feel about therapy?
4. What flaws do you see in the argument for a pluralistic approach? If you were going to criticise it, what would you say?

3 Building a Collaborative Therapeutic Relationship

This chapter discusses:

- The centrality of client–therapist collaboration to pluralistic thinking and practice.
- The dialogical nature of an effective therapeutic collaboration.
- Practical strategies for building a collaborative therapeutic relationship:
    - providing pre-therapy information;
    - reviewing the therapeutic work;
    - negotiating around the therapeutic frame;
    - 'metacommunicating': talking to clients about the process of therapy;
    - building collaborative rituals;
    - tailoring the style of relating to the individual client;
    - attending to different client and therapist voices.
- The concept of 'collaborative capacity'.

From a pluralistic standpoint, the nature of a helpful therapeutic relationship hinges on the concept of collaboration: a *mutual* involvement by therapist and client in the helping relationship (Tryon & Winograd, 2002). Pluralism, in the sense of being informed by a multiplicity of ideas and practices, is not helpful if it is allied to an expert-driven approach to therapy. If it is the therapist alone who decides on which therapy interventions and theories to use, then the strengths, capabilities and preferences of the person seeking help are likely to be oppressed and silenced – it is another form of 'monism'. By contrast, when the client and therapist are able to work together to create facilitative experiences, a situation is created where the client is able to renew already existing personal resources, and augment them with new learning. As Bohart and Tallman (1999: 224) put it, 'a mutual, equal, active collaboration between two intelligences in which two streams of expertise enrich one another and blend'. This is not about 'empowering' clients, but respecting, recognising and responding to the power they already have.

Working collaboratively is based on an image of two (or more) people working together to carry out a task. This idea of collaboration is very similar to many everyday situations in which people work together. For example, a father and grandmother make arrangements for a child's birthday party. Tennis partners decide on their strategy for dealing with an opposing team. Two plumbers work out how to approach the task of fitting a new bathroom. There are a huge number of examples that can be imagined of situations in which people may have a shared goal, and then need to decide on how to make best use of each individual's knowledge, skill, experience and time in order to achieve that goal. Although therapy may have its own distinctive goals (see Chapter 4), it can still be viewed as part of a much wider category of collaborative action. If a person felt able to accomplish a therapeutic task on their own, they would just get on and do it. By seeking out a therapist, they are acknowledging that some kind of collaborative action is necessary.

As we have seen in Chapter 2, there has been a great deal of research indicating that collaboration and the strength of the therapeutic alliance are the most significant predictors of eventual good outcome, and there is little doubt that the client–therapist relationship represents one of the cornerstones of productive counselling. No matter how insightful a therapist may be in terms of understanding and explaining the client's problems, or how skilled they may be in delivering specific therapeutic interventions, if the client feels that the therapist is not on the same wavelength, or is not reliable, caring or trustworthy, then they are unlikely to make a commitment to facing difficult issues and making life changes.

Despite the general consensus among counsellors and psychotherapists that the establishment of such an alliance is the basis of effective practice, there is little agreement around what therapists can or should actually *do* to make such a relationship happen. Within the counselling and psychotherapy literature, there exist a range of competing ideas about how to make sense of the part that the relationship plays in therapy. This has produced some interesting debates between adherents of different schools of thought (see, for example, Shlien 1984; see also Kahn, 1997 for analysis of competing concepts of therapeutic relationships), but has, in our view, inhibited the emergence of an integrated, pragmatic approach to this issue.

This chapter provides an outline of some of the practical things that therapists can do to maximise the chances that a collaborative relationship will be formed between them and their clients. What follows should not be regarded as a definitive list. We have tended to focus on those strategies that are particular to a pluralistic way of working, and not on the many others that have been described, in extensive detail, elsewhere (for instance, empathy, unconditional positive regard and congruence, see Rogers, 1957). In the spirit of pluralistically-informed 'wiki-knowledge', it would be enormously valuable if ways could be found to pool the collective wisdom and inventiveness of clients and therapists around this issue, in order to broaden the repertoire of relationship-building possibilities.

When reading the ideas presented below, it is also important to keep in mind that not all of these strategies will be appropriate for specific therapists or settings. There is an enormous diversity of therapists and therapy settings, and what works for some people may not necessarily work for others.

Box 3.1: Relationship-building is the therapist's responsibility

In everyday situations, when two people meet and become close friends or colleagues, there is an expectation of *mutuality* – both participants actively contribute to the deepening of the relationship. If there is an imbalance, for example where one participant is too pushy or demanding, it is likely that the relationship will fail. The situation in therapy is quite different. Bedi, Davis, and Williams (2005) interviewed a sample of clients, and asked them to describe events in therapy that had lead to a strengthening of their relationship with their therapist. These clients were able to describe a large number of 'relationship-building' events. However, very few of these events had been initiated by the client. It was very clear that, for these clients, looking after the relationship was the responsibility of the therapist. This finding makes a lot of sense. For the most part, clients do not know the 'rules' of what is possible in therapy, and are not in a good position to take the initiative in terms of relationship patterns. Also, clients have an expectation that their counsellor or psychotherapist will take care of them.

In the Bedi et al. (2005) study, it is also interesting to note that many of the relationship-building episodes that participants regarded as most significant were those where the therapist had demonstrated, in their actions, a genuine care for the client. For instance: 'the therapist allowed me to choose which chair I wanted to sit in'; 'the therapist taught me a grounding technique', 'the therapist said, "call anytime, or just come in anytime, and there will be someone here, even if I'm not here"'. This is consistent with other recent findings that clients particularly value therapists who are willing to 'go the extra mile' (McMillan & McLeod, 2006), who offer a 'really, genuine caring' that is '"over and above" what they had expected from a professional therapeutic relationship' (Knox, 2008: 185). The message from these finding is that collaborative therapists need to be alert to apparently minor and routine acts of reaching out, which may have great significance for individual clients.

Dialogue as the Basis for Effective Collaboration

In the following sections of this chapter, a series of practical strategies for building collaborative relationships with clients are discussed. To be implemented effectively, each of these strategies needs to be based on a willingness to engage in *dialogue* with clients. A pluralistic approach to therapy requires striving to reach a point where there is mutual inter-action between client and therapist. It is through dialogue that something new can emerge for the client, arising from the inter-play between their own strategies for dealing with problems and the ideas and practices of the therapist.

Dialogue can be described as a form of interpersonal engagement in which each person is both *receptive* to the other, and capable of *expressing* towards the other something of their own genuine, multifaceted being (Cooper, 2005; Mearns & Cooper, 2005). In person-centred terms (Rogers, 1957), dialogue involves a profound empathic attunement to the other, an acceptance of the other's reality, and the ability to actively convey this understanding and acceptance to the other in a manner that is authentically personal. Dialogue has a 'yes, and…' quality (Moore, 2005): each partner building on what the other has said and being mutually impacted upon in the encounter (Cooper & Spinelli, in press). Here, communications are presented as 'offers' that the other is free to modify, develop or reject (Moore, 2005), rather than as fixed or given truths. Dialogue can be contrasted with a monological 'no, but…' conversational stance (Moore, 2005), or with a 'talking or reloading' form of communication, 'where we're impatiently waiting for the other person to finish so that can quickly lob back our already-prepared conversational grenade' (Moore, 2005: 81). Buber (1947b: 69) also talks about the many non-dialogical forms of communication, for instance *speechifying*, where 'people do not really speak to one another, but each, although turned to the other, really speaks to a fictitious court of appeal whose life consists of nothing but listening to him'.

Therapy that seeks to be grounded in dialogue reaches beyond many of the assumptions about the therapeutic relationship that typically inform current theory and practice. For example, most therapists are exceptionally skilled listeners, and are able to create relationships where clients may feel heard and understood. From a pluralistic stance, however, there is a danger that this kind of empathic process can be monological rather than dialogical – the client tells his or her story, but learns little about the therapist's personal response to that story. Other therapists are highly competent at 'telling' – either by offering an interpretation of the client's actions or by initiating an intervention. Again, though, this kind of process is monological rather than dialogical if it does not accommodate the client's active involvement in co-constructing a new understanding or co-creating a new change strategy.

Genuine dialogue between two or more people is difficult to achieve, and relatively little has been written in the therapy literature about how to make sense of this vital process (though see Cooper & Spinelli, in press). There are several sources of ideas about dialogue that are of particular relevance for pluralistic practitioners. Perhaps the best place to start is the paper 'Dialogue', by the existential philosopher Martin Buber (1947a). It is not an easy read but, as with Buber's (1958) classic text *I and Thou*, is a wonderfully rich, poetic and soulful contemplation on the nature of human relating. Buber's work has been developed into a dialogical system of psychotherapy by Maurice Friedman (1985), as well as the contemporary gestalt psychotherapist Richard Hycner (1991; Hycner & Jacobs, 1995). Valuable resources can also be found within the person-centred literature, for example in the writings of the Austrian person-centred therapist Peter Schmid (2001, 2007), in the concept of 'relational depth' (Mearns & Cooper, 2005), and in Carl Rogers's own dialogue with Martin Buber (Anderson & Cissna, 1997). Similar ideas can be found in contemporary psychodynamic thinking, where it has become commonplace to talk about a 'two-person' relationship in therapy (see Kahn, 1997), where both client and therapist are actively present, in contrast to the 'one-person' relationship in which the client is present but the person of the therapist remains hidden.

Although these humanistic, person-centred and psychodynamic ideas are useful for pluralistic therapists seeking to work dialogically with clients, they tend to suffer from the fact that they were developed in the context of somewhat non-dialogical traditions of practice, with the result that contemporary readers need to be able to somehow separate out these different strands of thinking. What may also be useful for therapists interested in the concept of dialogue, therefore, is the work of the Finnish therapist Jaakko Seikkula. This work is particularly significant for two reasons. First, it places dialogue at the heart of therapy, rather than viewing it as a desirable but not strictly necessary add-on. Second, his approach has been shown to be effective with a highly challenging client group – people diagnosed with schizophrenia (Seikkula, et al., 2006).

Recommended reading

Buber, M. (1947). Dialogue. In *Between Man and Man* (R. G. Smith, Trans.) (pp. 17–59). London: Fontana.

Cooper, M., & Spinelli, E. (in press). A dialogue on dialogue. In L. Barnett & G. Madison (Eds.), *Existential Psychotherapy: Legacy, Vibrancy and Dialogue.* London: Routledge.

Seikkula, J., & Trimble, D. (2005). Healing elements of therapeutic conversation: Dialogue as an embodiment of love. *Family Process*, *44*, 461–475.

Strong, T. (2000). Six orienting ideas for collaborative counsellors. *European Journal of Psychotherapy, Counselling and Health*, *3*, 25–42.

In his understanding of the meaning and role of dialogue, Seikkula draws heavily on the writings of the philosopher Mikhail Bakhtin (1973). A central assumption that informed Bakhtin's way of thinking about human interaction and communication is the notion that there are always multiple voices (internal and external) involved in any conversation. A further assumption is that every statement that is made in a conversation is directed towards a real or imagined audience, and if the audience does not respond in some way, that voice will be silenced. As Bakhtin (1975: 127) put it, 'there is nothing more terrible than a lack of response'. Finally, dialogue and conversation do not merely consist of an exchange of ideas, but are an embodied 'performance' in the present moment – the physical presence of each speaker, for example their expressed emotional state, conveys a great deal of meaning. The implications of these ideas for psychotherapy practice are explored in detail in Seikkula and Trimble (2005) and Seikkula and Arnkil (2006). In summary, what is recommended is that therapists who are seeking to promote dialogue need to be willing to do their best to respond to *all* of the voices with which the client speaks (and all of their own voices). The accomplishment of dialogue is built on curiosity, patience, tolerance of uncertainty, repeating statements so that they can be heard in their full meaning, and finding a rhythm that best reflects the shared emotional experience of both (or all) participants. From a pluralistic therapy perspective, this kind of process can be understood as one that enables, as far as possible, the resources of both client and therapist to be brought to bear on the 'problem': each voice within a 'polyphonic' dialogical space represents a valuable resource.

Box 3.2: Being willing to be actively involved in the therapeutic process

In a recent research study, Sundet (in press) interviewed clients using a family therapy clinic in Norway about what they had found helpful in their therapy. One of the main themes to emerge was that of *helpful participation.* Clients did not like their therapist to be passive, but preferred them to be actively involved and willing to share their professional knowledge and personal voice, and to 'do things'. What they were looking for was a sense of *generosity* on the part of their therapists – an openness to giving of themselves within the therapeutic work.

Practical Strategies For Building A Collaborative Therapeutic Relationship

There are many practical ways in which therapists can promote an ethos of dialogue and collaboration within therapy. The list of strategies described in the following sections is not intended to be prescriptive or comprehensive. Some clients will inevitably find that some of these approaches make more sense to them than others. Also, it is important for therapists to develop their own personal style, which may involve the creation of further collaborative strategies not mentioned here.

Providing pre-therapy information

There is no reason to assume that clients come to therapy with an expectation that they will be involved in collaborative conversations around what they want to happen in therapy, their ideas about change process, and so on. Some clients may expect that their views will be taken into account, but many others will expect that a therapist will behave like a doctor or teacher, and essentially tell them what to do. Research indicates that it is good practice in counselling and psychotherapy to provide clients with information in advance of beginning therapy – and even in advance of taking part in an intake or assessment interview – increasing overall outcomes and reducing drop-out rates and anxieties (Guajardo & Anderson, 2007; Hoehn-Saric, et al., 1964). It is useful, as a means of establishing the principle of collaboration from the start, if this information emphasises and explains that their active involvement is essential, and that their therapist will want to know about their ideas around what would be helpful for them. An example of pre-therapy information for clients is provided in Appendix A (see page 182). This material is not copyright, and readers are welcome to edit and adapt it for use in leaflets and information sheets for clients in their own practice settings. It can be helpful to repeat and reinforce this information during any assessment or intake interviews that are conducted with clients. This kind of face-to-face meeting allows the client to ask questions and the interviewer to provide examples of collaboration that are relevant to the client's situation. In some counselling agencies, the intake interview may itself include collaborative elements, for instance discussion around the timing and frequency of counselling, the number of sessions and choice of counsellor (see Negotiating the therapeutic frame, on page 43). These conversations set the scene for later collaboration around therapy process issues.

Exercise 3.1: What *you* can offer clients

If you are a practising or training therapist, take 10 minutes or so to write down on a piece of paper what you feel you can offer a client. For instance, you may feel that you can offer them a chance to be 'listened to and heard', perhaps 'emotional support', or maybe 'techniques for dealing with stress and anxiety'. Once you have done this, spend another 10 minutes or so reflecting, with or without a partner, on the extent to which you currently share this with prospective clients. Do you feel that you can be more transparent with them about what you can offer?

Box 3.3: Using intake/assessment sessions to lay the groundwork for collaborative pluralistic work

In many therapy settings, the client meets with the therapist, or with an intake interviewer, before the therapy begins. The role of this kind of meeting, and the issues to be addressed, will vary according to the particular organisation in which therapy takes place (see Mace, 1995). However, no matter what else might need to be covered, it is valuable for therapists working in a pluralistic way to use the opportunity of a first meeting with a client to initiate a dialogue around a range of topics that are central to this way of working:

- the intention of the therapist to be flexible and be guided by the client's preferences and choices;
- the therapist's belief in the client's strengths and resources;
- how useful it is for the therapist when the client is able to offer feedback on the helpfulness or otherwise of therapeutic activities that have been carried out;
- what the client wants from therapy – what their goals are;
- the idea that it may be helpful if these goals are broken down into smaller steps or tasks;
- what would be best for the client (and possible for the therapist) around the timing and scheduling of sessions;
- the therapist's 'menu': what is on offer.

It is unlikely that any of these issues will be fully explored or resolved during an assessment or intake session, or even in a series of such meetings. What is

(Continued)

essential, instead, is that the client receives a clear message about the importance of their active contribution to therapy, and the therapist begins to tune into the client's preferences and goals.

Reminders and reviews

Our own way of working is to remind clients on a regular basis that we are interested in their ideas, preferences and feedback. This is particularly important in early sessions, as a way of reinforcing the principle of collaboration. Some strategies for using reminders and reviews include the following conversational leads:

- (At the start of a session). 'I'd like it if we could take a few moments to just think about what you want to get from our session today, and what we might do to achieve that…'
- 'I know this is probably very boring, and you have heard me say this many times before, but it is really helpful if you can keep letting me know about what you find helpful or unhelpful in the counselling, and any ideas (anything at all!) that you have about things that we could be doing or talking about that you think would be useful for you. As I have said, I have lots of ideas about what might be useful, but in the end its whether they work for you that is the important thing.'
- 'We just have a couple of minutes left today. I'd find it useful if we could look at what you got from today's session, whether there was anything missing, or anything else that you'd like to say about it.'
- 'We have had six sessions now. My own sense is that what we have been talking about has been helpful for you. However, I was wondering if we could specifically take a few minutes next week to review things, so I can get a feel for where you want to go next in terms of these issues. Would you be willing to give that some thought before our next session?'

It is essential, as far as possible, to try to develop these conversational leads into passages of dialogue. Clients are usually tentative or uncertain in expressing their ideas and preferences, and may need some help to draw out their thoughts. At the same time, these thoughts may not be particularly well developed, and the client may feel embarrassed or 'put on the spot' if they feel they are being interrogated or made to feel stupid by not being readily able to explain what they want. In addition, it is crucial to keep in mind that the other side of dialogue is a willingness on the part of the therapist to share what they are thinking. For example, in a conversation stimulated by the first statement above ('I'd like it if we could take a few moments to just think about what you want to get from our session today, and what we might do to achieve that…'), it will usually be facilitative for the therapist, at some point, to share what they are thinking (for instance, 'I realise that the way we have been approaching issues is to talk them through … I have enjoyed doing that with you, and my sense is that is has been helpful for you, but at the same time I remember what you said at our first meeting about being a very practical person, and I was just wondering whether the counselling had been practical enough for you … does that make sense?'). If the therapist is not willing to be open in this way, then the client may be left guessing what the counsellor really wants or thinks and then trying to comply. This is not at all helpful and is the antithesis of collaboration.

Negotiating the therapeutic frame

There are many aspects of therapy practice that are taken for granted by practitioners and counselling agencies, in terms of being pre-defined and specified by the therapist or agency, but which in principle can be open to collaborative negotiation. These aspects include:

- the duration of counselling sessions;
- frequency and timing of sessions;
- choice of therapist;
- location of therapy;
- individual therapy or involvement of family members;
- contact between sessions;
- payment;
- client involvement in research and data collection.

An invitation to consider these issues can help a client to begin to think about the wider issues of what they want from therapy and how they can get what they want. This type of conversation can be introduced by saying something along the lines of 'My/our normal practice is (weekly meetings at the same time, etc.) … but I/we also realise that this may not be ideal for some people, so we are open to looking at alternative ways of organising the counselling, in so far as we are able to accommodate them…'. For example, some people find a 50 minute session is too long for them. By contrast, other people seem to need longer sessions, for example if they are intending to explore very painful material and want to be reasonably 'together' by the time they leave the building and go home. Some clients find it helpful to receive a letter or email following each session (White & Epston, 1990), while others may not like this procedure. Both of us work in services in which clients are told that they can change their therapist if they feel that the person to whom they have been allocated is not the right person for them. All of these areas of practical decision-making represent discrete, concrete issues around which collaboration can take place. By opening up at least some practical arrangements for negotiation (and renegotiation), a therapist or counselling agency is signalling the importance it attaches to collaborative decision-making. And because it can be easier for clients to engage with collaborative discussion around such concrete practical issues, as compared with more abstract therapy concerns (for instance, 'Do you want to talk about your early childhood or develop practical coping skills?'), the negotiation around the frame of therapy can be a useful model or template for subsequent collaboration around therapy goals and methods.

As with negotiation and collaborative dialogue around any other aspect of therapy, however, it is essential that the therapist is aware of, and realistic and transparent about, the limits of what they can offer the client. If, for instance, an agency requires therapists to work within 50-minute time slots, it is unlikely to be helpful for a therapist to ask a client whether they would prefer longer sessions. Rather, being clear about the boundaries of the work, and being open to how clients might feel about this, is more likely to be constructive in taking things forward.

Outcome monitoring

In recent years, one therapeutic strategy that has demonstrated a remarkable ability to enhance therapeutic outcomes – while also reducing drop-out rates – is the use of systems that track, and provide feedback on, client progress (Lambert, 2007; Miller, Duncan, Sorrell, & Brown, 2005). Here, clients complete a brief outcome measure every time they attend counselling or psychotherapy, such as the 10-item CORE–OM (see Box 3.4 on page 45). The scores are then processed (either by hand or by computer) and fed back to the therapist prior to the following session. If the client is found to be 'not on track' (i.e., not improving or deteriorating), the therapist is notified and advised to carefully review the case and to consider possible strategies for addressing the problem, such as discussing this with the client and working on the therapeutic alliance.

Such research suggests that a very useful form of collaborative activity between therapist and client may be to openly reflect on, discuss and address issues regarding the client's progress in therapy, particularly when the client does not seem to be improving. This may be hard for therapists to do ('Does it mean that I am a lousy counsellor?') and, in some instances, there is the potential that it could be demotivating for a client; but the evidence overwhelmingly suggests that, in general, it is much better to address difficulties and a lack of progress in therapy than to carry on regardless. (Contrary to the old adage, there is very little evidence to suggest that clients need to get worse before they get better and, in general, a deterioration in client's symptoms is a very strong predictor that they will continue to get worse and/or drop out of therapy (Lambert, 2007).) And while therapists may feel that they only need to address this when they can see that a client is struggling, the research also indicates that, in most instances, therapists are very poor at knowing when negative outcomes are likely (Lambert & Ogles, 1997). This highlights the importance of using 'objective' measures, which are less likely to be influenced by the therapist's perceptions or hopes, and also of regularly inviting clients to review the work and comment on its helpfulness.

Duncan and colleagues (2004: 113–115) give an excellent example of using feedback data from outcome measures in a collaborative way to help turn around a client's progress in therapy. Steven was a gentle and spiritual man in his 30s who had been experiencing chronic depression. Over the first few sessions, he and his therapist worked psychodynamically, exploring the various experiences in Steven's childhood that may have been connected to his current difficulties. Steven had participated in such therapy previously, and indicated that he was very happy with this way of working, but his scores on a measure of psychological distress got gradually worse – particularly in terms of social and interpersonal functioning. The therapist raised this with Steven, who acknowledged his decline, but both were at a loss to explain it. They talked about what to do, and eventually decided that they should bring in a 'reflecting team' – a strategy commonly used in contemporary family therapy whereby a group of therapists discuss the issues in the presence of the client. Steven listened to the team's 'free-for-all of unedited speculations and suggestions' about what he should do, and expressed considerable interest in the idea that, rather than 'rooting around in his past' for something that might explain his depression, he and his therapist should work on bringing his positive characteristics to life. They started to do so, and subsequently Steven's level of psychological well-being began to improve, with sustained improvements a year after therapy had ended. Duncan and colleagues conclude that: 'With Steven, the presence of the [outcome] data helped circumvent a negative outcome by pushing the therapist to explore alternatives in the process.'

Box 3.4: What (free) measures can I use to monitor and evaluate my practice?

Today, many of the best tools for measuring counselling and psychotherapy outcomes are freely available, with clear guidance on how they can be used in practice. Leading the way in the UK is the Clinical Outcomes for Routine Evaluation – Outcome Measure (CORE–OM), which is a well-validated, client-completed measure of global psychological distress (see www.coreims.co.uk). A second very popular and well-validated global outcome measure, developed in the USA and somewhat briefer, is the Outcome Rating Scale (ORS) (download via www.scottdmiller.com). The ORS is accompanied by an easy-to-use measure of the therapeutic alliance, the Session Rating Scale (SRS). Another measure that is used extensively in the UK, including sites in which the Improving Access to Psychological Therapies (IAPT) Programme has been implemented, is the Patient Health Questionnaire (PHQ–9), which specifically focuses on symptoms of depression. Its 'sister measure', for symptoms of generalised anxiety, is the General Anxiety Disorder Assessment (GAD–7) (both measures can be downloaded from, and completed on, a range of internet sites). An alternative means of helping clients track improvements in mental health and well-being, particularly suited to clients who have experienced severe psychological difficulties, is the Recovery Star (www.mhpf.org.uk/recoveryStar.asp). For more qualitative outcome assessment approaches, a range of innovative measures and procedures are available (see www.experiential-researchers.org). For children and young people, probably the best validated family of outcome measures is the Strengths and Difficulties Questionnaire (see www.sdqinfo.org), which has child-, parent- and teacher-completion versions and is available in a range of languages.

Metacommunication: micro-collaboration in action

A further strategy for enhancing the level of collaboration in a counselling relationship is to pay attention to the interplay of intentions and purposes of both client and therapist, in the moment-by-moment flow of the counselling process. This can be accomplished through the use of *metacommunication* (Rennie, 1998). Most of the time, counselling discourse consists of talk about problem-related topics that are of concern to the client. The client talks about something that is bothering them and the counsellor responds. Alternatively, the counsellor may ask questions or initiate a therapeutic intervention and the client responds. Metacommunication refers to moments in the conversation where one or other of the participants stands aside or above ('meta') the flow of conversation and makes some kind of comment about what has been said or done. Metacommunication is communication about communication.

Although the concept of metacommunication originates in the work of one of the founders of interpersonal therapy, Donald Kiesler (1988), its broader significance for therapy practice only came to be appreciated as a result of research carried out by David Rennie (1990, 2002). In these studies, an audio recording was made of a therapy session, and then played back to the client. The client was invited to pause the recording whenever they could recall what they had been thinking or feeling during the actual counselling session, and to report these recollections to an interviewer. What Rennie (2000, 2001) discovered through this technique was that there were three key qualities that characterised the client's experience of the process of therapy. First, clients had a strong sense that, at times, they were on a 'track' – they were talking about something that was meaningful, and knew that what they were discussing was meaningful and would lead somewhere. Second, clients described a strong sense of *agency* or purposefulness – they were aware of their plans and intentions on a moment-by-moment basis. Third, clients described themselves as being highly *reflexive* – they made judgements and found meaning in relation to what was happening. Within this kind of experience, the therapist played a kind of ambiguous role. Sometimes, the therapist would say something, or be present in a useful way, that facilitated their progress down the track that they were following. At other times, the therapist would act in ways that would be confusing or intrusive, and throw them off their track. At yet other times, the client would pretend to respond to unhelpful interventions by the therapist, while covertly pursuing their preferred track. Finally, almost none of this was apparent in the recording of the therapy session. The agency and reflexivity of the client was rarely voiced, with the result that there were many instances where the client and therapist were, in effect, talking at cross purposes. Of course, this kind of experience, or being on a track, being purposeful and reflective, also occurs in the awareness of the therapist, and typically is not voiced on that side either.

Exercise 3.2: What clients don't say

If you currently are, or ever have been, in therapy, take 10 minutes or so to reflect on, or discuss with a partner, the things that you are not saying, or did not say, to your therapist. These could be about your life experiences, about the therapist, or about the relationship between the two of you (note, research suggests that around 50% of clients have kept one or more secrets from their therapists, around half of these being of a sexual nature – Hill, Thompson, Cogar & Denman, 1993). Now spend 10 minutes or so on the following questions:

- As a client, why do/did you not disclose these things to your therapist?
- What might your therapist do/have done to help you feel more able to disclose these things?

Rennie (1998) made a massive contribution to counselling and psychotherapy theory and practice by suggesting that therapists and clients might be able to hold more useful conversations if they were to engage more frequently in metacommunication that brings into the open the hitherto hidden aspects of how each of them was feeling about what was happening, and what they were planning to do about it. Rennie proposed that there are four different types of therapist-initiated metacommunication:

1. The therapist reveals the reasons for their communication.
2. The therapist reveals the impact on them of the client's communication.
3. The therapist enquires into the purpose behind the client's communication.
4. The therapist enquires into the impact on the client of the therapist's communication.

An example of the potential impact of these ways of talking is provided below. The situation that is described arose in John's practice. The client (a young woman who lived away from home and had developed a successful career) was talking about how hard it was for her to stand up to her father when he behaved in a controlling way.

Client: He just insists that we come through for the weekend, no matter what else we might have arranged. There's no way to avoid it. He phones up, and he always just gets what he wants.

Counsellor: And it's just the same as it has always been, ever since you were a little girl.

Client: I know, I just can't do anything about it.

This was not a very effective or helpful interaction in terms of enabling the client to make progress in her relationship with her father. One of the reasons why it was ineffective was that there was a lot unsaid, which could have been brought into the open through the use of metacommunication. In the excerpts that follow, the same interaction is replayed, with the addition in each case of a different form of metacommunication (in italics).

Type 1 metacommunication: The therapist reveals the reasons for their communication

Client: He just insists that we come through for the weekend, no matter what else we might have arranged. There's no way to avoid it. He phones up, and he always just gets what he wants.

Counsellor: And it's just the same as it has always been, ever since you were a little girl. *I was just thinking, as you said that about your dad, that it reminded me about how he was about your music lessons. We have talked a lot about how you can make sense of difficult stuff that's happening now, as a re-run of what is was like as a child.*

New client response: *I know. Yes, that's been useful. But it's not what I want to do today. What I want now is to stay with what happened when he phoned yesterday. I was so angry and I didn't say anything!*

Type 2 metacommunication: The therapist reveals the impact on them of the client's communication

Client: He just insists that we come through for the weekend, no matter what else we might have arranged. There's no way to avoid it. He phones up, and he always just gets what he wants.
Counsellor: And it's just the same as it has always been, ever since you were a little girl.
Client: I know, I just can't do anything about it.
Counsellor: *When you said that, I felt just a bit frustrated. It's like you understand what is happening, and we have talked a lot about what you can do differently, but you seem somehow paralysed. And I feel paralysed too.*
Client: *I... just don't have the will power to stand up to him ... I get angry but I don't have the courage to let him have it.*

Type 3 metacommunication: The therapist enquires into the purpose behind the client's communication

Client: He just insists that we come through for the weekend, no matter what else we might have arranged. There's no way to avoid it. He phones up, and he always just gets what he wants.
Counsellor: *He gets what he wants, and you don't seem to be able to do anything about it [empathic reflection]... what do you want to do now about all that? Do you have a sense of how we could work on that together?*
Client: *Yes, I think so ... it's about how angry I felt last time he called...*

Type 4 metacommunication: The therapist enquires into the impact on the client of the therapist's communication

Client: He just insists that we come through for the weekend, no matter what else we might have arranged. There's no way to avoid it. He phones up, and he always just gets what he wants.
Counsellor: And it's just the same as it has always been, ever since you were a little girl.
Client: I know, I just can't do anything about it.
Counsellor: *Before we move on, I'd like to just check out something, if that's OK. When I said that, just now, about it being just the same as when you were little – I wondered how you felt about what I said. I wondered about whether you were annoyed by what I said – you kind of ignored it and looked away.*
Client: I was a bit annoyed. Not with you so much, but its just that we've talked that one to death. What seems more important to me now is what I felt the last time he called...

In each of these examples, the use of metacommunication contributed to more effective collaboration. The client was able to say that the counsellor's assumption that it would be helpful to do 'meaning-making' work, linking current events to childhood patterns, was not what she wanted to do. And the implied openness on the part of the counsellor, in the form of an invitation to reflect together on what might be helpful allowed the client to acknowledge that what all this was really about was getting angry with her father. The risk, if metacommunication had not been introduced, could have been that the client may have felt obliged to follow the therapist's lead and talk about childhood events that she just did not view as relevant.

The use of metacommunication is a central aspect of a collaborative, pluralistic approach to counselling. It provides a way to begin to access the possibilities that exist at each moment during a therapeutic conversation, in relation to *purposes* and impacts. Expressing purposes is a matter of sharing, from both sides, notions of what might be helpful. Talking about impacts allows evaluation and monitoring of what has been helpful.

Box 3.5: Creating a 'culture of feedback'

From a pluralistic standpoint, dialogue over the goals, tasks and methods of therapy, metacommunication and the use of feedback measures is about far more than just one-off negotiations or discussions. Rather, it is about trying to create a 'culture of feedback' (Duncan & Miller, 2008), whereby the client feels increasingly comfortable in telling the therapist what is helpful, and is not helpful, for them. That is, by inviting clients to give feedback through talking about the kinds of methods they might prefer, or through completing measures (see Box 3.4 on page 45), the hope is that they will come to feel that the therapeutic relationship is one in which the giving (and, perhaps, even receiving) of feedback is acceptable and welcomed.

Building collaborative rituals

A ritual is a routinised sequence of activity that demands the focused attention of participants, and has the function of externalising and reinforcing important dimension of meaning and relationship. All human cultures include their own distinctive healing rituals. It is possible to understand counselling and psychotherapy in this light – as meaningful healing rituals within contemporary society. Therapy occurs in a special place, at a special time, and within a therapy session there will be certain regular features, such as the therapist's opening statement, the sharing of a dream, a phase of two-chair work, the negotiation of a homework assignment. It can be useful to build collaborative rituals into this structure. In the previous section, metacommunication was described as a strategy for enhancing collaboration on a moment-by-moment basis. In addition to this ongoing willingness to engage in dialogue, it is also possible to create predictable moments when both client and therapist know that collaboration around the goals and tasks of therapy will take place. For instance, the use of client feedback tools (see above) can be the basis for collaborative ritual: at the start of a session the client completes an outcome or goals scale, hands it to the therapist, who reads it, and then invites discussion of the implications of the client's answer for their work during the remainder of that session. A similar ritual may take place at the end of the session. Some therapists tell their clients from the outset that they wish to review the progress of the therapy after each set of six sessions. Within some traditions of family therapy and narrative therapy, a reflecting team (Andersen, 1987) may be used to interrupt the flow of client–therapist interaction, and initiate a pause where collaborative reflection will take place. These are just some of the ways in which the intention to work collaboratively can be highlighted and reinforced through the use of rituals.

Box 3.6: Can you metacommunicate too much?

Given the pluralistic assumption that any method has the potential to be both helpful and harmful to clients, even pluralistic methods, such as metacommunication, can be seen as having the potential to get in the way of therapy at times. For instance, a client may feel:

- that too much responsibility is being put on them;
- overwhelmed by the range of possibilities presented;
- that they 'just want to get on with it' and feel frustrated or bored by talking about talking;
- uncomfortable giving such personal feedback to the therapist;
- that they are put on the spot;
- that the therapist's request for feedback is a sign that the therapist 'does not know what they are doing', which may then undermine their confidence in the therapy.

Much more research is needed to find out when metacommunication is, and is not, helpful. However, as with any method, a pluralistic therapist needs to be sensitive to the value that metacommunication seems to be having with a particular client, and be willing to adjust accordingly.

Tailoring the therapeutic relationship

In developing a collaborative relationship with clients, it may also be very important for therapists to be able to vary their style of relating, such that it can most closely match an individual client's needs and preferences. As we have argued in Chapter 2, different clients are likely to vary enormously in their ways of being, such that the kind of therapeutic relationship that one client finds involving and helpful may be experienced by another client as alienating and off-putting. Duncan and colleagues (2004: 35) write: 'there is no single, invariably facilitative, type of relationship', and, drawing on empirical research by Bachelor (1995), they go on to state: 'Some clients want a friendship; some, expert advice; and some, a collaborative endeavour.' Based on such evidence, Arnold Lazarus (1981, 1993, 2005) writes that a genuinely effective therapist needs:

> [A] flexible repertoire of relationship styles and stances to suit different clients' needs and expectations. This would include decisions about the therapist's level of formality and informality, the degree to which he or she discloses personal information, the extent to which the therapist initiates topics of conversation, and in general, when and how to be directive, supportive or reflective. (Lazarus, 1993: 405)

Lazarus (1993) describes such a therapist as an 'authentic chameleon': authentic in the sense that they do not pretend to be a different kind of person with different clients, but chameleon-like in the sense that they are willing to be flexible within the limits of their personality and competences. Lazarus adds to this that, even with the same client, a therapist can be flexible in their style of relating depending on the client's needs at a particular point in time. From a pluralistic standpoint, we might add that a flexible approach to relating means acknowledging that, for some clients, a therapist's relational style may be much more important than to others. In our experiences, for instance, we have worked with clients who are acutely sensitive to each and every relational manoeuvre, while a few clients seem to be relatively nonplussed about our relationship with them.

Recommended reading

Lazarus, A. A. (1993). Tailoring the therapeutic relationship: On being an authentic chameleon. *Psychotherapy, 30* (3), 404–407.

Another term that has been used in the psychotherapy literature to describe this flexible approach to interpersonal relating is 'responsiveness' (Stiles, Honos-Webb, & Surko, 1998). By this, Stiles and colleagues mean a willingness to allow our behaviour to be influenced by the client and the emerging context. They contrast this with a 'ballistic stance' (think of throwing a ball which, once released, carries along its trajectory) in which we carry through on a course of action regardless of the changing nature of our social environment.

So how can a therapist develop their awareness of the kind of relationship that a client wants or needs? One strategy is to try to intuit this from the client's communications and actions, or to try to learn to trust one's inner felt-sense of what a client seems to be wanting. However, what the research tends to show is that therapists, in general, are not particularly good at knowing how their clients' experience or perceive things, especially with respect to the therapeutic relationship (see Cooper, 2008: 2). So although it may be useful for therapists to note, and reflect on, their implicit understandings of what clients want, it may also be very important for them to check this out with clients, and talk explicitly to them about it. This is something that might be most helpfully undertaken in a first session. For instance, a therapist might ask, 'What kind of therapy do you think you'd find most helpful – something challenging and direct, or something more supportive?' Or perhaps, 'I get a sense that you are really looking for a lot of encouragement and reassurance in our relationship, is that right?' If a client has been in therapy previously, this may be a particularly good starting point for finding out what kind of relationship a client is most likely to find helpful or unhelpful. A therapist might ask, for instance, 'What have you found helpful in counselling before?' or 'It sounds like you really valued the relationship where the psychotherapist was challenging with you. Is that something that you are also looking for here?'

Even with such direct communication, however, it can still be difficult for clients to ask for what they want, as research on 'client deference' would seem to suggest (Rennie, 1994). For this reason, inviting clients to complete forms or answer structured questions can also sometimes be helpful – creating a 'third space' in which the client may feel freer to express their genuine preferences. In their Multimodal Life History Inventory, for instance, Lazarus and Lazarus (1991) ask clients, prior to the commencement of therapy, to describe their ideal therapist. Another tool that Mick has been developing, in collaboration with Maria Bowens and David Johnston, is a 'Therapy Personalisation Form' (TPF). An initial version of this is presented in Appendix B (see page 186) and is free for therapists and researchers to copy and use (download from www.pluralistictherapy.com), though practitioners should bear in mind that it is still very much in development. The idea of the TPF is that it is something that can be given to clients at regular intervals during the therapy or prior to a review, for them to reflect on how they are experiencing the therapeutic relationship and whether there are any ways of working that they would prefer. Clients are asked, for instance, to indicate whether they would like the therapist to 'Show their personality and humour more' or 'Be more formal'; 'Be more challenging' or 'Be more gentle'. The dimensions on the measure were developed by asking therapists about the different ways in which they felt they could vary their practice, and are deliberately dichotomised so that clients cannot simply ask for more of everything. A slightly modified version of this, the TPF-A, can also be used at the start of therapy to see what kind of relationship clients might want in the first place.

Here, as with all aspects of the pluralistic approach, it is important to note that the intention with such a tool is not that, once the therapist gets the feedback, they then *comply* with whatever the client wants. Rather, the measure is best considered a 'frame for a conversation' (Chris Evans, personal communication, 2009) – a stimulus for stimulating, or restimulating, a dialogue between therapist and client on what may most meet a client's needs. For instance, Jonah, a client of Mick's, completed the Therapy Personalisation Form at the end of session 30. He indicated that most aspects of the therapy were 'just right' for him, but on Dimension 7 (challenging versus gentle), he indicated that he would like Mick to be a bit more challenging (a score of 2 in that direction). Mick invited Jonah to talk more about his responses at the beginning of the next session, and Jonah clarified that while it wasn't a 'big thing', he would sometimes like to be focused a bit more and not allowed to drift so much. This did not lead to any dramatic shifts in Mick's work with Jonah but, subsequently, Mick *was* quicker to check out with Jonah if he felt Jonah might be going off his point, or if he wasn't quite sure what Jonah was talking about.

Alongside the use of such explicit strategies for tailoring the therapeutic relationship, it can also be very important to pick up on what clients may say or intimate about the kind of therapeutic relationship they would prefer. In the first few sessions with Meena, for instance, Mick felt that it might be useful to share with her some of his own thoughts on how her depression and binge eating seemed to have evolved. During session three, however, Meena said to Mick that she felt interrupted by his 'insights', and at session five she specifically asked him to 'listen more and say less'. For Mick, this was a somewhat bruising experiencing. However, he consciously attempted to adapt his way of working, intervening much less and sticking primarily to close, empathic reflections. As a consequence of this, the therapeutic relationship improved markedly, and Meena began to get much more of what she wanted out of the therapy.

As Mick's experience with Meena demonstrates, it is not always easy to receive feedback from clients – particularly when it is negative – and there is always the danger of responding in defensive or self-justifying ways. Even asking for feedback may be anxiety-evoking for many of us. We may worry, for instance, that clients will think that we are no good, will not like us, or would prefer to see a 'more effective' therapist, and this may make us more reluctant to seek out a client's view. Our personal experience, however, has generally been the opposite. Clients' feedback, in the main, tends to be surprisingly positive, and this has been very useful in reassuring us that our work is along the right lines. And where difficulties or criticisms have been raised, the concrete nature of feedback makes it possible to respond to them and improve our practice – far better than trying to address amorphous and indefinable fears!

What the example of Mick's work with Meena also demonstrates is that, to be able to work with clients in a pluralistic way, it may be necessary for therapists to be aware of their own 'relationship repertoire' (see Exercise 3.3) and find ways to extend the relational possibilities that they offer to clients. There are some models of relationship that can provide useful frameworks to guide this type of personal development. Howard, Nance, and Myers (1987) analyse therapist behaviour in terms of two general dimensions: *directiveness* and *supportiveness*, which combine to form four therapist *relational styles*:

- *High direction/low support.* The therapist is in charge of what is happening. This style is appropriate when the client is unwilling or unable to move him/herself toward the goals of therapy.
- *High direction/high support.* The therapist adopts a teaching/psychoeducational role, in relation to a client who has indicated a willingness to learn. This is a relational style commonly found in CBT approaches.
- *Low direction/high support.* The therapist using this style is essentially accompanying a client who is engaged in a process of exploration and growth. This is the relational style associated with person-centred counselling.
- *Low direction/low support.* The therapist functions mainly as an observer of the client's progress. This relational style is characteristic of classical psychoanalysis.

Research carried out by Howard et al. (1987) has shown that the majority of therapists are comfortable and confident in only one or two of these relational styles. Other valuable relationship models can be found in Clarkson (1990, 1995) and Josselson (1996).

A final point on tailoring the therapeutic relationship is that even the degree of collaboration may need to be adjusted for individual clients. While the research discussed in Chapter 2, for instance, suggests that many clients will appreciate – and benefit from – being collaboratively involved in the shaping of their therapy, there may be others who will do better with a more therapist-led approach. As with shared decision-making in medical settings (see Chapter 2), then, it may be useful to think of collaborative activity as existing on a spectrum: from primarily therapist-led to primarily client-led (Borrell-Carrio, et al., 2004). Here, what may be most important is that the therapist has the flexibility to work from a variety of points on this spectrum, and that they are also sensitive to the level of collaboration that clients may be indicating they want.

Exercise 3.3: *Your* relationship repertoire

1. Look back over the four relational styles identified by Howard et al. (1987). To what extent do you consider yourself comfortable and confident in each of these styles?
2. To explore your relational repertoire in more detail, have a look at the dimensions on the Therapy Personalisation Form in Appendix B. For each one, circle the extent to which you feel you are able to vary your style of relating. For instance, on Dimension 7, if you feel very comfortable working in a gentle way with clients, but really don't like being challenging, draw a circle from the midpoint (0) to 5 (Be more gentle).

Spend 10 minutes or so reflecting on, or discussing with a partner, the relational styles/spectra of practice that you really do not feel comfortable in. What would you do if a client said that they really wanted to work in one of these ways?

Attending to different client and therapist voices

Earlier in this chapter, it was suggested that dialogue implies an openness to the multiplicity of voices 'within' an individual: the various positions that they might take, or areas of experience from which they might speak (see, for instance, Berne, 1961; Mearns & Thorne, 2000; Rowan, 1990; Rowan & Cooper, 1999). From this perspective, responding to a person (or presenting oneself as a therapist) as if they constituted a single, unitary 'voice' may have the effect of closing down collaborative possibilities. The more voices that are included in a conversation, the greater the degree of potential collaboration.

For example, Jenny was a client who described herself as depressed and stuck in her life, and who mainly talked in a rational, rather hesitant manner. She described herself as lacking in energy, and for many sessions this lack of energy was exhibited in the way she talked to her therapist. For John, who was her counsellor, it was easy to respond to this voice with an empathic therapist voice that invited collaboration and exploration around Jenny's goals. This process seemed to be useful to Jenny, in some respects, but did not lead to any significant shift in her sense of herself as depressed and worthless. Over a period of time, some other voices entered the conversation. John found within him a voice that felt a bit more like a caring father than a therapist, and gradually allowed himself to use it. For her part, Jenny occasionally revealed flashes of a 'feisty little girl' voice, that was quite rebellious and naughty, and very occasionally also a hurt and vulnerable voice. Each of these additional voices made a major contribution to the resources available, on both sides, for collaborative action. For example, John's caring parent voice was able to suggest things that might be 'good for' Jenny, while the part of her that entered the dialogue as a naughty little girl was able to stand up to him, and to other authority figures in her life. The emergence of these voices did not mean that their work together came to be dominated by psychodynamic assumptions about childhood experiences. Far from it – Jenny's preferred way of working was primarily centred around the use of CBT-type homework activities. But, through the introduction of different voices, the collaborative discussions around what the homework might consist of, and reviews of its outcomes, became much richer, and somehow more reflective of the whole being of each person.

Helping Clients To Develop Their 'Collaborative Capacity'

In this chapter, we have argued that developing a collaborative therapeutic relationship is essential in ensuring that the client's expertise and understanding are drawn on, such that the therapeutic work is most tailored to meeting their individual wants and needs. However, the development of a collaborative relationship may also be a valuable therapeutic method in itself, helping clients to develop their ability to work effectively in tune with others. Many of the most widely used theories of therapeutic relationships, such as the concept of relational depth (Mearns & Cooper, 2005), refer to this benefit of collaboration – they are focused on enabling the person to develop a general capacity for 'collaborativity,' rather than on actually working side-by-side to make life changes or fulfil therapeutic goals. Further information on these theories can be found in Feltham (1999), Kahn (1997) and McLeod (2009b).

For Meena, for example, a particularly helpful aspect of her therapy was her experience of challenging Mick (see page 52), and feeling that this was heard and responded to. Previously, Meena had tended to bottled up her feelings of frustration and irritation with others, assuming that they would respond punitively to her if she communicated them. This, however, left her feeling powerless, and she would tend to withdraw from relationships on the basis that she could never get what she wanted. Her experience of challenging Mick, then, helped her to feel that she *did* have ways of changing relationships if she was unhappy with them, and consequently she came to feel more confident and willing to relate to others.

As with any therapeutic task (see Chapter 5), not all clients will need to develop their collaborative capacity. There are some clients, for instance, who already possess a well-developed ability to work with others, and are not particularly interested in exploring any barriers to collaboration that might arise in their relationship with their therapist. For these people, renegotiating a working relationship, or readjusting the balance of effort, is quite simple. They are good at this kind of thing. What they are looking for in therapy is someone to act as a support, a catalyst, a devil's advocate, or whatever, while they resolve a problem in their life. By contrast, there are other people who enter counselling who have terrible difficulties around collaborativity. These are people who have developed a deep sense of mistrust of others, whose inner lives are cluttered by voices that they hear, or who have a style of relating to others that is structured around control and coercion. For these clients, there may need to be a lot of attention devoted to questions such as 'How are we going to communicate with each other?' or 'How do we decide what to do?' The majority of people who enter counselling are somewhere in the middle of this spectrum – they basically know how to collaborate with others, but occasionally get into difficulty.

It should not be underestimated, however, how hard it can be to help clients develop their collaborative and relational capacities. People with major difficulties in relating to others (sometimes diagnosed as 'borderline personality disorder') tend not to exhibit much change following counselling or psychotherapy (Castonguay & Beutler, 2006a). Why is this? There is some evidence that people who benefit most from therapy are more likely to be those who already possess a fair capacity for collaborativity, at least in the sense of possessing quite strong social networks or using talking to others as a coping mechanism (see Cooper, 2008: Chapter 4). While it may be, then, that some people who really need to learn about how to relate to others (at least in the eyes of those who know them) may benefit from an in-depth therapeutic relationship, others may be more likely to find an answer using alternative approaches, rather than looking for a 'talking cure'.

Summary

At the heart of a pluralistic approach to counselling and psychotherapy is a commitment to a mutually involved, collaborative client–therapist relationship, based on dialogue. There are many practical steps that therapists can take to enhance this level of collaboration. Therapists can provide clients with pre-therapy information; regularly invite clients to reflect on, and review, the therapeutic work; negotiate over different aspects of the therapeutic frame; and review and discuss with clients their progress in therapy. Within the pluralistic approach, communicating about the process of communication – metacommunication – is also considered a valuable means of enhancing levels of collaboration, as is tailoring the therapeutic relationship to the individual client. Collaboration is not only important because it draws on, and utilises, clients' expertise, but because it can help clients develop their capacity to collaborate with others in everyday life.

Questions for reflection and discussion

1. To what extent do you agree with the view that a collaborative client–therapist relationship is essential to effective therapy? If you think it is important, Why?
2. What factors do you think are most likely to facilitate a collaborative relationship between client and therapist? What factors do you think are most likely to get in the way?
3. How do you feel about asking clients to complete outcome measures at every session and reviewing progress? What do you see as the value of such a practice and in what ways do you think it has the potential to negatively effect therapy?

4 Client Goals: The Starting Point for Therapy

This chapter discusses:

- The reasons why clients' goals are the orientating point for pluralistic thinking and practice.
- What goals are, and how they can be related to each other.
- The different kinds of goals that clients can have for therapy.
- How therapists can help clients to articulate their goals.
- The therapeutic value of goal dialogue.

In the pluralistic approach developed in this book, the most basic starting point is clients' goals: what individuals *want* from their lives and from the therapeutic work. This starting point arises out of the humanistic, progressive philosophy on which this pluralistic approach is based (see Chapter 2). A pluralistic perspective regards one of the core characteristics of human experience as that of having a sense of an intended or preferred future, and of striving to create a meaningful and rewarding life. Of course, different people may have very different ideas about what a meaningful and rewarding life might look like. But all people organise their lives around some sense of a future, however vague that image might be. There are many words that can be used to describe this dimension of human life: wants, dreams, striving, desire, purpose, self-actualisation, becoming, integration, and other terms. In pluralistic therapy, the concept of 'goal' is used as a means of referring to this key aspect of lived experience.

As we have seen in Chapter 2, outcomes in therapy tend to be best when client and therapist have a shared understanding of the goals for therapy. There is also good evidence that people are more productive when they work towards specific, and relatively challenging, goals (Locke & Latham, 2002). However, these are not the central reasons why client's goals are the *starting point* for a pluralistic approach. Rather, it is because it is only by orienting themselves to what the client wants that a therapist can begin to work in a collaborative way. This is not to assume that clients arrive in therapy with clearly articulated goals that can readily be translated into therapeutic tasks. Far from it. One of the most common difficulties that clients report at the outset of therapy is that they feel 'stuck' in their lives, and have lost sight of what a better future might look like. Other clients have been so oppressed and silenced in their lives that they hardly believe that they can be allowed to want anything, or to put their wants into words. But even those clients who struggle to articulate their goals for therapy have still made their way to the therapy room for some reason. People do not stumble into counselling and therapy appointments by accident – there is always some kind of hope for a better future.

This chapter begins by explaining why the concept of goal is a core element of a pluralistic approach to therapy. It then goes on to look at what goals actually are and the different dimensions along which they can vary. The next part of the chapter considers the pragmatics of working with client goals in therapy – something which has received surprisingly scant attention previously (Strong, 2009). The chapter closes by reviewing the therapeutic value of talking about goals.

Why Goals are Central to a Pluralistic Approach

Thinking about therapy in terms of goals reflects four important themes within a pluralistic perspective on therapy. First, as discussed above, seeing therapy as goal-orientated implies a particular concept of the person: as an active *agent*, engaged in constructing their lives and relationships. Second, a focus on the *client's* goals is a reminder that the client is a separate other person, with their own views. Third, working in an explicit goal-orientated way represents a deliberate *ethical* stance, around informed consent. Finally, paying attention to goals is a *pragmatic* strategy for activating the resource and energies of the client. These facets of goal-orientated therapy are expanded in the following sections.

In emphasising the importance of goals, a pluralistic therapy practice is not seeking to deny the relevance and value of times when the focus of therapy is on the immediate process that is taking place in the therapy room; or on the more spontaneous processes of growth and change that a client may undergo. Indeed, as Michalak and Holtforth (2006: 359) write, 'when the therapist single-mindedly fixates on a certain goal, he or she runs the risk of losing contact with the here-and-now experience of the therapeutic situation'. Pluralism is not a philosophy of 'either/or', but instead invites inclusion, of 'both/and'. Thus, in some therapies, there may be quite long periods when goals are not explicitly mentioned. However, if goals are *never* mentioned, it may be that a vital aspect of the client's experience is being excluded from consideration.

The agentic client

The pluralistic approach is rooted in a desire to conceptualise, and engage with, people in deeply valuing and respectful ways. For this reason, it starts from the assumption that people are active, agentic, choice-making beings, and not passive 'sponges' that simply soak up the world around them. Here, then, is an understanding of people as beings who act towards their future in purposeful ways, and this understanding puts people's goals as a central orientating element of their being. This is not, of course, to suggest that everything people do is consciously thought out, planned and implemented with military precision – in many cases, people's goals will be vague, poorly worked out, and possibly unconscious (see below). It is also not to suggest that the value of any activity comes from whether or not it reaches its 'objective': in many instances, what people do on the way will be far more important. What it does assume, though, is that people are essentially *meaning-ful* beings (Frankl, 1986): that they are always orientated towards some end.

Exercise 4.1: Exploring your own goals in life

1. Working on your own, or with a partner, take 15 minutes or so to think about what, for you, are the main goals in your life. Below are some possibilities that you may wish to consider:

- happiness;
- being loved by people;
- a vibrant and full existence;
- being a powerful leader;
- becoming financially secure;
- fame;
- duty;
- making the world a better place ;
- achieving spiritual enlightenment;
- making the most of your potential;
- feeling good about yourself;
- freedom from anxiety and worry;
- having good relationships with others;
- being closer to God;
- making others feel loved and cared for.

2. How would it be, or is it, for you to work with clients who have similar goals?
3. Now read back over the above list and note which goals, if any, you feel somewhat judgemental or critical towards. How would it be for you to work with clients who held those goals as most important in their lives?

Privileging the client's perspective

A second reason why *clients'* goals are an orientating point within the pluralistic approach is because, from this ethical standpoint, there is a desire to privilege the client's perspective – including their views on what makes life meaningful and satisfying for them – over and above those of the therapist. This means that, within a pluralistic approach, the orientation of the therapeutic work is towards what the individual client wants it to be, and not towards any goals that the therapist holds for the client or believes to be valid for all individuals (whether this is rational thinking, actualisation, or spiritual awakening). This is not to suggest that therapists' beliefs about what clients may need, want or find helpful cannot play a valuable part in the therapeutic process but, from this standpoint, they must always be *in the service of* helping to articulate the *client's* wants. Here, it may be worth remembering Bohart and Tallman's (1999: 16) metaphor of the therapist-as-home-decorating-consultant (see Chapter 2): someone who can facilitate, advise and encourage their client, but would be going well beyond their role if they started to tell their clients what kind of décor they actually wanted.

Given this emphasis on helping to clarify the client's goals, a useful developmental exercise for therapists may be to spend some time thinking about *their* own goals in life, and how these may get in the way of, or facilitate, an understanding of their client's goals (see Exercise 4.1).

Recommended reading

Brian Little is a psychologist who has developed a methodology for exploring the structure of what he calls 'personal projects' (everyday life goals). Guidelines for using this technique, along with relevant research articles, can be found on his website: www.brianrlittle.com. An example of how this way of thinking about goals can be applied in therapy can be found in K. Samelo-Aro (1992). Struggling with self: The personal projects of students seeking psychological counselling. *Scandinavian Journal of Psychology, 33*, 330–338.

This emphasis on starting with clients', rather than therapists', goals also means that diagnoses (e.g., 'major depression', 'generalised anxiety disorder,' 'substance abuse disorder') take a secondary role in the pluralistic approach. This makes it quite different from an 'evidence-based' practice standpoint (e.g., National Institute for Health and Clinical Excellence, 2009), which holds that clients should be 'treated' according to the therapies that have been shown to be effective for their 'disorders'. Here, from a pluralistic standpoint, the question is not 'What do diagnosticians think is best for a person?' but 'What does the person himself or herself want?' Of course, a person may want to be treated in a way that clinical diagnosticians recommend, and this is entirely in keeping with a pluralistic approach; but they may also not want that, and a pluralistic approach holds open this possibility. The fact that clients within any one diagnostic grouping often exhibit very different therapeutic goals (see Box 4.1 on page 61) supports the argument that we should be wary of orientating therapy exclusively around a client's diagnosis.

Box 4.1: Do clients with the same diagnoses have the same therapeutic goals?

Research suggests that clients with the same diagnosis may want quite different things from therapy. For instance, Rajkarnikar (2009) looked at the specific problems that clients diagnosed with social anxiety wanted to work on in therapy, through an analysis of their responses to the Personal Questionnaire problem description form (Elliott, Shapiro & Mack, 1999, see page 73). Across 24 participants, she found 207 different problems, with around half of the problems rated by external judges as 'definitely not' related to social anxiety. When these problems were coded into 21 categories, 'Low self-esteem and confidence' was found to be the most common type of problem that clients wanted to work on, but even this was figural for only 87.5% of clients. Meanwhile, 'typical' social anxiety problems, such as avoiding social interaction and performance anxiety were relevant to 62.5% and 50% of clients respectively, while around 10–20% of clients wanted to work on problems like sexuality issues, work-related problems or irritability. This suggests, then, that clients under a similar diagnostic label can demonstrate considerable heterogeneity in what they want, and find helpful, from therapy.

A study of clients' therapeutic goals in a Swiss university outpatient clinic found much the same thing (Holtforth & Grawe, 2002). Moreover, while this study found that clients' goals were strongly influenced by their diagnosis (for instance, depressed clients were more likely than anxious clients to set goals around their current relationship), there was considerable similarity in goals *across* diagnostic groupings, with many of the clients' goals unrelated to their particular diagnosis. Holtforth and Grawe (2002: 96) conclude from their research that, 'therapists should be well prepared to deal with the full range of treatment goals because patients present with combinations of treatment goals, not only with single or isolated goals'.

From a standpoint which aims to privilege a client's perspective, it is also essential to find out what clients want from therapy (if anything) because, without that, a therapist has no way of knowing whether or not the therapy is likely to be helpful. This is different from many mainstream therapeutic perspectives, including more humanistic approaches, such as person-centred therapy (Rogers, 1957), which tend to hold that their therapeutic stance will, necessarily, bring about therapeutic personality change, provided that certain basic conditions are fulfilled. From a pluralistic stance, however, every therapeutic method has the potential to be harmful as well as helpful, and the therapist cannot know this in advance. So finding out what a client wants, and seeing whether the methods that the therapist can offer fit with this, is an essential first step in beginning therapeutic work.

The client's right to choose

A third reason why the pluralistic framework orientates itself around clients' wants – and not their thoughts, feelings or actions – is because this may be the most direct way of engaging with, and responding to, their rights as self-determined, agentic subjectivities. In other words, if we want to work with people in a way that deeply respects their being, it would seem essential to respect, and respond, to what they ask for. The more that these wants are ignored, sidelined, or treated as secondary to their emotions, cognitions or behaviours, the more we are moving away from an acknowledgment of the Other as a human being with the capacity, and right, to self-determination towards a more paternalistic standpoint (see Isaiah Berlin, Chapter 2).

A strengths-based approach

A fourth reason why the pluralistic approach orientates itself around clients' *goals*, as opposed to their diagnoses, problems or pathologies (e.g., Pinsof, 2005), is because it is a somewhat more positive reading of where clients are at, which leaves greater room for appreciating their potentialities and possibilities. Here, the question is not 'What is wrong with a client?' but 'Where are they trying to get to?' Of course, in many instances, what clients want to achieve is to get rid of their problem, and these are entirely legitimate goals within the pluralistic approach. However, by starting with goals, it also becomes possible to acknowledge and conceptualise therapeutic wants that may be less problem-centred and more growth-orientated (Rowan, 2004): for instance, 'I want to develop my creativity', or 'I'd like to look at ways of making my relationship and sex life even better'.

The Nature of Goals

Goals can be defined as 'a projected state of affairs that a person or a system plans or intends to achieve' (Wikipedia, 2009). Goals may be conscious and deliberately chosen (for instance, 'I've decided that I will lose weight for next summer'), or we may barely be aware of them (for instance, 'I desperately want everyone to love me'). Either way, for a range of existential and humanistic theorists (e.g., Bohart, 2001; Frankl, 1986; Heidegger, 1962) – as well as leading cognitive psychologists (e.g., Carver & Scheier, 1990; Markus & Nurius, 1986) and integrative therapists (e.g., Beitman, Soth, & Bomby, 2005) – they are one of the key determinants of our thoughts, feelings and behaviours, underlying everything that we experience and do.

The structure of goals

For cognitive theorists such as Carver and Scheier (1990), who have developed Powers' (1973) 'control theory', human goals can be conceptualised as existing in a hierarchical structure. That is, we have 'higher order' goals and 'lower order' goals, with the latter acting as strategies by which we strive to achieve the former. For instance, if your immediate

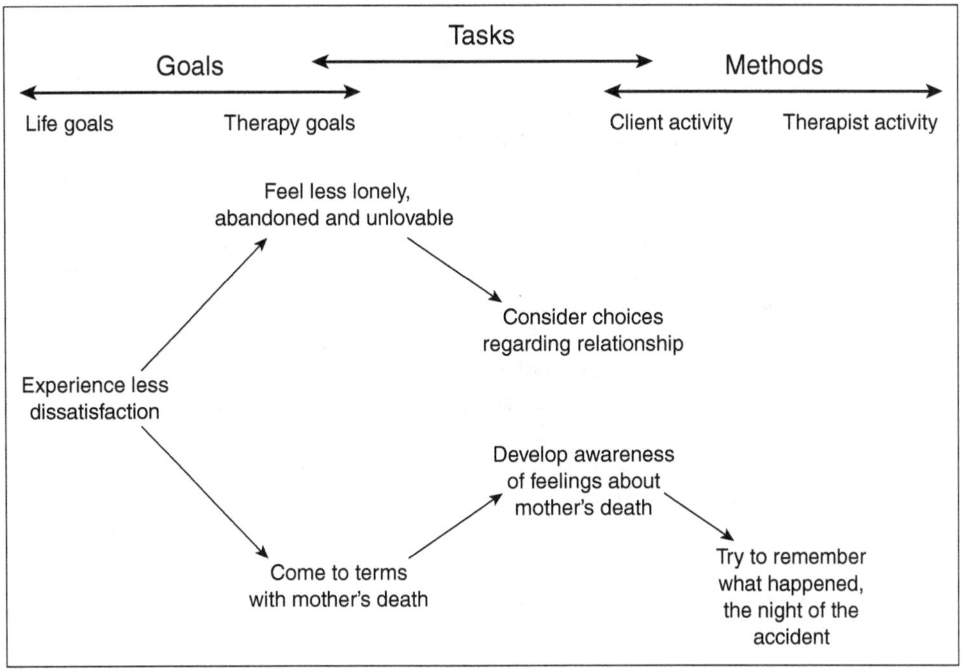

Figure 4.1: Neville's goals, sub-goals and sub-sub-goals

goal is to learn about the pluralistic approach, this might be in the service of a higher order goal, such as successfully completing your counselling training; and this might, itself, be in the service of an even higher order goal, such as doing a meaningful job – which is, then, a means of trying to achieve the highest order goal of living a satisfying life.

Such a structure can be useful when we think about clients and what they might want from therapy. For instance, Neville was a young man who, at the highest level of goals, wanted to experience less unhappiness and dissatisfaction in his life. How did he want to achieve this in therapy? By feeling less lonely, abandoned and unlovable, and by coming to terms with the death of his mother when he was young. This, then, set the goals for his ongoing therapeutic work. For instance, to help Neville come to terms with the death of his mother, he worked on developing his awareness of how he had felt, as a child, about his mother's death in a car crash; and to help him feel less lonely in his life, he worked on developing his understanding of what choices he could make with respect to his partner, with whom he was having an 'on-off' relationship. For each of these sub-goals, there were then 'sub-sub-goals' that Neville worked on. For instance, to explore how he felt about his mother's death, he focused on trying to remember, as accurately as he could, what happened the night he was told about her death. Such a hierarchy of goals is another way of thinking about the goals/tasks/methods domain structure of the pluralistic framework, as introduced in Chapter 1 (Figure 1.2 on page 11): clients have goals, tasks are ways of achieving these goals, and methods are ways of achieving these tasks. Note, as indicated in this map, we think it is sometimes useful to distinguish between higher order 'life goals' and those goals that may be more specific to the therapeutic context ('therapy goals') (Mackrill, in press).

As with all pluralistic work, it is important to note that, in reality, the exploration and negotiation of these goals and sub-goals is vastly more intricate, complex and subtle than this analysis might suggest. For instance, the therapist (Mick) did not begin the work by saying, 'OK, so your goal is to feel more lovable, what sub-goal could we work on so that you can achieve that target state?' Rather, an awareness of what the client wanted from therapy and some discussion of how Neville might get there served as a very loose map to help orientate the work, and to try to ensure that Neville got out of therapy what he wanted.

Both across clients and within clients, as in the case of Neville, the pluralistic approach assumes that multiple goals may exist. Some of these may be synthesisable, or reducible down to a smaller number of higher order goals (perhaps even one), but the pluralistic approach holds open the possibility that, at the highest level, a person may have a diversity of mutually non-reducible goals. This is consistent with the psychological research that suggests that people tend to have several, often unrelated, core meanings in their lives (Baumeister, 1991) as opposed to one single, 'grand' or integrative 'higher meaning'. It is also consistent with many therapists' everyday clinical observations, in which clients may present with 'several very heterogeneous goals' (Holtforth & Grawe, 2002: 80). Indeed, one study at a university psychotherapy clinic found that clients had between one and eight goals for therapy, usually of quite different types, with an average of 3.25 per client (Holtforth & Grawe, 2002).

In a situation where a client has identified multiple goals, it may be helpful to explore whether any of these goals are contradictory, or in tension with each other. For example, Ian was a client who described three main goals at the start of therapy: (i) leaving his wife and finding a more satisfying relationship with someone else; (ii) being a better Dad for his children; and (iii) getting a better-paid job. In exploring the feasibility of using therapy to pursue these goals, Ian realised that his career-change goal was less of a priority for him at that moment, and also that the distress and frustration in his life arose from the fact that he regarded goals (i) and (ii) as being mutually incompatible. For Ian, therefore, a core theme in therapy centred around not how certain goals might be achieved, but on the meaning and implications of making a choice between two goals, each of which reflected deeply-held yet (for him) incompatible values.

Unconscious goals

In working with a client's goals, it is important to recognise that there may be direction and purpose in a person's life of which they are not consciously aware. This is not to disregard the significance of the goals that a person is able to put into words, but to suggest that in some instances there may be intentions that are implicit in a person's actions, and which they may only come to appreciate over time. Psychodynamic perspectives on therapy, and in particular the concept of *transference* and *countertransference*, can provide valuable conceptual tools in terms of being able to identify implicit or unconscious goals. Jennifer was a client who had been sexually abused in childhood, and wished to use therapy to help her to come to terms with what had happened, and to get rid of painful and frightening memories of what had happened. Over the course of several months, however, Jennifer seemed to find it hard to commit herself to therapy. Although she said that she liked her therapist, and was satisfied with the way that the therapist was working with her problems, she still missed several sessions, and on occasion could be quite sarcastic towards her therapist, or remain silent and withdrawn for lengthy periods. At the same time, the therapist had a strong sense that it was essential that she should remain consistently accepting and caring in her responses to Jennifer, no matter what the provocation. Eventually, the therapist invited Jennifer to consider the possibility that some 'testing out' might be taking place, and if it was, then what it might mean. What emerged from this discussion was an appreciation on both sides that Jennifer wanted a relationship in which she could feel unequivocally valued and 'special', and was trying to find out whether her therapist was someone who could provide this. Up until that conversation, the idea that 'finding a relationship in which I can feel valued and special' had not been a goal that Jennifer would have been capable of putting into words. However, once verbalised, it made a lot of sense to her, and then could join her other therapy goals in informing the work that she and her therapist would do together.

Recommended reading

The following papers provide clear examples of how to understand and work with unconscious goals in therapy:

Bugas, J., & Silberschatz, G. (2000). How patients coach their therapists in psychotherapy. *Psychotherapy, 37*, 64–70.

Curtis, J. T., et al. (1988). Developing reliable psychodynamic case formulations: An illustration of the plan diagnosis method. *Psychotherapy*, *25*, 256–265.

Approach goals versus avoidance goals

It can be useful to think about goals as existing on an 'approach–avoidance' continuum, or in terms of 'positive' and 'negative' goals. A positive or approach-orientated goal is something that a person is striving to achieve, for example, 'to ask someone out on a date' or 'to be able to take a flight on a plane'. By contrast, a negative or avoidance goal refers to some kind of event or state the person is seeking *not* to happen, for example 'to be less anxious', 'to get out of my marriage'. Negative/avoidance goals can be understood as descriptions of *problems*, whereas positive/approach goals can be viewed as descriptions of solutions or possibilities. At the start of therapy, clients usually talk about what they want in terms of problems. This is because their life at that point is experienced as 'problematic' – they are distressed by something, and want that unpleasant situation to end or be resolved in some way. However, on the whole, therapy is not particularly effective at *stopping* things, or assisting a person to *not* do something. Almost all effective therapy techniques aim to enable the person to construct new understandings and patterns of behaviour, in other words to be helped to move towards positive goals. In one study, Elliot and Church (2002) found that clients who made mainly avoidance statements at the start of therapy had poorer eventual outcomes than those who articulated their aims for therapy mainly in terms of approach goals.

One of the implications of the approach–avoidance distinction is to remind us that, in the early part of therapy, clients may find it hard to engage with the notion of positive goals. From a pluralistic perspective, it may not be helpful to *expect* clients to be able at the outset to engage in 'goal-attainment scaling', where they identify their intended outcomes or targets for therapy, specify the behaviours that will indicate steps on the road to achieving these targets, and then make ratings of progress on a week-by-week basis. This kind of structured goal-driven therapy, which is outlined in Cytrynbaum, Ginath, Birdwell, and Brandt (1979) and Kiresuk, Smith, and Cardillo (1994) may be appropriate for some clients, and welcomed by them. For other clients, the requirement to identify goals and targets may be experienced as irrelevant and even oppressive, because it does not reflect where they are in relation to their process of change. Similarly, any approach that is wholly *problem-focused*, and does not allow clients scope to view their therapy aims in terms of positive goals, likewise runs the risk of failing to be sensitive to individual needs and preferences. From a pluralistic perspective, it is important to give permission for both positive and negative goals to be explored.

Achievability of goals

A further dimension to be taken into account, when considering a client's goals, is the degree to which they are achievable in therapy. For example, some goals are not achievable because they require other people to change. Joe, a 15 year-old schoolboy, came into counselling because he wanted a group of kids in the playground to stop bullying him. Jeff, a 50 year-old man, came into counselling because he wanted his wife to pay more attention to him. In both cases, using these goals as a guide to what might happen in therapy would have lead to frustration or failure. Joe and Jeff, and their counsellors needed to reframe these goals in terms of outcomes that they could accomplish through their own actions ('being able to stand up to the bullies'; 'being able to ask my wife for what I want from the relationship'). Other goals that are sometimes mentioned by clients are not achievable because they require help from a completely different kind of source. For example, Jack stated that one of his goals for therapy was 'to be able to get rid of the evil spirits that lived in his house'. His therapist was not willing to work with this goal. As far as the therapist was concerned, there were specialists in exorcism who might be able to help Jack with evil spirits. As a therapist, it could be that he might have a role to play in supporting Jack in contacting an exorcist. But the actual exorcism was well outside his area of competence. Finally, there are goals that are not achievable because they are too hard. Jonah was terrified about a job interview he had the following day, and wanted to be able to feel completely relaxed about it. This goal was not realistic, given the time that was available. Other clients can have a problem that they not only want to learn to cope with, but to completely eliminate from their life. For example, Jerry had a longstanding, severe drink problem and wanted to be able to drink what he wanted, when he wanted, without fear of going on a bender. Jerry's therapist was unwilling to agree to this goal because, based on his personal experience and reading of the research evidence, the chance of success was too low.

Within a pluralistic orientation, the issue of achievability of goals acts as a reminder that therapy is a collaborative activity. It is not helpful for a client if their therapist believes that the goals that they have identified are unrealistic and unachievable, but then keeps their mouth shut. With some clients, the issue of 'setting oneself up to fail' or 'never being good enough' can represent major life themes, with the result that the very act of talking about the achievability of their goals, in a way that is challenging as well as empathic, can be highly facilitative.

The narrative context of therapy goals

In this chapter, and in much therapy practice, therapy goals are usually described through summary labels, such as 'get myself to let go of the past' or 'moving on from anger and thoughts of self-harm'. These labels can be regarded as functioning as a shorthand title for a much more detailed story that the client has told about how their problem or goal is embedded in a particular life situation. It is vital for a therapist to be curious about the meaning of any goal statements that a client makes, because it is likely that the 'headline title' has a complex set of meanings that are known by the client, but may only be dimly perceived by the therapist. For example, when Andy was asked in an initial assessment interview to summarise his goals for counselling, he said that what he wanted was to 'move on from anger and thoughts of self-harm'. For Andy, this statement was meaningful in ways that his therapist only began to appreciate after several weeks. For instance, the idea of 'moving on' reflected Andy's sense of his life as a journey, the anger referred to certain patterns in his relationship with his partner, and 'self-harm' was about his long-term struggle to live with a debilitating health condition (self-harm meant 'not looking after myself well enough'). In other words, the meaning of his therapy goal could only be understood in the context of his life story as a whole.

Recommended reading

White, M. (2007). *Maps of Narrative Practice.* New York: W.W. Norton (pp. 27–37). A fascinating discussion of the suggestion that therapists should be willing to act as 'investigative reporters' in their efforts to make explicit the implicit meaning in the ways in which clients talk about their problems and goals.

The goal horizon

The goals that a person holds can be viewed as reflecting their horizon or boundary of what is possible. The goal defines what is imaginable for them. Once the person gets close to accomplishing a goal, then whatever lies over that horizon, or on the other side of that boundary, begins to become visible or imaginable. One client, Margaret, felt desperately alone because she and her husband seemed to have grown apart over the years as a result of the stresses of combining work and childcare. Margaret's goal for therapy was to be able to get close to her husband again, and enjoy his company. Her therapy worked out well for her, and she found what she needed to do to re-establish contact with her husband and life partner. As this piece of therapeutic work came to a close, however, she began to be aware of the emergence of another issue, another horizon – the question of her commitment to her own spirituality. At the start of her therapy, the question of spirituality was far from Margaret's thoughts, even if an outside observer who knew something about the course of her life might have been curious about what had happened to diminish an active spiritual quest that had been meaningful for Margaret in her early adult life.

There are two implications for therapists of the concept of the goal horizon. First, it is not useful to get 'too far ahead' of clients, in the sense of trying to anticipate what might come next for them. Better to take things one at a time. Second, one of the surest indicators of when a client has accomplished what they need to do in relation to a therapy goal is that they start to talk about something else.

The ideas introduced in this section – goal structure, conscious–unconscious, approach–avoidance, achievability, narrative context, and goal horizon – are not intended to be understood as comprising a 'theory of goals' or a model of how to work with goals. Instead, they are offered as *sensitising* concepts – ways of conceptualising goals that may contribute to the capacity to engage in facilitative conversations around the meaning of goals for clients (and their therapists). Further distinctions and evidence from the psychological field (see Box 4.2 below) can also be useful when therapists start to think about what kind of goals to set with clients.

Box 4.2: What makes goal-setting effective?

Over the last four decades, Edwin Locke and colleagues, American psychologists, have undertaken an extensive programme of research into goals and goal-setting, and many of their findings are of relevance to the therapeutic setting of goals. Their principal findings, summarised in Locke and Latham (2002) are as follows:

The setting of goals can lead to improved performance because it:

- directs attention towards goal-relevant activities;
- energises people;
- prolongs effort;
- leads people to discover and use task-relevant strategies and knowledge.

In addition, research indicates that the setting of goals is most likely to be effective when:

- the goal is *challenging* (unless this becomes too anxiety-evoking);
- the goal is *specific* rather than vague;
- people are *committed* to achieving the goal;
- the goal is seen as being *important*;
- the *rationale* for the goal is clear;
- the goal is *close by* and achievable, rather than far away;
- the goal is *consistent* with a person's genuine values, wants and personal needs ('self-concordant'), rather than being driven by external demands or internal feelings of guilt or embarrassment;

- a person's goals are *not in conflict* with one another;
- *feedback* is given on progress in relation to the goal;
- an action plan is formulated to achieve the goal (see Tasks, Chapter 5).

(Cox & Klinger, 2002; Koestner, Lekes, Powers & Chicoine, 2002; Locke & Latham, 2002; Michalak & Martin Grosse, 2006).

What Kind of Goals do People Have?

According to *therapists* in the Collaborative Research Network of the Society for Psychotherapy Research (Orlinsky & Rønnestad, 2005d; see also Chapter 1), the goal that is most important to help clients realise is 'Have a strong sense of self-worth and identity' (Orlinsky & Rønnestad, 2005d: 227). This is followed by 'Improve the quality of their relationships' and 'Understand their feelings, motives and/or behavior', with 'Develop courage to approach new or previously avoided situations' also frequently endorsed. In addition, more experienced therapists felt it was important to help clients achieve a goal of integrating 'excluded or segregated aspects of experience'.

In contrast, a detailed taxonomy of *clients'* goals for therapy was developed by Holtforth and Grawe (2002). They analysed the treatment goals, as jointly defined by therapists and clients, from around 300 clients over about 20 years at the University of Bern therapy outpatient clinic. Twenty-three goals were identified, which could be categorised into five main types of goal: Interpersonal goals, Coping with specific problems and symptoms, Personal growth, Wellbeing and functioning, and Existential issues. Figure 4.2 gives the percentages of clients who presented with each of these goals. As can be seen here, outpatient clients, most frequently, presented with goals of an interpersonal type (though Coping with specific problems and symptoms was most common for an inpatient sample – Holtforth, Reubi, Ruckstuhl, Berking, & Grawe, 2004), with the most frequent specific goals, in descending order, being to do with assertiveness, fears or anxiety, connectedness/intimacy, current relationship and attitude towards self. A similar study in a UK primary care population again found that clients' most common goals for therapy were either to do with Coping with specific problems and symptoms, or of an Interpersonal nature (McBeath, 2007).

In an earlier study, Braaten (1989) constructed a questionnaire of personal development goals, with five goal dimensions:

- *Interpersonal dependency*. Sample statements: stop blaming others too much, become more responsible for myself;
- *Interpersonal intimacy*: express positive feelings more freely towards others, feel freer physically to touch others;
- *Social assertiveness*: dare to state my case more assertively with others, learn to express anger more spontaneously;
- *Self-individuation*: learn to appreciate quiet reflection by myself, stop escaping the freedom to be myself;
- *Self-acceptance*: become more self-accepting, stop condemning myself when I fail.

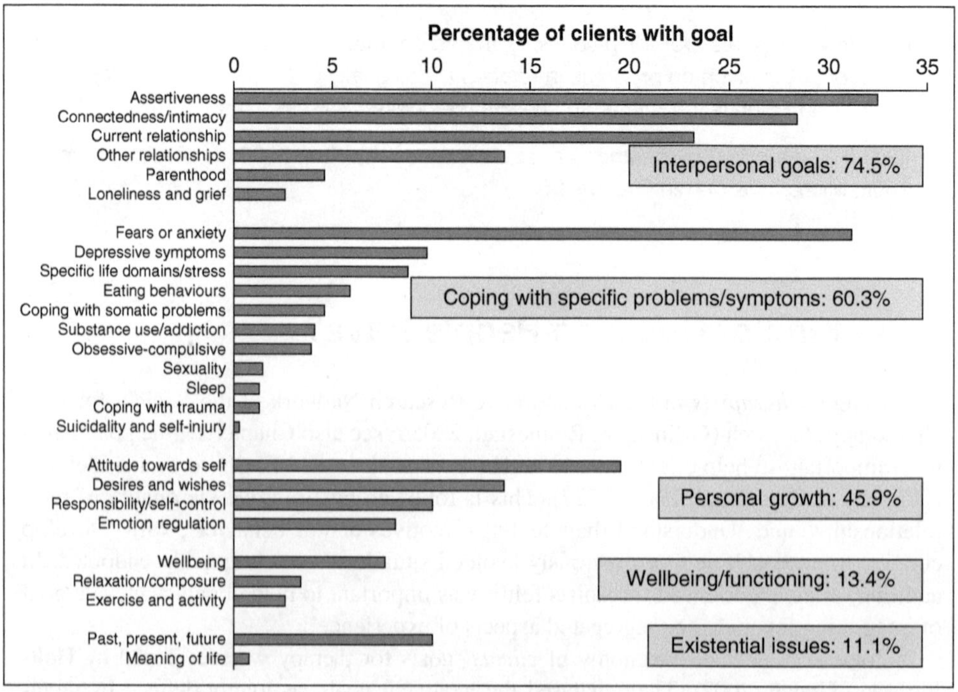

Figure 4.2: Taxonomy and frequency of clients' goals for therapy (source: Holtforth & Grawe, 2002)

Exercise 4.2: What goals can you help a client to achieve?

Working in pairs or on your own, take 10 minutes or so to think about the goals that you, as a therapist, are most able to help your client achieve (you may want to use the list of goals in Exercise 4.1 on page 59 as a starting point). Now take another 15 minutes or so to see if you can map out the different things that you can offer to clients to help them achieve these goals (for instance, listening intently so that they can develop greater self-awareness).

Braaten (1989) found that both people receiving treatment for mental health problems and those who were designated as 'healthy controls', reported similar personal development goal profiles. The difference between those participants with psychological problems and those who lead satisfying lives was not that they had different personal goals, but that the latter were more comfortable and confident around the degree to which they had been able to attain these goals.

The research into personal goals demonstrates that there exists a rich vocabulary for talking about goals. This vocabulary encompasses a set of goals that are linked to symptom relief in respect of psychological problems such as anxiety or depression, but is clearly much wider in scope. From a pluralistic perspective, then, the language of goals enables clients who find meaning in psychiatric categories to make use of these ideas when identifying their goals (e.g., 'my goal in therapy is to become less depressed'), while also creating an appropriate conversational space for clients who do not view their difficulties in psychiatric terms. Finally, compared to standardised symptom checklists and questionnaires such as the CORE–OM or the BDI–II, a language of goals allows clients to express their troubles in a form that is personalised and flexible.

The Process of Working With Client Goals

Allowing therapy to be informed by the client's goals is not a one-off activity that takes place at the beginning of counselling. Instead, it is better viewed as a *process* that changes shape and focus at different points during therapy. Indeed, research indicates that many clients are likely to develop new goals over time (Schulte-Bahrenberg & Schulte, 1993). In this respect, it can be helpful to adopt an attitude of being *mindful* of the client's goals. Even when what is happening in a therapy session may not have been explicitly negotiated in terms of its relevance to the client's goals, it can be valuable for both therapist and client to retain a background awareness of the intended direction of travel that has been agreed.

Helping clients to articulate their goals

Research suggests that therapists and clients can 'operate on very different wavelengths as far as their ideology about goals for therapy' (Dimsdale, Klerman & Shershow, 1979: 3). For example, Dimsdale and colleagues found that psychiatric staff in an inpatient setting consistently ranked 'insight' as the most important goal for therapy, while the clients themselves ranked this as *least* important, instead prioritising adaptation and symptom relief.

This means that a therapeutic approach which orientates itself around clients' goals needs to ensure that, right from the very start of therapy, clients have an opportunity to talk about what they want from it and that 'goal metacommunication' (see Chapter 3) takes place. This may happen naturally. For instance, a client may say in their first session that what they want from therapy is a chance to feel less anxious and to have better relationships with their partners. However, in many instances, clients may not, spontaneously, say what they want from therapy or from their lives. This may be for a number of reasons: they may feel that it is inappropriate, irrelevant or rude to tell the therapist what they want; they may assume that the therapist knows what they want or need; they may not be aware of what they want; or they may have so many things that they want to get off their chest, or be so overwhelmed with anxiety, that what they want from life and from therapy is of little salience.

In such circumstances, it is unlikely to be helpful for a therapist to push the question of what a client wants from life or from therapy. Research indicates that one of the most important tasks at the beginning of therapy is to help clients feel welcomed and understood (Cooper, 2008), and directly or persistently asking clients what they want the moment they walk through the door may be experienced as unhelpfully probing, interrupting or blunt. However, from a pluralistic standpoint, at some point during an assessment or initial session, it is generally useful to explore with a client what they want from therapy. For instance, a practitioner might start off by asking:

- 'Do you have a sense of what you want from our work together?'
- 'What do you hope to get out of therapy?'
- 'So I wonder what's brought you here?'
- 'What kind of things would you like to change in your life?'
- 'What do you see as the goals for this therapeutic work?'
- 'Where would you like to be by the end of therapy?'
- 'If you were to say just one word about what you wanted from this therapy, what would it be?'
- 'What would have to be minimally different in your life for you to consider our work together a success?' (Duncan, et al., 2004: 69)
- 'What will be the first sign for you that you have taken a solid step on the road to improvement even though you might not yet be out of the woods?' (Duncan, et al., 2004: 69)

Therapists can then work with the client – through the use of basic counselling skills such as reflection, summaries, probes, etc. – to help clarify their answers to these questions. Such a dialogue regarding the goals of therapy may be very brief but, from a pluralistic standpoint, it is essential in helping the therapist (and client) to orientate themselves to what the client wants. It then also serves as the basis for beginning to identify appropriate tasks and methods for the therapeutic process (see Chapters 5 and 6).

Structured goal-articulation methods

Over the years, a number of formal, form-based techniques have been developed to help clients articulate their individual goals for therapy – although, in most instance, this is in terms of the *problems* or *difficulties* that they wish to work on (Rodgers, 2010). All these forms have been developed primarily for research purposes – evaluating the outcomes of therapy in more individualised ways – but are also suitable for therapists to use in their everyday practice. Practitioners sometimes worry that the use of such forms will be experienced by clients as intrusive or impersonal but, in our experience, clients generally find them facilitative, helping them to focus on what they want from therapy and their main difficulties.

At the most basic level, clients can simply be asked what their main goal(s) is/are for therapy, and these can be written down (e.g., Kiresuk & Sherman, 1968). If such a form were to be used for ongoing monitoring of therapeutic progress, clients could also be asked to rate how close they were to these goals: for instance, on a 1 to 7 scale from '*Not at all achieved*' to '*Completely achieved*'.

Alternatively, clients may be asked to identify the main difficulties that they want to work on in therapy, or what they see as their main problems. The Goals Form, used at the Tayside Centre for Counselling, for instance, allows clients to formulate what they want from therapy in either negative terms (as problems) or more positively (as goals) (see Appendix C on page 189 and at www.pluralistictherapy.com). A one-page form is used, which was developed from an initial template devised by Deane, Spicer, and Todd (1997). The most recent version of this instrument includes questions about the achievability and salience of each goal. Clients are invited to complete this form before the beginning of each counselling session, and the counsellor retains a file of previously-completed forms to enable comparison with the client's goal/problem statement and ratings from earlier sessions. Different counsellors working in the Centre have evolved their own style of making use of the information in the Goals Form. Also, clients differ in the level of their involvement in wanting to discuss what they have written in the form. However, for both clients and therapists, the Goals Form serves as a reminder that the client's goals are the starting point for therapy, and it helps to anchor each session in the client's current definition of their goals. One of the most useful aspects of the Goals Form, compared to some other goal-rating techniques, is that it allows the clients' understandings of their goals to evolve and become more differentiated. This is because clients restate their goals at the beginning of each session.

An alternative method for eliciting and recording client problem/goal statements is the Simplified Personal Questionnaire Procedure, developed by Robert Elliott and colleagues (Elliott, et al., 1999). Full instructions for the procedure are available online at www.experiential-researchers.org. The procedure begins with a brainstorming session, in which the client is asked to list as many problems in their life as possible. The therapist/researcher then works with the client to reduce these down to ten or so statements which truly reflect the client's experience of what is problematic in their lives: for instance, 'Forgotten how to share life with people', 'My confidence is low' or 'I get anxious about things outwith my control'. Each of these is written down on separate index cards. Next, the client is asked to sort these cards in terms of the priority of these problems, with the most important concern first, then the next most important, etc. Finally, these problems are transferred to a form, where the client is asked to rate each problem on a 1 to 7 scale, indicating how much this problem has been bothering them over the last seven days (from *Not at all* to *Maximum possible*).

There are several other instruments that have been developed to enable clients to articulate their goals, including MYMOP (Paterson, 1996) and PSYCHLOPS (Ashworth, et al., 2004). Along with the instruments outline above, any of these procedures can be used both to identify goals or problems at the start of therapy, and also to monitor a client's progress towards these goals as the therapy develops. Here, at the beginning of each therapy session, or perhaps just at the last therapy session, a client can be asked to rate themselves according to how close they feel towards their goal(s), or how much they feel that their problems are still bothering them. From personal experience, such ongoing monitoring represents a useful means of helping clients see how their therapeutic work is progressing, and also serves to keep their therapeutic goals in mind.

What happens when clients cannot articulate their goals?

As discussed at the beginning of the chapter, and as the research indicates (Strong, 2009), clients may struggle at times to respond to therapists' invitation to identify goals. It is not unusual, then, for questions like 'What do you want to get out of this work?' to be met with a blank stare, or a client may say that they have never thought about this, or that they are just there because a friend/partner/GP told them to go.

In such circumstances, it may be useful for a therapist to try to explore this question a little further. For instance, they may ask the client about their goals in a different way, invite them to spend a few minutes thinking/talking about it, explain to them why it may be helpful to know what they want from therapy, or simply reflect back the fact that the client does not know what they want. It may also be useful to invite the client to think about their highest order goals (e.g., 'What's most important for you in life?', 'Where would you like to be in ten years time?') as a way of helping them think about how they are hoping that therapy can take them there. If it is assumed, as in this pluralistic approach, that all behaviour is ultimately meaningful, then there will be some rationale for the client coming to therapy that will eventually emerge. However, as the research indicates (Strong, 2009), this can often take an extended period of shared negotiation, with many turns by therapist and client before a clearer sense of the client's wants comes to light.

Below is an example from about 40 minutes into a first session of therapy with a young woman, Saskia, who came to see Mick with severe depression, anxiety and social isolation. When initially asked about what she wanted from therapy, Saskia found it difficult to respond, but as the dialogue proceeded, so a number of important goals came to light:

Mick: Where you would like to move forward to?

Saskia: I don't know what to ask, I mean, obviously, 20 sessions is not a long time. Um... I don't really know, I don't want to hope for too much. Em... It's hard to say.

Mick: What are the main things that you'd like, perhaps, to be a bit different?

Saskia: Well certainly the relationship thing's a big thing because, you know, I'm 22 now and I haven't been with anyone for a long time... *[Client talks about her desire for a stable relationship.]*

Mick: So getting somewhere maybe to the point where you're closer to being in a relationship sounds like a good place – maybe a good place to get to.

Saskia: And maybe, also, I dunno, there's always this problem of, um... understandably I think there is this problem of jealousy and envy. [*Mick*: Uh huh] And it's all about comparison and, er, setting myself up for a failure... *[Saskia goes on to talk about her tendency to compare herself against others, and how she would like to stop doing this.]*

So, to say – to ask me where I would like to be – I dunno, healthier, anyway – I know that's very vague and general.

Mick: Physically, do you mean, or...?

Saskia: Both ways, both ways... [*Saskia talks about her current lack of exercise. Mick and Saskia then go on to talk about whether she would like to be in employment. Saskia says that she would like to be doing some work as a teaching assistant.*]

Mick: So if you were like, two of three years down the line, and you had a life that was working with children, and you were in a relationship, that would feel good?

Saskia: Aw, that would be awesome.

If, however, such a line of exploration seems to be making the client feel uncomfortable, anxious or confused (i.e., threatening a rupture in the therapeutic alliance), it may be best to leave this issue and consider coming back to it at a later time. This would particularly be the case if the client seems, otherwise, to be satisfied or engaged with the therapeutic work; or if the therapist is getting a strong (albeit unspoken) sense from the client of what they want and feels well-orientated in the work. However, if the client cannot articulate what they want from therapy, and if the therapist is also really not clear what the client wants, then this may be something important to come back to and to try to discuss sooner rather than later.

In some cases, it may become evident that the client really does not want anything from therapy (this is different, of course, from a client who really cannot articulate what they want from therapy). If this is the case, and if, as is likely, the client is not particularly engaged with the therapeutic process or satisfied with it, it would probably make sense for the therapist to begin discussing with the client about the appropriateness of therapy at the present time. From a pluralistic standpoint, this can (and should) be done in an entirely non-pathologising and non-judgemental way: different people need different things at different points in time, and it is quite legitimate that some people at some points in time will not be helped by therapy. For instance, if it emerges in discussion that a client's real need is to make sure that their housing benefit is in place, it may be much more helpful to them to work with a housing support officer than a psychologically-trained practitioner.

What happens when therapists 'disagree' with clients' goals?

In some instances, as Duncan and colleagues (2004) point out, clients' goals will not fit our own sensibilities about what they need. It may even be that we feel critical or hostile towards the goals they set out for themselves. How does a pluralistically-informed therapist respond in such circumstances?

First, it may be helpful for the therapist to reflect on their own beliefs and assumptions (see Exercise 4.1 on page 59) and consider, perhaps in supervision, whether this is where their reaction is coming from. Is it, for instance, that the client has articulated a goal which the therapist, at some level, does not feel to be worthy? A therapist who holds happiness as the highest possible goal in life, for instance, may find it difficult to accept a client's goal towards faith.

Even if this is not the case, it may be best for the therapist to allow themselves, as far as possible, to trust the client's goal (provided that it is not likely to hurt themselves or others). Duncan and colleagues (2004) give the example of a 'mentally ill' young woman, Sarah, who lived in a supervised residence and repeatedly expressed a desire to be a cheerleader for the local team. The therapist found it hard to accept this goal and wanted to orientate Sarah towards greater socialising and exercising, but once he started to go with Sarah's own goals, he began to see how helpful it was for her to explore her own passion: an area in her life in which she experienced a great deal of expertise. After a while, Sarah went ahead and organised a cheerleading squad for a local basketball team, something that helped her re-integrate into her community and develop a greater sense of self-efficacy.

Based on such examples, Duncan and colleagues (2004: 69) write about the importance of accepting clients' goals at 'face value', 'because those are the desires that will excite and motivate the client to initiate action on his or her own behalf'. From an ethical standpoint, it would also seem important to be able to trust and value a client's own articulation of their goals, rather than holding a position of 'I know what this client wants even if they do not say it themselves'.

At the same time, there is a reality that the goals that clients propose for therapy may be 'rather vague or unrealistic' (Berking, Holtforth, Jacobi & Kroner-Herwig, 2005: 316). They might also 'not be appropriate to help the patient in the long term' (Berking, et al., 2005: 316). Another way of putting this latter point is that the lower-order goals that a client proposes may not seem particularly useful at helping them achieve their higher-order goals. For instance, Stig came to therapy wanting to improve his relationship with his partner and, to achieve that, he wanted to learn to be better at stopping his anger. Over the first few sessions, however, it became quickly apparent that the more he tried to push down his anger, the more frustrated and irritated he became, and the more he took things out on his boyfriend. In such circumstances, within a pluralistic approach, it is entirely appropriate for a therapist to help a client explore whether their goals will really help them get what they want; and it is also appropriate to challenge clients on how realistic their goals are, or to encourage them to clarify the nature of their goals. Like the home decorating consultant, a pluralistic therapist may be most effective when they robustly challenge the client's view, but this can all be done without ever questioning or undermining the client's highest order wants and values.

In some instances, it may be that a therapist feels that a client's goals are quite legitimate, clear and realistic, but just does not feel that they have the knowledge, skills or motivation to help them in this. For therapists, clarifying for themselves what they feel they *can* help clients achieve (see Exercise 3.1 on page 41) may be useful in identifying when this may be the case. Here, it may be important for the therapist to discuss this with the client, and explore the possibility of onward referral to someone who may be more able to help them towards their goals (see Box 4.2 on page 68) (again, in the pluralistic framework, the need to refer on is absolutely not a reflection on the therapist's competence – we cannot be all things to all people all of the time). However, if the client is finding the work useful, then this is a key factor to consider, and onward referral may not be appropriate. It may be, for instance, that the therapist has misunderstood what the client wants from therapy, or that they are underestimating their capacity to be helpful to the client. Either way, however, opening up this dialogue may be useful for both therapist and client in deepening a sense of what the client wants from therapy.

Box 4.3: Making onward referrals

There is surprisingly little in the counselling and psychotherapy literature on how to successfully refer a client on to another practitioner (though see Leigh, 1998). Perhaps this is because, from a schoolist standpoint, therapists of different orientations have tended to assume that what they offer will be helpful to most – if not all – clients. From a pluralistic standpoint, however, different therapists will be of lesser or greater help to different clients, depending on the degree of alignment across goals, tasks and methods. This means that a key skill for pluralistically-informed therapists is being able to refer clients on to a more appropriate practitioner (therapist or otherwise) in a constructive – i.e., sensitive, supportive, informed and helpful – way. Research on how to do this is badly needed, but some initial suggestions are outlined below:

- Try to be as aware as possible of what you can and cannot offer clients, so that you have a clear sense of when onward referral may be appropriate.
- Try to be accepting of your limitations as a therapist, so that you do not experience the need for onward referral as a sign of personal failure, but as an indication of your commitment to helping clients as fully as possible.
- Wherever possible, try to refer onwards in a collaborative way with the client, so that it feels that it is a decision being made together, rather than something being imposed on them.
- Clients may well experience onward referral as a sign of rejection – for instance, that they are not 'good enough' or are 'beyond help' – so it may be important to emphasise to a client that an onward referral is a consequence of *your* limitations as a therapist, and not any failing in them as a client.
- Try to be aware of what other options might be available to the client (for instance, specialised services, low-cost counselling, couples counselling), so that you have suggestions to hand if the need for referral emerges.
- For further discussion and advice on onward referral, see Leigh (1998).

As a final point, although it may not be immediately obvious that there is a disagreement over the goals of therapy, if difficulties or ruptures are starting to emerge in the work, it is always worth reflecting on the degree of accord over what the therapeutic work is trying to achieve. Is it the case, for instance, that the therapist is trying to help their client get more in touch with their feelings, while the client is wanting some practical solutions to their problems; or might it be that the therapist is wanting to 'cure' the client, when the client is more concerned with coming to terms with their difficulties? This is something that can be very useful for therapists to discuss in supervision, and perhaps bring back to the therapeutic relationship. A therapist might say, for instance, 'I have a sense here that I am really trying to help you get more in touch with your emotions, and I am wondering whether, maybe, you're actually looking for something else. What's your sense...' Through reflecting on the degree of goal-agreement in supervision, a therapist may also come to see that they really have very little idea of what a client wants from therapy and this, again, can be a useful insight to bring back to the therapeutic work.

The process of goal differentiation

During pluralistic therapy, clients have an opportunity to learn about their goals. They are invited to articulate their goals, and to identify ways to attain these goals. They engage in dialogue with their therapist, where they are able to appreciate more fully how their goals are perceived by another person. They can revisit and monitor their goals on a regular basis. All of these activities can contribute to a gradual *differentiation* within a client's understanding of where they stand in respect of their goals.

Eva was a client who received counselling for several months. During a pre-therapy intake and assessment session, she was not able to identify a clear-cut goal for her counselling. Instead, when invited to describe her goals, she gave an account of an intolerable life situation that she wanted to escape:

> I was abused when I was a child. I then married very young, to a man who was a heavy drinker and was physically abusive to me. For the first time in my life I am alone, with no one to tell me what to do, not anyone to ask how things are done. My two daughters have rejected me. My mother died this year, and my only companion, a pet cat, is seriously ill.

After 16 sessions, she used her Goals Form to record the following statement:

> My giving love seems to invite abuse. I want to develop strengths to recognise warning signs of manipulation. I want to learn to say 'no'.

This new statement includes the identification for the first time of specific 'wants', and a sense of a preferred or desired future that was implicit in her pre-therapy response. The new statement also incorporates an appreciation of causal links ('my giving love *invites* abuse, *therefore* I want to develop strengths'). In later sessions, Eva's goals became even more clearly differentiated, as she became able to identify specific changes she could make in specific situations.

The goal statements made by Eva reflect two processes that can occur in good outcome therapy. First, the client begins to shift from avoidance/problem statements towards approach/goal statements. Essentially, this process seems to be one in which the possibility of a preferred future begins to take shape. Second, the client starts off with generalised statements of distress, and begins to be able to break down their problem into cause-and-effect sequences that link the causes of the problem, the current difficulty, and things that can be done to make the situation better. Of course, in individual cases, the sequence can follow different pathways. But, on the whole, when an effective collaborative relationship is established, and the client begins to accomplish their therapeutic goals, then this kind of pattern can often be observed. The implication for therapists is that it is important to keep up to date with the client in relation to what their goals are *now*, rather than continuing to hold on to a goal statement and therapeutic contract or formulation that might have been agreed several weeks previously (though see Box 4.4). The use of a monitoring instrument such as the Goals Form, or regular reviews with a client, makes it easier to keep track of the ways in which a client's goals may be gradually mutating over time.

Recommended reading

Michalak, J., & Holtforth, M. G. (2006). Where do we go from here? The goal perspective in psychotherapy. *Clinical Psychology: Science and Practice, 13*, 346–365. Valuable review of recent research into the role of goals in therapy and implications for practice.

Box 4.4: Is goal flexibility always a good thing?

As part of a collaborative, pluralistic approach to therapy, we have argued that therapists, in general, should be flexible around goals, allowing them to evolve and become more differentiated as the therapy progresses. However, Schulte-Bahrenberg and Schulte (1993) suggest that it is not always a good thing for goals to change in therapy. They suggest four types of goal change:

1. *Expansive* – new goals and aims are taken up (see The goal horizon, page 67);
2. *Adaptive-constructive* – goals are revised or more finely differentiated to better suit the client's needs (see The process of goal differentiation, page 77);
3. *Resigned* – original goals are recognised as being unattainable, and less ambitious goals are adopted;
4. *Destructive* – goals that are potentially attainable are given up on too early.

The implication of this analysis is that, while therapists should be open to changes and developments in clients' goals, it is unlikely to be helpful if goals are consistently modified and revised 'willy-nilly', without any discussion or exploration. Not only may this convey an impression of uncertainty and lack of competence, but it may also leave the client feeling that the therapist does not believe in their capacity to achieve the goals they set for themselves.

The Therapeutic Value of Goal Dialogue

A final point in this chapter is that talking to clients about what they want from life and from therapy, in itself, may be a valuable therapeutic method. This is in three respects. First, if people are not aware of what they want from life, it may be very difficult for them to get it, so the more that clients can develop their ability to reflect on their life goals, the more they may be able to achieve these possibilities. This, in many respects, is consistent with the basic premises underlying existential (e.g., Frankl, 1986) and person-centred (e.g., Rogers, 1959) therapies, which encourage clients to reconnect with their meanings in life or their 'organismic valuing process' so that they can choose towards more genuinely satisfying and fulfilling ways of being. Second, and closely related to this, is the hypotheses that people may not get what they want from life because they are not very good at asking for it or talking about it (cf. assertiveness). They may feel, for instance, that other people will perceive them as demanding and selfish if they ask for what they want ('I want never gets'); or they may be fine at asking for what they want but find it very difficult to listen to the wants of others. Hence, goal dialogue in therapy gives clients the opportunity to develop their skills in expressing, and negotiating around, wants, with the possibility that they will then become more effective in attaining their goals in everyday relationships with others. It may also help them to feel less guilty about having wants in the first place. Finally, talking about goals can inspire hope in clients (Lazarus, 1981; Snyder, Michael & Cheavens, 1999). As research indicates, a sense of hopelessness and an inability to see a future are often a key feature of psychological distress (Higginson & Mansell, 2008). Helping clients to identify goals may therefore be beneficial by reminding them of their dreams, hopes and possibilities (Mackrill, 2010).

Summary

The pluralistic approach takes clients' goals as the basic starting point for therapy. This stance reflects the humanistic philosophical underpinnings of the approach, which emphasises clients' perspectives, rights, strengths, and capacity to be agentic. Goals can be defined as a projected state of affairs that a person intends to achieve, and can be conceptualised as existing in a hierarchy: from the highest-level life-meanings to the most concrete, contextually-based aims. Clients may have several discrete goals for therapy, and these are most commonly to do with interpersonal issues and their specific problems or symptoms. Therapists are not always good at knowing what clients' goals are, and therefore it is important, within the pluralistic approach, to ask clients what they want from therapy early on in the process, either in informal or structured ways. In many instances, clients do not find this an easy question to answer, but they can be helped to explore it further. If therapists find themselves disagreeing with clients' goals, they may find it useful to look at their own prejudices and values, and try to trust the client's sense of what they want. However, within the pluralistic approach it is also quite appropriate for therapists to challenge clients and to help them clarify what it is that they really want in their lives and from therapy. If difficulties emerge in the therapeutic work, it may be helpful for therapists to reflect on whether they, and their clients, share the same goal.

Questions for reflection and discussion

1. What are the possible advantages and disadvantages associated with taking the client's goals as the primary orientating point for therapeutic work?
2. 'Everything that human beings do or experience is directed towards goals.' Discuss.
3. How important do you think it is for a therapist to know what a client wants from therapy? Would you be able to work effectively with a client if you did not know what they wanted?
4. If you have had the experience of being a client in therapy yourself, then what opportunities did your therapist create for talking about your goals? How helpful was your therapist's approach in relation to this issue? What did your therapist do that was helpful for you, and what would you have wanted him or her to do differently, in respect of exploring your goals for therapy?

5 Tasks: Focusing the Therapeutic Work

This chapter discusses:

- The concept of therapeutic tasks: the particular routes by which clients can reach their goals.
- The kinds of therapeutic tasks that clients frequently undertake.
- How the concept of tasks can be used to develop the therapeutic work.
- How theory and research can be used to develop an understanding of appropriate tasks.
- Case formulation from a pluralistic, task-orientated perspective.

Andrew was a young man in his mid-20s who had moved away from his home in a rural town, and had found employment as a retail worker in a large city. He came into therapy, on the advice of his GP, following the death of his mother. It was hard for him to talk, but gradually he reported that he felt despair, and was experiencing frequent panic attacks. He had been very close to his mother, but had a poor relationship with his father and brothers. When asked about his goals for counselling, he said that the main thing was to 'survive', then to be able to 'move on' in his life and to 'eventually be happy'. Andrew used the first two sessions of therapy to unburden himself, and tell John his story. It became apparent that he was in a very difficult point in his life – the present moment was almost intolerably painful, and none of his hopes for the future seemed realistic or achievable. As with many clients, there was a sense of almost paralysis at the scale of what needed to be done if Andrew was ever to attain his goal of being happy. What was clear was what Andrew wanted and hoped for in therapy. He was in a state of profound personal crisis, he felt hopeless, and knew that he needed to move forward in his life. John wanted the work in therapy to be grounded in his sense of what might be helpful, but Andrew was in no state to stand back, reflect and arrive at anything that might resemble a plan of actions. In any case, he had never been in therapy before, and said that he knew nothing about counselling. He had little appreciation of the options open to him. At the start of the third session, John asked him if it would be acceptable to him if John talked for a bit about how John thought they might proceed. John said to him that he did not want to cut across anything that Andrew wanted to talk about at that moment, but that if he thought it might be useful for him, John wanted to share his response to Andrew's situation. Over the space of about

20 minutes, with various pauses for discussion between them, John outlined a set of possibilities for their work together:

- exploring how various life events had affected him in the way they had, in order to make sense of his current difficulties;
- concentrating on specific incidents that continued to haunt him, so that he could come to terms with these particular events;
- doing some problem-solving, planning and decision-making around areas of life that Andrew found stressful;
- making behavioural changes, for example finding ways to stop his self-destructive gambling addiction;
- coming to terms with a life without his mother and family base – opening a new chapter in his life;
- developing strategies for dealing with difficult feelings and emotions, for example when he lost his temper with other people;
- finding, analysing and acting on information, in relation to a possible new career;
- taking better care of himself;
- working out how to maintain some kind of relationship with his father.

As John talked through these ideas, he wrote them on a piece of paper, which he then handed to Andrew so he had them in front of him. John's formulation of this set of possible therapeutic tasks was based on a combination of both *content* and *process* information. In Andrew's story, there was plenty of evidence of difficulties around patterns of feeling and relationship. Andrew had also identified some key tasks – for instance he stated that 'I need to get a different job'. Finally, John paid attention to the *way* in which Andrew talked, and the quality of his being in the room – for instance his story was continually punctuated with self-deprecating statements, and he conveyed an acute sense of emotional pain.

In the conversation that developed during this therapy session, and following sessions, Andrew was able to decide where to start, in terms of the areas that were an immediate priority for him, in contrast that those that could wait. This process gave both John and Andrew more confidence about what they were trying to do together. They became able to focus on specific issues, while knowing that other issues had not been forgotten. They also had a shared sense of the whole picture, the context in which they were working.

The Concept of Therapeutic Tasks

A client's goals, as discussed in the previous chapter, can be viewed as specifying the contract or agreement around what they want from therapy *as a whole*. In the session-by-session process of therapy, however, such goals may be at a level that is too global or abstract to effectively orientate the therapeutic work; and, indeed, research shows that a well-formulated action plan is a key factor in helping people to achieve the goals that they set for themselves (Koestner, et al., 2002). For this reason, within the pluralistic framework, we also find it useful to think about therapeutic 'tasks'. Tasks, as illustrated in the work with Andrew, are the particular ways in which clients can achieve their goals. With Andrew, for instance, the hope was that he could move on in his life ('goal') by exploring how different life events had affected him ('task') and making behavioural changes ('task').

Within the pluralistic framework, tasks occupy a space between 'goals' and 'methods'. The goals of therapy are defined by the client, and are linked to their more general life goals. The methods of therapy are much more specific, concrete and fine-grained. Tasks are in between: the specific routes by which the client can get to their destination. Tasks can also be thought of as *foci* for the therapeutic work, or the different *phases/stages* of the work, or as different *plans*. Broadly speaking, these are all ways of referring to the same fundamental activity of breaking down the effort of therapy into achievable/digestible chunks.

The concept of tasks is particularly relevant to therapists who want to work in a specifically pluralistic way. For therapists who are working in a more specialised manner, however, the concept of tasks can also be useful in terms of thinking about their work with clients. It can also be something that specialised therapists may want to discuss and negotiate with their clients: 'What is it that we want to do in our work now?' 'Where shall we take things?' 'What is it that you would like to focus on for this session today?'

Box 5.1: Other perspectives on the concept of therapeutic tasks

In the 1980s, Les Greenberg and his colleagues (Greenberg, Rice & Elliott, 1993) conducted a programme of research and theory-building with the aim of identifying the main therapeutic events that occurred within their process-experiential model of therapy (later called emotion-focused therapy). What they discovered was that, when therapy was effective for the client, specific sequences of task activity could be observed, in response to specific 'markers' of emotional distress. Another influential task-orientated model that many therapists have found valuable is the 'tasks of mourning' approach developed by William Worden (2001). Arising from many years of clinical experience in working with people around bereavement issues, and immersion in the relevant theoretical and research literature, Worden's (2001) model suggests that, following the loss of a significant other, a person is faced with four tasks: accepting the reality of the loss; working through the pain of grief; adjusting to an environment in which the deceased is missing; emotionally relocating the deceased and moving on in life. These tasks refer to foci that clients can readily identify as being directly relevant to their therapeutic goals – they have a high degree of common-sense credibility for people seeking counselling for bereavement issues. The literature on emotion-focused therapy, and around the Worden model, represents valuable resources for pluralistic therapists seeking to deepen their understanding of the different tasks that clients may embark upon, and that may be useful for particular clients at particular points in time.

A Taxonomy of Therapeutic Tasks

A pluralistic perspective requires the adoption of an inclusive approach to considering the types of task that may arise in counselling and psychotherapy. The following list, however, represents a preliminary attempt to construct a taxonomy of tasks that occur across a wide variety of clients, many of which were apparent in the work with Andrew:

- making meaning: talking through an issue in order to understand things better;
- making sense of a specific problematic experience;
- problem-solving, planning and decision-making;
- changing behaviour;
- negotiating a life transition or developmental crisis;
- dealing with difficult feelings and emotions;
- finding, analysing and acting on information;
- undoing self-criticism and enhancing self-care;
- dealing with difficult or painful relationships.

Exercise 5.1: Tasks in your own therapy

If you have been a client in counselling or psychotherapy, take 15 minutes or so to reflect on, or discuss with a partner, what the main tasks were for you in this work. Are they covered in the list above or are there other tasks that you think need adding?

An important implication of this position is that all therapists who wish to practice in a pluralistic way need to possess at least a basic level of competency in relation to facilitating completion of each of these tasks. This is discussed more fully in Chapter 8.

An advantage of thinking about therapy in terms of tasks is that it makes it possible to hold a fine-grained discussion around the specific methods that may be used to complete that task. For example, Siobhan was a client who came into counselling because she said that she 'hated herself', and wanted to achieve more self-acceptance. Through exploring how this goal might be accomplished, Siobhan and her counsellor identified three main therapeutic tasks: to change her pattern of eating behaviour (she regularly engaged in binge eating episodes), to be less critical of herself when interacting with her boyfriend, and to make sense of how her difficulties had developed. She decided that the first task (changing eating patterns) should take priority, and be the main focus of each counselling session, while the other tasks would receive less attention each week, but still be discussed. Her counsellor then invited Siobhan to talk with her about *how* her compulsive eating might be modified (i.e., which method(s) might be used). Together, they discussed methods that the therapist was familiar with, along with strategies that Siobhan had found helpful in the past. They agreed on a package of methods that included keeping an eating diary where she recorded details of her emotional states when she felt the need to binge, working out at the gym three times each week, no more than one evening of overtime work each week (she had coped with long hours by eating junk food), enlisting her boyfriend to cook healthy meals, and contracting to speak to her boyfriend immediately about any urge to binge eat. This package comprised some ideas that the therapist believed would be helpful (awareness of emotional states and using social support), other ideas that Siobhan herself had found useful in the past (working out in the gym and feeling good), and further ideas that emerged when they talked together (the realisation that long working hours were associated with self-destructive eating). From a pluralistic standpoint, this combination of methods stands a greater chance of success than would an intervention based in any single therapy approach because it is uniquely tailored to the strengths and preferences of this particular client–therapist dyad.

As illustrated in the work with both Siobhan and Andrew, one thing that we have found particularly helpful is to collaboratively set out, and tackle, tasks on a *one-by-one*, sequential basis. The idea that therapy may consist of step-by-step progress towards an ultimate goal can activate hope and commitment in the client. This is partly because it may make the client's goals feel less distant and more achievable. Also, someone who has struggled for years to overcome a major personal problem will either not believe, or be frightened by, the idea that they might suddenly be changed.

Adopting a task-orientated perspective also encompasses a set of tasks that are not specifically focused on achieving the client's goals, but instead are concerned with ensuring that an appropriate therapeutic environment is being maintained (see Boxes 5.2 and 5.3).

Box 5.2: Maintenance tasks: taking care of the therapeutic space

In any therapeutic process, there is a set of *background* or *maintenance* tasks that need routine attention in order to ensure that the therapeutic process does not grind to a halt. The key maintenance tasks include:

- ensuring that there is a suitable physical space for therapy (soundproofed room, tissues at hand, etc.);
- arranging the duration and timing of sessions;
- monitoring the quality of the therapeutic relationship, and addressing any 'ruptures' that may occur – for instance, if the client becomes angry and resentful;
- dealing with ethical and boundary issues and dilemmas – for example, a client is unlikely to feel safe in therapy if they are worried about the confidentiality of what is being discussed;
- addressing the possibility of risk to the client, therapist or other people.

For reasons of space, the perspectives and practices associated with effective work around these maintenance tasks are not examined in any detail in this book. These

(Continued)

professional practice issues are typically discussed in depth during basic counsellor and psychotherapist training, continuing professional development courses, and ongoing clinical supervision.

In relation to the context of a pluralistic approach to therapy, what needs to be taken into account is that there are times when these 'maintenance' tasks will need to shift from the background into the foreground, almost always at the instigation of the therapist. Because of the inbuilt professional therapist–client power imbalance, it is usually very hard for clients to take the initiative to say anything about whether they hate the therapy room, are worried about confidentiality, or even are thinking about jumping off a bridge. The skill of being a therapist involves the development of a capacity to pick up whether any of these challenging situations is on the horizon, and an ability to respond in an effective manner.

Box 5.3: A pluralistic approach to working with suicidal clients

Working with clients who are suicidal presents particular challenges for any therapist. The disclosure of suicidal intentions opens up the possibility that the counsellor may feel that it is necessary to take control and intervene, for example by setting in motion a procedure that could lead to involuntary hospitalisation. In addition, the therapy itself may be focused on highly destructive and hopeless parts of the self, with little leverage in terms of possibilities for positive change. Finally, there is the impact on the therapist himself or herself, of accepting responsibility in a situation where something tragic might happen, and dealing with personal feelings around the meaning of suicide.

A pluralistic perspective is particularly helpful in relation to this area of therapy practice. There is evidence that one of the most valuable strategies for overcoming a suicidal crisis is simply to remain in therapy, to keep talking (Reeves, 2010; Winter, Bradshaw, Bunn, & Wellsted, 2009). A pluralistic emphasis on collaboration, and on the identification of specific tasks, provides a useful framework for engaging in dialogue with clients around suicidal intentions and activities. There is evidence that suicide is a complex phenomenon – there are multiple pathways and types of suicidal person (Lindner, Fiedler, Altenhofer, Goetze & Happach, 2006; Strike, Rhodes, Bergmans & Links, 2006). A range of alternative ways of making sense of suicide have been developed within different schools of therapy, including the notion of destructive inner voices (Firestone, 1986, 1997), the interpersonal theory that the person sees themselves as a burden to others (Stellrecht, et al., 2006), cognitive-behavioural concept of reasons for living (Linehan, Goodstyen, Nielsen & Chiles, 1983), and medical model concepts of risk assessment (Cochrane-Brink, Lofchy & Sakinofsky, 2000; Joseph, 2000). There are a number of methods that have proved valuable in relation to responding to suicidal crises, including: suicide helplines and websites (Baker & Fortune, 2008); no suicide contracts, commitment to treatment statements and crisis response plans (Rudd, Mandrusiak & Joiner, 2006); outreach work and sending caring letters (Comtois & Linehan, 2006); and self-help reading (Jamison, 1999). There are also resources that can help therapists to reflect on their own emotional response to suicide (Richards, 2000; Trimble, Jackson & Harvey, 2000). Awareness of the plurality of perspectives and strategies that have been developed by therapists and other professional groups, in response to the challenge of suicide and serious self-harm, provide the basis for pluralistic practitioners to find the approach to working with suicide that is most effective for each individual client in the specific situation within they find themselves.

Using Theory and Research to Mediate from Goals to Tasks

A useful strategy for thinking about the possible tasks that might be involved in making progress towards a goal is to make use of relevant theories of, and research as to, what is likely to help clients. There are many examples, particularly in CBT, of therapy protocols that have been developed for particular 'disorders', such as cognitive therapy for depression (Beck, et al., 1979). From a pluralistic perspective, such protocols are viewed not as fixed treatment plans to be delivered in a standardised fashion, but as 'offerings' (Moore, 2005) for collaborative discussion. Usually, published protocols or treatment manuals tend to be based on one specific theoretical model. A wider appreciation of potential tasks, in any specific case, can be achieved by considering alternative or competing models. For example, Angela was a client who was highly fearful in social situations. A psychodynamic theoretical perspective might suggest that it would be necessary for Angela to be able to gain insight into the childhood origins of her fears (*meaning-making* task). From a behavioural theoretical perspective, it would be useful for Angela to develop new coping skills, such as relaxation and breathing techniques (*behaviour change* task). From a humanistic perspective, Angela's fear might be understood as indicating an interruption or failure in her progress towards individuation or actualisation (*life transition* task). Undoubtedly, there are other valuable theoretical offerings that can be suggested for Angela's situation. The point here is that each of these perspectives generates different ideas about the tasks that might be helpful for Angela in moving beyond a life of persistent fear and anxiety. Ultimately, the test of these theories lies in what works (either on its own or in combination) for this particular case, in terms of making sense to the client.

In nearly all instances, such theories are based on particular understandings of the development (aetiology) of psychological distress. For instance, a psychodynamic perspective would hold that clients like Angela are unable to 'contain' their fear because of specific childhood experiences, while a cognitive perspective might attribute Angela's anxieties to cognitive distortions and a misperception of threat. From a pluralistic perspective, such aetiological theories provide a rich body of understandings for therapists and clients to draw on when working to identify appropriate therapeutic tasks and methods. That is, if client and therapist can work out what led to the development of a client's problem, it might provide some very useful clues as to how that difficulty can be resolved.

For example, Mick worked with a young man, Marcel, who had come to therapy to overcome a fear of speaking in public (see Cooper, 2009). He had had a previous episode of counselling, and much of that work was focused around some experiences of abuse he had suffered as a boy. In the first two sessions, this was also the focus of the work, but in the third session, when Marcel was asked how he was finding the therapy, he said that he was really not sure whether he wanted to go into the abuse again: 'I just can't be bothered with it any more', he said, 'Is it just going to be there and I have to accept it?'

Mick replied: 'I guess part of the question is how much it is related to the problems that you are experiencing at the moment, and that is what we don't really know.' Mick and Marcel then explored a range of possible understandings for why Marcel might be experiencing his difficulties, summarised by Mick towards the end of the third session as follows:

> One is that ... it is about stuff that happened in your past that has made it really difficult for you and has really inhibited you and made you really anxious [*psychodynamic understanding*]. Another one is that it's something that you're just not good at it and you may as well give up and it's not really that much about your past [*biological explanation*]. I guess there is another one, that you're talking about there, that is about a pattern that you have got into, or a cycle, that isn't so much ... that is not so much caused by things in your past, so much as you've started avoiding doing that kind of talking, and because you've avoided doing it you've built it up as something that is more and more frightening, and actually if you started doing it a bit more you would, as you are saying, that 'It's not actually that bad ... it's bearable' [*behavioural explanation*].

'I'm just thinking about those,' answered Marcel, 'it could be a pattern of behaviour I've just got into...'

Based on such an understanding, the focus of the work turned towards helping Marcel undo this cycle of behaviour through the task of confronting his fears: developing practical strategies so that he no longer avoided speaking in public, and helping him develop more positive and supportive 'self-talk' around in these situations. By the end of 17 sessions, Marcel's fears of public speaking had substantially attenuated.

In this work with Marcel, Mick drew on a number of established theories about the aetiology of psychological distress, but, working pluralistically, these theories were introduced into the dialogue as offerings and possibilities rather than as given truths. They were also introduced in a way that tried not to favour one theory over another. Instead, the aim was to hold open a series of possibilities that different clients might find useful at different points in time. And, indeed, just to illustrate this point, when a similar set of potential understandings was introduced into the therapeutic dialogue with Tammi, who also experienced fears of talking in public, she immediately became drawn towards a more psychodynamic account: that her fears were linked to a humiliating and neglectful relationship with her mother. Hence, Tammi spent much of her therapy with Mick talking through painful childhood experiences: a very different focus from the work with Marcel, but with similarly successful outcomes.

Identifying Tasks as a Process of Collaborative Case Formulation

The process of developing a shared understanding of a client's problems, and deciding on appropriate tasks, can be seen as one element of a broader process of 'case formulation'. A *case formulation* can be defined as a summary statement of the way that the counsellor or psychotherapist makes sense of their work with a client. A case formulation will usually encompass the following issues:

- Current issues/presenting problems/stated goals.
- Underlying causes/vulnerability (why does the person have these problems?)
- What are the mechanisms/actions/processes through which these difficulties are maintained? How do these mechanisms connect the underlying and the current problems?
- Why now? What has precipitated the need for help now?
- How can the problem be tackled in therapy? (treatment plan)
- What are the obstacles to therapy? What are the client's strengths?

Historically, the practice of case formulation has been associated with the cognitive-behavioural tradition in counselling and psychotherapy. However, case formulation, in some guise, is used in all forms of therapy (Eells, 2007; Johnstone & Dallos, 2006). There has been a tendency for practitioners within experiential, person-centred and psychodynamic traditions not to be trained to construct explicit formulations linked to treatment plans, because of the emphasis in these approaches of working with the immediate, here-and-now process taking place in the therapy room. Nevertheless, even in these approaches, practitioners would be expected to be able to explain to their clinical supervisor what they think is happening in the client's life, and how they understand the therapeutic options that are open to them.

Pluralistic counselling and psychotherapy requires engaging in a *process* of ongoing case formulation and reformulation. The aim is not to established a fixed treatment plan at the start of therapy, and then stick to it no matter what transpires, but to *offer* the client a possible framework for deciding on what might be helpful, and then *inviting* the client to adapt, modify or rewrite this template so that it more closely reflects their preferences and needs. There are many effective strategies for conveying a formulation to a client, including initiating a conversation on the topic, using a narrative approach (Omer, 1997), making diagrams, and offering a written report (Ryle, 2005; Ryle & Kerr, 2002). Different clients may prefer different types of communication, as will different practitioners – engaging in conversation around such matters is part of a pluralistic collaborative approach.

Agreement around tasks will often comprise the central focus of the formulation process. This is because, from a client perspective, tasks will often represent the most tangible and concrete aspect of what is being discussed. Clients may be hazy around how they make sense of their difficulties, how to describe their goals, and what methods might be best suited to them. By contrast, a client will often have a clear appreciation of the steps that they need to take to make a difference in their life (i.e., the set of therapeutic tasks), and the order in which they would want to tackle them. For example, in the case of Andrew, introduced earlier in this chapter, he was clear that the immediate priority for him was to work on how to make his life less stressful, and then how to get a new job, and that, as far as he was concerned, making sense of his life would need to wait until he was 'in a better place to think about that stuff'.

Conclusion: The Therapy 'Menu'

A key aspect of a pluralistic approach (see Chapter 3) is that the therapist should be able to explain to the client how they see their therapy as working, and enlist the client's involvement in deciding how to proceed in relation to what they would find most helpful at that particular point in time. In our experience, the concept of 'task' is extremely valuable in respect of being able to do this, because tasks can be described in ways that make intuitive sense to clients. The explanatory power of a task perspective also has implications for public appreciation and understanding of the role of counselling and psychotherapy: the list of tasks presented in this chapter provides a straightforward, non-pathologising description of what therapy has to offer.

A useful metaphor here is the idea of the therapy *menu*. The list of tasks outlined in this chapter is the kinds of things that a therapist can provide. The notion of a menu evokes an understanding of therapy as a service industry, but also an understanding that what is involved is something very basic – an act of feeding and responding to a person's needs. The idea of a menu is highly congruent with a pluralistic vision of human relationships and culture. In advanced industrial societies, we have access to restaurants that offer many different types of menu. We understand that we have a right to choose the items from the menu that we prefer, and that (usually) we can specify variants on the menu. In Appendix A (see page 182), there are some suggestions about how the idea of a therapy menu can be communicated to clients.

Exercise 5.2: Your therapy restaurant

Take 20 minutes or so to reflect on, or discuss with a partner, the following questions. It is not to be taken too seriously, but it might give you some interesting insights into how you think about the therapy you offer:

- If the therapeutic service that you offered your clients was a restaurant, what kind of restaurant might it be? (for instance, specialist, fusion, take-away)
- What would your menu be like? (for instance, extensive, just a few items)
- What, specifically, would you put on your menu? (for instance, 'An opportunity to talk and be listened to', 'home-grown wisdom', 'Skills for dealing with life'?)
- What is your 'signature dish'?
- How much would you charge?
- What do you think your clients would make of your restaurant?
  - What might they like?
  - What might they complain about?

Summary

Tasks are the routes taken by client and therapist in order to achieve the client's therapeutic goals. The concept of tasks provides a way of thinking, and talking, about counselling and psychotherapy in an everyday, non-pathologising language, and a way of enabling therapists and clients to decide together on the focus of therapy within each session. A preliminary taxonomy of generic tasks can be constructed, though it is unlikely that it will ever be complete. Therapists and clients can identify potentially appropriate tasks from drawing on theories of treatment and distress but, from a pluralistic perspective, they need to be tailored to the client's sense of what will be most effective for them.

Questions for reflection

1. What does the term 'task' evoke for you? What are the advantages and disadvantages of this metaphor as a way of making sense of the process of therapy?
2. What other therapeutic tasks can you think of that are not included in the taxonomy above.
3. What are the therapeutic tasks with which you feel most confident and competent as a therapist? What are the tasks that are currently outside your competence, or with which you lack confidence in tackling with clients?

6 Methods: Resources for Facilitating Change

This chapter discusses:

- The concept of methods: the specific activities that the client and the therapist undertake to accomplish therapeutic tasks and goals.
- The many different methods that can be used in therapy.
- The different sources from which therapeutic methods can be derived:
    - therapeutic literature and tradition;
    - cultural resources;
    - personal knowledge.
- Specific strategies for negotiating around methods in therapy.
- The importance of monitoring the effectiveness of methods.
- The development of method competency in both therapy practitioners and clients.

What are the *specific* things that clients can do to complete tasks and achieve their goals? Within the field of counselling and psychotherapy as a whole, different therapeutic approaches (cognitive-behavioural, psychodynamic, person-centred, and so on) have been organised around quite specific, singular ideas about how to make a difference. By contrast, from a pluralistic perspective, we have argued that there are *many* ways to make a difference. Within this model, the actual procedures or actions that a therapist and client jointly perform in order to make a difference are called *methods*. This can be broken down further into *client activities*, the specific things that clients do, and *therapist activities*, the specific things that therapists do. This distinction may be particularly helpful when we think about the things that clients can do which may not necessarily require the input of a therapist (see Box 6.4 on page 105).

From a pluralistic perspective, it is not particularly helpful to think about 'brand-name' therapy orientations (e.g., psychodynamic, CBT) as methods. This is because, if methods are defined as collaborative client and therapist activities, then each of these orientations encompasses a plurality of methods. From the client's perspective, there may be one or two CBT-based methods that work for them, along with some methods from psychodynamic practice, and some from gestalt therapy. A truly pluralistic therapy, that seeks to be as responsive to the client's sense of what will be most useful for them, always needs to be prepared to deconstruct existing therapy orientations and treatment packages in order to find the specific method that seems best for this specific client in relation to the specific therapeutic task on which they are engaged at any specific point in time.

Everything that a therapist says or does in the presence of a client can be viewed as a therapist activity in so far as their words and actions have an impact on the client's attention and the way that the client experiences the therapist and the therapeutic relationship. Even when a therapist might believe that they are not using a specific technique or intervention, they are nevertheless influencing the client, and being influenced in turn.

A Multiplicity of Methods

In thinking about the abundance of potential therapeutic activities, Mahrer (2007: 12) invites therapists to imagine 'a vast public marketplace that stretches over several city blocks and includes hundreds of shops and stalls, each containing methods'. Haruki, for instance, was a student in his first year at university who suffered from 'performance anxiety' – a crippling fear of speaking (or even worse, presenting a paper) in a tutorial group or seminar. When he came to see John, he was clear that his life as a whole was satisfactory, and that all he wanted from counselling was to achieve his goal of 'being able to take part in seminars'. After some discussion, it appeared that there were three main therapeutic *tasks* (see Chapter 5) that would need to be tackled in order for Haruki to achieve his goal. These were: (a) *making sense* of why this pattern had developed – Haruki did not want a 'quick fix', but felt that he needed to have an understanding of the problem in order to prevent it re-occurring in the future; (b) learning how to control the powerful and debilitating panic that overcame him in seminars; (c) moving beyond just 'coping', and having a positive image of how he might actually be successful and do well as a 'presenter' (this was part of a broader *life transition* task that was tied in to his hope of entering the teaching profession). As the counselling proceeded, each of these three themes tended to be focused on in separate sessions.

During one of the early sessions that focused on the task of dealing with his panic feelings, John and Haruki talked together about the various ways that Haruki thought that it might be possible for them to address this issue. John wrote down the ideas that emerged on a flipchart. Haruki began by saying that the only thing that came to mind for him was that he believed that he needed to learn to relax. John then asked him if there were any other situations that were similar to performing in seminars, but which he was able to handle more easily. He could not immediately identify any scenario of this type, but later in the session he returned to this question, and told John that he remembered that he always took the penalties for his school soccer team, and dealt with his anxieties by running through in his mind some advice that he had received from his grandfather, about following a fixed routine. John then asked him if he would like to hear some of John's suggestions about dealing with panic. John emphasised that these were only suggestions, and that it was fine for him to reject them if they did not seem useful. John mentioned three possibilities. One was to look at a model of panic, as a way of understanding the process of losing emotional control. The second was to use a two-chair method to explore what was going on in his mind, in terms of what he was internally saying to himself at panic moments. The third was to read a self-help booklet on overcoming panic.

Haruki thought that all of these methods, by this time written up on the flipchart, had some potential value for him, although he acknowledged that the 'two-chair stuff sounds a bit scary'. Over the next two sessions, Haruki and John tried out each of these methods, along with suitable homework tasks (for example, practising relaxation skills and speaking to two people, whom he respected, who would give him advice on how to deal with seminar nerves). Haruki fairly quickly became a lot more confident in seminars.

What was happening during this piece of therapy? From a pluralistic perspective, both Haruki and John were working together to bring what they could to the table, in terms of ideas and resources. Some of these ideas, such as learning relaxation skills and applying them to a hierarchy of situations, were drawn from CBT. Although the 'consulting trusted others' idea came from Haruki, as they developed it together, John gave it a narrative therapy spin (John's background), in respect of ideas about 're-membering'. The two-chair exercise came from gestalt therapy and emotion-focused therapy (EFT), although it was probably not implemented wholly according to the EFT manual. Both Haruki and John had a fairly clear idea of what they were trying to achieve – an ability to function in seminars. These sessions were enjoyable for both of them because they had been able to create a space in which they could try out different strategies and not feel defeated if one of them turned out to be ineffective.

Sources of Methods

Ultimately, all of the methods used in therapy derive from the immensely rich cultural heritage of the history of human being. Each and every idea and practice that is described in a therapy or psychology textbook has its origins somewhere in everyday life. Having said that, it is useful to think about methods for change, healing and growth as located within three broad and overlapping categories:

- Techniques, ideas, strategies and practices that are described within the *counselling and psychotherapy literature* – either formally or informally – and which are supported by professional structures of training, supervision and research.
- Practices that exist within *culture and society*, but which are not usually described as 'therapeutic'. These practices might include such activities as playing music, art-making, walking, adventure, caring, reading, meditation, sport, political involvement, and much else.
- Practices that are *idiosyncratic and unique to individuals* – personal knowledge.

What needs to be acknowledged is that both clients and therapists have access to all three categories of method. Most people, not just trained therapists, have some notions about what happens in therapy, and the different methods that can be used. Everyone has some personal experience of life-enhancing and life-changing activities that arise through being a member of a culture and through living a life.

There is not enough space in this book to include a comprehensive list of methods of healing, change and renewal that have been used in therapy, or which might be used. The list would just be too long. Instead, some examples of the most widely-used methods are summarised in the following sections, which describe a core repertoire of methods that can be used in most therapy situations.

Methods derived from the therapy literature

The counselling and psychotherapy professional community has generated a vast number of books and articles over the last century, outlining a staggering array of ideas about how to help people to change. However, it is possible to identify five main strategies for change within this literature. These are:

- conversation;
- structured problem-solving;
- creating new experiences;
- making use of existing strengths;
- directively intervening to alter information-processing.

Each of these categories of method will be discussed in turn.

Conversation

The most widely used therapy method, and in most therapy situations the 'default mode' of practice, can be defined as 'just talking'. Conversation is a powerful human tool that has evolved over millennia as a means through which people can come together to make sense of experience and enlist help and support from others. It is possible to address any therapy task by allowing the person to talk about their problem, reflect on what they have said, and make decisions about new actions that they can undertake. Effective use of conversation as a therapy method requires an appreciation of the many different ways in which talk can be organised and structured.

For example, many therapists make use of the person-centred conversational strategy of *empathic reflection* as a way of helping their clients to explore the meaning of issues. For some clients, however, this way of talking may be experienced as strange, threatening and alienating – they need more of a structure in order to feel safe enough to open up. It may be useful to check this out with a client, for example by saying something like: 'I was just wondering there – is the way we are talking about this OK for you? I realise I am not saying much. That's because I want to give you the space to say whatever is important for you. But if you thought it would be better for you, I could say more, or ask specific questions. What do you think?'

There can be situations where the conversational technique of *Socratic questioning*, widely used in cognitive-behavioural therapy, may be valuable: 'I'm thinking that it might be useful to try something here. What we agreed was to talk about your situation for a bit to start to get some perspective on what has been happening to you when you get really worried. What I'm thinking now is that, as you are talking about these worries, there seem to be a lot of assumptions that you are making, that I think might not be helpful for you. I'd like to challenge some of these ideas? Does that make sense? Would it be OK if we just stayed with the worries and looked a bit more closely at these assumptions? Would it be all right with you if I asked you a few questions about this?'

Another conversational strategy that can be useful is to pay attention to the *metaphors* and images that are generated by the client: 'When you said that just now, about how your life with Don is like pushing a boulder up a hill, I was just struck by how that image just seemed to capture the whole dilemma for you. I'm thinking that it might be helpful to just stay with that image for a minute. Would that make sense for you?'

Yet another conversational strategy that is employed by many therapists is the use of *interpretation* – intentionally placing the client's statement in a wider meaning context. For example: 'I've been listening to what you have been saying about how you find it hard to trust your colleague at work, and it reminded me of how hard it was for you to trust me at the start, in the first sessions we had, and what you said last week about how unreliable your Dad always was. Is there a connection there that you can see yourself, or I am reading too much into this?'

These are just some of the many ways that conversation can be used to facilitate exploration, reflection, meaning-making, learning and decision-making. Note how, from the standpoint of various single orientation practices, some of these methods are strongly prescribed, while others are actively proscribed. But from a pluralistic stance, they are simply different forms of conversation, with no clear demarcating lines between 'good' and 'bad' forms: all have the potential to be helpful or unhelpful with different clients at different points in time.

Structured problem-solving

There are some therapeutic tasks that call for the client and therapist to work out a *plan* of action that can be implemented over a period of time. This kind of method views the task in hand as similar to a *project*, and draws on ideas about problem-solving and project management that are found in industry and commerce. Structured problem-solving is a key method within cognitive-behavioural approaches to therapy. The therapist collects information from the client about the problem and how it has arisen, and the client's goals for change. This information is then assembled into a *case formulation* (see Chapter 5), which is like a blueprint for the project, outlining the action that needs to be taken first of all to reduce or eliminate the problem behaviour, and then to establish the preferred pattern of responses. This plan is then implemented in a structured fashion, week by week, usually through agreed homework assignments that the client carries out between sessions, and then reviews with the therapist at their next meeting. This kind of method is popular with many clients because it gives them a sense of being able to do something practical and positive to change their situation. Also, many of the activities that are involved are similar to problem-solving strategies that are widely used in other walks of life, such as creating a timeline, setting targets, risk assessment, filling in monitoring forms, making lists of advantages and disadvantages of alternative strategies, and SWOT (strengths, weaknesses, opportunities and threats) analyses.

Recommended reading

Lazarus, A. A. (1981). *The Practice of Multimodal Therapy.* Baltimore, MD: Johns Hopkins University Press. Valuable introduction to multimodal therapy, outlining a wide range of methods that can be used by pluralistic therapists. For a clear and concise summary of multimodal therapy, see S. Palmer (2000).

Westbrook, D., Kennerley, H. & Kirk, J. (2007). *An Introduction to Cognitive Behaviour Therapy: Skills and Applications.* London: Sage. Provides authoritative and easy-to-read access to a widely used, research-based therapy orientation that has generated a large number of methods of structured problem-solving and behavioural experimentation.

Creating new experiences

A useful idea from psychoanalytic theory is the notion of therapy as a 'corrective emotional experience' (Alexander & French, 1946). There are some people who miss out on the childhood experience of being in a relationship in which important aspects of their emotional life are allowed expression. For example, a child whose mother or primary caretaker is physically or emotionally absent or unavailable may never learn what it is like to feel emotionally safe. Such a person can then grow up never quite trusting others. For this person, their relationship with their therapist represents the possibility of having a new experience, characterised by trust and safety. This kind of process can be understood in terms of the pluralistic notion of method. It is a matter of saying to the client (along with other things) something along the lines of: 'One of the steps you are saying that you want to take in your life is to stop being so suspicious of other people, and feel that you can trust them. I guess there are many ways we could work on that. But maybe one of the options would be to just be aware of what is happening between you and me. What would it take for you to feel safe with me? What could I do to help that to happen, if it's something that you would like to be able to do?'

Another type of therapy task that involves the creation of new experiences occurs when a person has developed a pattern of avoiding certain situations. For example, Sheila has a fear of enclosed spaces, and will not enter a lift or travel on the underground. If this problem is to be addressed successfully, there is no getting away from the fact that, at some stage, Sheila will need to undergo the new and scary experience of being in a lift or in an underground train carriage. Within cognitive-behavioural therapy, the concept of *exposure* is used to describe this type of method – the aim is to work with the client to create a graded sequence of actions that will eventually make it possible for them to be exposed to their most feared scenario or situation (see Westbrook, Kennerley & Kirk, 2007).

There are many other therapy methods that involve the creation of new experiences. For instance, 'two-chair' work in gestalt therapy and emotion-focused therapy (Greenberg, 2002), which invites the client to engage in a dialogue with a significant other person (e.g., one's mother or father) or part of self (e.g., my inner critic), is in itself a new experience, and can lead to further new experiences such as the expression of long-buried sadness, disgust or anger. Other examples of therapy methods that involve the creation of new experiences arise in relaxation training, assertiveness training and mindfulness techniques. Here, the client is introduced to what is, for them, a new way of being in the world.

Making use of existing strengths

A significant set of therapy methods, that have been given particular emphasis in recent years by solution-focused therapists and narrative therapists, centre on ways of enabling the client to make use of their existing knowledge, skills and personal attributes. The key move in these methods is first to encourage the client to remember or notice their personal strengths, and then to reflect on how these abilities can be applied to help them to deal more effectively with their current problems. For example, the client may be invited to try to remember times in the past when they were able to overcome a particular problem, to note current instances where they functioned effectively ('exceptions'), or to imagine a time in the future when they have overcome their problem (and then to explain how they achieved this success). A simple way to enter this territory, and yet something that is challenging for many clients, is to ask a person to make a list of their positive qualities. In a wonderfully innovative therapy episode, Madigan (1999) worked with a client who was depressed to send letters to people he knew, to invite their thoughts on how he had in the past, and could in the future, make a positive contribution to society. Group therapy can be a powerful arena for enabling clients to become aware of their strengths, by receiving feedback from other group members around how honest, sensitive, etc., they have been in the group, and to practise these qualities in their interactions with others.

Exercise 6.1: Learning to pay attention to your client's strengths and resources

When clients seem to be bogged down in intractable problems, it can be all too easy to lose sight of their personal strengths and resources. For 5 minutes before each therapy session with a client, take some time to list the client's strengths and resources, which you have learned about in earlier meetings, and reflect on possible ways that these strengths might be applied in achieving the client's goals for therapy. As soon as possible following the session, take another 5 minutes to reflect on how effective you have been in enabling the client to access their strengths. A focused self-supervision activity of this kind was found by Flückiger and Holtforth (2008) to lead to enhanced therapeutic outcomes and a stronger therapeutic alliance.

Recommended reading

Flückiger, C., Wüsten, G., Zinbarg, R. E. & Wampold, B. E. (2010). *Resource Activation: Using Clients' Own Strengths in Psychotherapy and Counseling*. Cambridge, MA: Hogrefe & Huber. An invaluable source of ideas about how to help clients to identify and make use of their personal strengths and resources.

Directively intervening to alter information-processing

A final category of therapy methods refers to techniques in which the therapist acts in a way that seeks to have a direct impact on brain functioning and cognitive processing in the client. This kind of method differs from the other categories of method described in previous sections in its level of therapist control. When a therapist engages with a client in conversation, problem-solving, creating new experiences or solution-finding, there is usually a high degree of collaboration or co-construction involved. By contrast, when a therapist uses hypnosis, emotional field techniques (tapping), or eye movement desensitisation and reprocessing (EMDR), the role of the client tends to be somewhat less active than in other methods that have been discussed.

Developing competence in formal therapy methods

The discussion provided above of these five domains of formal therapy methods should be viewed as no more than a general introduction to these different practices. A useful overview of therapy methods can be found in Seiser and Wastell (2002). Information about training courses and workshops on therapeutic methods are advertised in professional journals such as *Therapy Today* (in the UK) and similar publications in other countries. Regardless of theoretical orientation or initial training, it seems that, in practice, the majority of therapists make use of a repertoire of methods that are drawn from a wide range of therapy orientations (see Box 6.1).

Box 6.1: Methods used by experienced therapists

A study by Thoma and Cecero (2009) examined the extent to which therapists make use of techniques and methods from approaches that are outside their core theoretical model. A survey questionnaire, describing 127 techniques drawn from all major therapy approaches, was completed by 209 experienced therapists in the USA. There was clear evidence that therapists from specific orientations tended to use techniques from outside their identified approach more frequently than they used techniques from the school of therapy with which they identified (see Chapter 1). It was also clear from analysis of the survey data that there seems to exist a set of core therapy techniques that are employed by most therapists, regardless of their espoused theoretical orientation. The 'Top 20' of these therapeutic methods are given below, in descending order of endorsement:

1. Trying to understand the world from the client's point of view (empathy) (humanistic).
2. Providing unconditional positive regard (humanistic).
3. Challenging maladaptive or distorted beliefs (cognitive-behavioural).
4. Being congruent/genuine (humanistic).
5. Reflection of feeling (humanistic).
6. Planning and encouraging alternative behaviours (cognitive-behavioural).
7. Assisting the patient to work through or apply insights to a range of life situations (psychodynamic).
8. Training the client to notice how thoughts, assumptions or beliefs cause different emotional responses (cognitive-behavioural).
9. Calling attention to here-and-now awareness (humanistic).
10. Teaching clients to recognise and change their shoulds, oughts and musts (cognitive-behavioural).
11. Scheduling or encouraging pleasurable activities (cognitive-behavioural).
12. Offering positive reframing to help a person change their narrative about a person or situation (cognitive-behavioural).
13. Facilitating the discovery of a sense of meaning and purpose (humanistic).
14. Exploring early childhood experience (psychodynamic).
15. Encouraging the client to examine their own role in the maladaptive family system (systemic).
16. Encouraging the client to be present to, or authentic with, the therapist (humanistic).

(Continued)

17. Exploring and interpreting emotional problems in terms of problematic interpersonal relationships (psychodynamic).
18. Giving the client feedback about their present-tense body language or manner of speech (humanistic).
19. Facilitating the client in focusing on present-tense internal feelings and sensations (humanistic).
20. Empathising with what the client is avoiding or minimising through empathic refocusing (humanistic).

An intriguing facet of this list is that humanistic methods are widely used by therapists of all schools, even though only 7% of those who responded to the Thoma and Cecero (2009) survey indicated that they belonged to this group. It may be that, historically, the distinctive identity of humanistic therapies, such as person-centred, gestalt and existential therapy, has dissolved as their ideas have permeated across the profession as a whole. It may be that a similar process is currently happening with CBT ideas and methods.

Some aspects of the most widely used of the formal methods described here (conversation, structured problem-solving, creating new experiences, making use of existing strengths) do not actually require any specific training. They are part of the commonsense, taken-for-granted knowledge base of all interpersonally sensitive, caring, helpful people in any culture. Yes, capability in these methods can be enhanced by training and supervision, and certainly practitioners have an ethical requirement to work within their competences, but not having received training in solution-focused therapy should not be an excuse for not being willing to be interested in a client's personal strengths. The fifth category of method (directively intervening to alter information-processing) does require specialised training. However, a client who is drawn towards one of these more directive methods may be helped to seek out and consult a more specialised practitioner, either as an adjunct to their ongoing therapy, or as an alternative. If a client believes that EMDR is what is needed to overcome deeply-ingrained post-trauma symptoms, then why deny that person the opportunity to give it a try? Why not do everything possible to help them to make best use of that technique, and to integrate its outcomes into their life?

Informal methods derived from the therapy literature

Like most artists, craftspersons and scientists (in fact, like most people who have ever lived), therapists are continually looking for ways to do their jobs better. What this means is that, alongside the innumerable empirically-validated manuals and protocols that have been published, there also exists a hugely creative and stimulating literature on 'informal' methods. These are techniques and strategies that have been devised by practitioners, but have never been assimilated into any of the brand-name theoretical approaches or included in manuals. Among the many valuable books that have been written by therapists about their idiosyncratic ways of working are *The Therapist's Toolbox* by Susan

Carrell (2001), *Constructive Psychotherapy* by Michael Mahoney (2005) and *The Gift of Therapy* by Irvin Yalom (2001). Here are some of the unique methods used by these therapists:

- visiting the client in their home to get a sense of their life outside the therapy room (Yalom, 2001);
- inviting the client to spend time in the therapy session looking into a mirror as a way of exploring issues around identity (Mahoney, 2005);
- when a woman client is agonising over a decision, ask: 'What would you say to a girlfriend who came to you with this story?' (Carrell, 2001).

These are just some of the many hundreds of idiosyncratic methods that have been described by practitioners down the years. It seems probable that there are even more methods that have never been written down, that are passed on within various oral traditions and communities of practice, or have been lost and forgotten.

Cultural resources as therapy methods

Earlier in this chapter, it was argued that all therapeutic methods are, ultimately, drawn from the vast repository of ideas and practices that exist within various world cultures and sub-cultures. From within that set of ideas, some ways of doing things become defined as belonging to the discourse of 'therapy'. However, this still leaves an almost endless list of activities that are available within a culture and are potentially 'therapeutic', in the sense of having the potential to have a positive impact on the capacity of a person to resolve a problem by allowing that person access to ways of making meaning, strategies for behaviour change, and a secure sense of identity and belonging (see Mahrer, 2007). Examples of *cultural resources* that can be used in therapy are given in Boxes 6.2 and 6.3.

Box 6.2: Making use of cultural resources: Angela's relationship with music and creativity

John worked for several months with a young woman, Angela, who was a professional woman in her 20s who felt dissatisfied with her life and had been diagnosed by her GP as depressed. Angela worked in the office of a large organisation, and was a valued and successful employee. Her longing, however, was to express her creativity, and to follow a different life path. One of the significant themes in Angela's childhood was her involvement in music. She had been an accomplished cellist, who had derived great pleasure from playing, but had eventually quit her musical career in a resentful protest against parental pressure to sit ever more advanced music exams. Now, many years later in therapy, she talked about joining a choir.

(Continued)

This activity became a source of joyfulness and pleasure, and gave her an opening in her life for her buried creativity. The choir also represented a kind of re-experiencing of earlier conflicts, when the choirmaster began to put pressure on her to take a solo part in a public performance – an event that she experienced as similar to these dreaded music exams of earlier years. Off and on, for a few sessions, the relationship between Angela and the choir, an important cultural resource in her life, became a key topic in therapy. As so often happens, this potentially life-changing cultural activity did not just slot into Angela's life in a neatly packaged manner – she needed to use the relationship with a therapist to see it through and make the most of it.

Box 6.3: The memory album: a cultural resource that was much more helpful than anything that happened in therapy

Jan was a straightforward, direct woman who had spent her life working in vital, but low-paid caring jobs and bringing up her children. Her immensely talented and much-loved daughter committed suicide at the age of 21. In the counselling room, Jan's emotional pain was palpable; it was there, it was the centre of her waking life. In counselling, Jan talked about many aspects of what had happened, and began to make some sense of it all. But the emotional pain remained. Jan's counsellor offered various ways of approaching the pain, but without any success. One week, she came in and mentioned that her daughter's friends were planning to bring round a memory book, filled with their pictures and stories. 'Do you think this is a good idea?' asked Jan. The counsellor said: 'Maybe you can show them how you feel, when you look at the book and read their words. Maybe you can listen to them and share your own memories a bit.' In the end, this is what worked for Jan, in so far as anything in the world could help at all: finding ordinary moments of connection with others who shared her loss.

Cultural resources should not been viewed as automatically or necessarily positive in their effects. For example, lifting weights after a stressful day at work can function as a means of relaxation, a boundary between home and work, and an opportunity to meet a wide range of new people. On the other hand, it can become an obsession and addiction, which reinforces a negative body image and is used as a way of avoiding authentic relationships. What is more useful is to regard cultural resources as providing a person with an array of *possibilities*. From the point of view of making use of these resources in therapy, some of the questions that arise include: What are the possibilities that the person associates with this activity? How might the person be supported and encouraged to make

Table 6.1: Coping strategies for dealing with depression

Most helpful interventions	Most widely-used interventions
1. Seeing a counsellor	1. Occasional drink
2. Physical activity	2. Pain relievers
3. Learn relaxation	3. Physical activity
4. Close friends	4. Close friends
5. Cut commitments	5. Family
6. Family	6. Vitamins
7. Get out more	7. Time off work
8. New recreations	8. Get out more
9. GP	9. GP
10. Read about problem	10. Cut commitments
11. Time off work	11. Massage
12. Massage	12. Read about problem
13. Psychologist	13. Special diet
14. Telephone counselling	14. Antidepressants
15. Antidepressants	15. Chemist
16. Psychiatrist	16. New recreations
17. Vitamins	17. Counselling
18. Social worker	18. Sleeping pills
19. Cut out alcohol	19. Naturopath
20. Clergy	20. Cut out alcohol
21. Psychotherapy	21. Antibiotics
22. Naturopath	22. Learn relaxation
23. Occasional drink	23. Psychologist
24. Special diet	24. Clergy
25. Hypnosis	25. Tranquillisers

use of these possibilities to achieve their life goals? What are the costs of involvement in this activity in terms of the balance of the person's life as a whole?

It is clear that most people who come to therapy are already using cultural resources to help them to deal with their problems. The Australian psychiatrist Anthony Jorm has conducted large-scale public surveys of the ways that ordinary people cope with everyday psychological problems such as depression. One of these studies (Jorm, et al., 2000) asked people about the strategies that they regarded as being most helpful in dealing with anxiety and depression, and the strategies that they actually had used. Their findings, listed in order of perceived effectiveness, are summarised in Table 6.1. The potential of many of these activities, in terms of their positive impact on mental health and wellbeing, and incorporation into counselling and psychotherapy, has already been widely recognised and subject to research scrutiny.

Exercise 6.2: What cultural resources do you draw on?

Spend 10 minutes or so reflecting on, or discussing with a partner, which of the resources in Table 6.1 you are most likely to use if you are feeling down, and which ones you find most helpful. Does this correspond to the lists in Table 6.1?

It is important to recognise that the list of cultural resources produced by Jorm, et al. (2000) is incomplete – it is never possible to cover everything in a survey questionnaire. Some of the other cultural practices that have been described by various writers and researchers as being potentially therapeutic include: art-making, cooking, education, gardening, meditation, consciousness-raising groups, music, pets, political involvement, voluntary work and watching television. One of the things we think is a particular strength of the pluralistic approach is that it provides a space for all of these possibilities to be considered helpful (or, potentially, unhelpful) without having to decide which is 'best' or having to distinguish such activities from 'proper therapy'.

How can counsellors and psychotherapists incorporate these kinds of methods into their practice with clients? One of the basic principles of what *not* to do is to attempt to 'prescribe' certain activities as useful. Marley (2009) interviewed people about their use of cultural resources when faced with crises in their lives. These participants identified a wide range of cultural activities in which they engaged, and which was similar to the Jorm, et al. (2000) list. However, what they said was that, at times of emotional stress, they did not feel strong enough to try anything new, and almost wholly relied on strategies that they had developed during happier periods in their life, typically during their childhood. In so far as they did seek out new sources of help and support during crisis periods, these tended to be activities, such as counselling, that provided a clear-cut structure and rationale, rather than activities where they would require confidence and initiative from them (qualities that they did not feel that they possessed at that time).

This finding is supported by the research that has been carried out into the use of self-help books ('bibliotherapy'). These resources have been shown to be of major value to people with psychological problems (den Boer, et al., 2004), and a substantial proportion of counsellors and psychotherapists suggest to their clients that they should read specific books (or watch certain movies) (Norcross, 2006). However, the evidence suggests that self-help reading is more effective when the client takes the initiative in choosing a book (i.e., they are using a coping strategy – reading – in which they already have some confidence), compared to situations where the book is prescribed by the therapist (Menchola, Arkowitz & Burke, 2007). What generally works best is for the therapist to be guided by the client, and to be willing to follow the client in their choice of reading material.

Exercise 6.3: Your own self-help materials

Take 10 minutes or so, on your own, to make a list of the books, films or other arts materials (e.g., painting) that you have found helpful or 'therapeutic' in your own life? Spend 10 minutes or so sharing your list with a learning partner. Reflect on the circumstances under which you might wish to make suggestions to a client regarding reading material or viewing films, and how you might handle this kind of conversation.

Recommended reading

Norcross, J. C. (2006). Integrating self-help into psychotherapy: 16 practical suggestions. *Professional Psychology: Research and Practice, 37*(6), 683–693.

Box 6.4: Client activities in the absence of therapist activities

Given the potential value of cultural resources, it is quite possible that clients will engage in helpful activities that are external – or even unrelated – to the therapeutic relationship. This is supported by empirical research, which suggests that 'clients do much of the work of change outside sessions' (Dreier, 2008: 17). For example, Sandra came to therapy with severe anxieties about her father's impending death. She wanted time to talk through these issues, and to try to prepare herself for what she knew was about to happen. Around the third or fourth session, Sandra started to mention how helpful she found it to go swimming: it was a chance for her to think about her father, to get in touch with some of her emotions, and also to make sense of issues that had been raised in her counselling session that week. Indeed, in session six, she cagily admitted that, in many ways, her swimming was more helpful to her than her meetings with the counsellor; although she added that the latter was a useful catalyst for the former, and also a space where she could explore things further.

As a therapist, such feedback is not always easy to hear. It can feel challenging to a therapist's sense of significance, and there may be a temptation to minimise the value of extra-therapeutic client activities, or else to re-interpret it as a relational communication. For instance, was Sandra indirectly expressing anger to her therapist? But from a pluralistic perspective, which holds that goals can be achieved through a multiplicity of methods, there is no need to place extra-therapeutic activities in competition with intra-therapeutic ones. Rather, it is assumed that both have the capacity to contribute to a client's progress: sometimes in highly interrelated ways (for instance, when a client undertakes homework that was agreed in therapy) and sometimes not.

Personal knowledge as a source of therapy methods: 'existential touchstones'

There is a further category of therapy method that is hard to describe, but nevertheless hugely important in practice. These are the individual, personal strategies that both clients and therapists have found to be of value in their lives. We have already discussed, above, the use of clients' resources and personal knowledges, but therapists' personal knowledge bases also have the potential to play a valuable role.

Dave Mearns (Mearns & Cooper, 2005: 137), co-author with Mick of *Working at Relational Depth in Counselling and Psychotherapy*, has observed that, in the process of undertaking sustained self-exploration in personal therapy and other arena, counsellors and psychotherapists can often become aware of areas of their lives within which they possess a great sense of certainty. These are 'events and self-experience from which we draw considerable strength and which help to ground us in relationships as well as making us more open to and comfortable with a diversity of relationships.' Dave has described these personal resources as 'existential touchstones': 'places that we can go to' in order to deeply understand our clients' experiences.

We can also think of existential touchstones as resources that we can draw on to deepen our understanding of the kinds of *methods* that clients might find most helpful at particular points in time. For example, after experiencing panic attacks for many years, Mick came to discover that one of his best strategies for dealing with them was to generate, prior to a potentially anxiety-inducing situation, as much 'adrenaline' in his body as he could (for instance, through vigorous exercise, or through imagining the worst possible outcome). That way, when he was doing the thing that he feared, he experienced much less shock and disorientation when his adrenaline levels started to surge, and was consequently less likely to spiral down into a panic cycle.

As a personal, 'home-grown' coping strategy, this is something that Mick would very rarely share with clients. However, when working with Marc, a young man who experienced severe anxieties at work, it seemed appropriate to draw on. Marc was a very skilled computer software programmer who would sometimes experience powerful panic attacks when meeting with his boss. 'I just have a sense she is looking through me,' he described, 'and I can feel I am trembling inside and then I just get worse and worse. I keep saying to myself, "She must think I'm a complete idiot," and then I get convinced that I'm going to lose my job.' Marc talked about the way that he had been trying yoga and swimming to see if it would help him with the anxiety: 'hammering it,' he said, 'trying to see if that would make a difference.'

Mick: Have you ever tried that in the morning, though?

Marc: [Pause] Before I go?

Mick: Yeah. I'm just thinking in terms of like, you know, if you get that kick of adrenaline, like, I wonder if – like, using exercise as a way of getting a real, kind of, kick of adrenaline...

Marc: And sort of replacing... [*Mick*: Well, maybe...] the body adrenaline with the exercise adrenaline?

Mick: I don't know that much about physiology but I just wonder if it would be worth trying, like, you know ... I think one of the things that happens in panic attacks is like, if your body is in quite a calm place, and then suddenly the adrenaline hits you, it really can really freak you out [*Marc*: Yup]. Whereas if you have been doing exercise you've kind of, been – you're body's a bit more used to feeling adrenaline [*Marc*: Yeah] so that, then, when you start feeling anxious, it doesn't feel like quite such a shock [*Marc*: Mm hm]. It's kind of, 'Oh yeah, I know what this is. This is just, kind of – ' because that's where you want [*Marc*: 'I recognise this...'] to get to: 'I recognise this, this is just, you know, this is...'

In drawing on such personal touchstones, therapists obviously need to be extremely careful not to assume that the methods they have found personally helpful will also be experienced as helpful by clients. In the example above, the client did, in fact, describe this exchange as 'Greatly helpful' (on a confidential form that he knew Mick would not see until the end of therapy), but there is clearly considerable potential here for clients to feel under pressure to agree, or comply with, the therapist's personal suggestions. Nevertheless, used judiciously, sensitively and in a highly tentative manner, the therapist's own personal touchstones, in the right circumstances, have the potential to be a further source of knowledge and insight into the methods that may be most helpful to clients.

Method Choice as Collaborative Activity

As will be obvious by now, from a pluralistic standpoint, it is essential that it is not the therapist alone who determines the methods to be used in therapy. Rather, as in the case of Haruki presented earlier in this chapter, this is something that should emerge from collaboration and dialogue between client and therapist. A more detailed example of this comes from a client whose goals were around 'eating in a more healthy way rather than secret bingeing'. The client had come to the stage where she understood that the next step or task for her was to 'gain a clearer understanding' of what it was that triggered her bingeing episodes.

Counsellor: That makes sense, to get a handle on sort of when and where it happens. As a way of getting a feel for how to do something different? Because, as you said, when we have talked about this, you keep coming back to that 'don't know'. And now it's like you are ready to look at it, you want to know where it's coming from…

Client: That's right. It's a bit scary. Like – being a bit more in control. It's not me.

Counsellor: Or … not the old you?

Client: OK. But what do you suggest?

Counsellor: About how to go about it?

Client: Yes.

Counsellor: Well – you know what I'm going to say here.

Client: Yes – what do *I* think?

Counsellor: What *do* you think? Do you have a feel for how to approach this? What would work for you?

Client: Maybe. I remember that a couple of weeks ago you said something about keeping a diary.

Counsellor: I remember that too. You didn't seem at all keen on the idea.

Client: I've warmed to it. It's like – I need to have something that I can do when I feel brave. When I come in here, when you just ask me to talk about these times … I just get embarrassed and upset.

Counsellor: So the diary is for you, but you could choose what to let me see? Or would I need to see it? Would you kind of bring it in and read bits to me? What would be best for you?

Client: I would hate for you to read it all. Can't go there. Not sure if I could read bits of it to you either.

This brief excerpt illustrates the process of jointly developing a method. The idea of keeping a diary seems, for both client and counsellor, to be a useful means of documenting and exploring 'binge triggers'. But there is still a lot of work to be done in terms of constructing a shared agreement around how this activity will be implemented. Keeping a diary can be categorised as a 'homework' method. There is an extensive research and clinical literature on the use of homework in therapy (Kazantzis, Deane, Ronan & L'Abate, 2005) which indicates that, most of the time, clients do not carry out homework tasks that they have previously agreed with their therapist. What this literature tells us is that the more that the client and therapist have arrived at a detailed joint understanding of what is involved in this method, and the reasons for carrying it through (i.e., how it may contribute to the fulfilment of tasks and goals), the more effective it is likely to be. The skill of the therapist lies in possessing a sufficient awareness of the possible ways that the method may unfold, and empathic attunement to what the activity may mean for the client. It is not a matter of the therapist 'prescribing' the method, but of facilitating a process of co-construction. And, of course, the method may require modification in the light of experience. Sometimes, the method takes off in an idiosyncratic direction. For instance, the client introduced above arrived at a point of keeping a diary, but then each week drawing two or three cartoon pictures for the therapist, of 'binge scenes'. That is what worked for her.

Below is a further example of collaboration over therapeutic methods from the psychologist Fabian Davis (2010: 33), who conducted in-depth interviews with mental health service users. This case narrative is a particularly powerful demonstration of the value that there can be for therapists in talking to clients about how they would like therapy to proceed, rather than making decisions on their behalf. Davis's interviewee 'was a young woman who believed she was the cause of the death of many around her and was the victim of childhood sexual abuse'. He writes:

> In her many counselling experiences she repeatedly reached a point of such emotional intensity that she was told she was not strong enough and therapy should stop before it caused harm. Fortunately, in her last therapy she was met with a different response. Her counsellor, rather than using professional power to cease therapy, asked my interviewee what could be done to get over this difficult period. After discussion it was agreed together that the client would take brief holidays from therapy at these points and return when ready to continue. After several periods of intensity and holidays the collaboration bore fruit. In time my interviewee no longer believed she caused the death of everyone around her and she returned to work. One key aspect of this process was the included person's (the counsellor's) preparedness to accede to the power of her client's own solution.

Initiating a dialogue over methods

In the earlier part of this chapter, an outline was provided of the many different kinds of methods that can be used within counselling and psychotherapy practice. It is seldom helpful for the client to try to engage in a lengthy discussion of all of the possible methods that might be used to address the particular therapeutic tasks that are on that person's agenda. Few clients are interested in the nuances of therapy technique. What is important, instead, is to facilitate joint decision-making in a manner that is both time-conscious and which also makes a contribution to the therapy process. Done well, this kind of conversation reinforces the capacity of client and therapist to collaborate, and adds to the client's sense of their ability to make choices and be in control of their life. Done poorly, on the other hand, it can confuse the client, undermine their confidence in the therapy, and use up value therapeutic time.

Typically, in a first session of therapy, following any contracting and boundary-setting that might be required, it is usual to identify the primary task as involving some kind of initial exploration or 'getting to know each other': the client is encouraged to tell their story and talk about their reasons for entering therapy. At this stage, it can be valuable to invite the client to talk about the methods by which they have dealt with their problem in the past, whether through formal therapeutic intervention or other means.

The entry into that discussion can be through a statement such as: 'As we agreed, the main thing for you right now is to find some way of not losing your temper when your partner comes home late from work. It seems to me that there are some different ways we could work on this. I have some suggestions, but I'd be really interested to hear if you have an idea of what would be helpful for you, in terms of becoming more able to deal with these flashes of anger…' It is essential to keep in mind that few clients will be able to come up with clear suggestions or strategies at this point. This is because most clients think that the therapist is the expert and 'knows best' (and as a result are reluctant to make suggestions, for fear of seeming 'stupid'). It is therefore necessary to be super-vigilant, at this moment and thereafter, for any hint that the client may have some idea of a preferred method, and to be willing to express maximum curiosity around what this method might be.

In the absence of the client making a proposal for how to tackle the therapy task, it is up to the therapist to make some tentative suggestions. *Three* may be a good number of suggestions. More than this number of suggestions runs the risk of confusing the client. Fewer suggestions runs the risk of closing down the discussion, by implying that there is only one way to approach the task. The type of statement that is appropriate at this stage might be:

> As I said before, there are different ways of approaching a problem like this. One way would be to just keep talking about it, and try to make sense of what is happening for you and why you react in this way. Another way might be to take a specific example of a time when you lost your temper with your partner, and really analyse what happened then, and how you could change that pattern. And then, a different approach might be to think a bit about times when they have come in from work and you *haven't* got angry, and see what we can learn from that. But these are just my ideas. I'm interested in what you think – whether any of these ideas seem useful to you, or whether there's some other way of going about it, that you think might be better for you….

It is important to be aware of what this kind of statement is trying to achieve. The client is not being offered a choice between person-centred/psychodynamic ('keep talking'), CBT (changing a pattern of thought–feeling–action) or solution-focused therapy (exception-finding). Instead, what is being offered is an opportunity to reflect on some potentially valuable change methods that happen to be informed by these well-established therapy approaches. The client may opt for one of them, and perhaps wish to pursue a fairly standard CBT protocol. Alternatively, the client may arrive at some kind of combination of these methods, that makes sense to them (e.g., 'I'm drawn to options 2 and 3 in your list – thinking about when I haven't got angry can help me to see how to change that boring old pattern…'). Or, the very idea that plausible alternative strategies exist may have the welcome effect of stimulating further consideration of the matter by the client, in respect of their own private ideas, and (even better) nudge them in the direction of positioning themselves as 'one who can do something about this problem' rather than as 'one who is helpless in the face of the problem'.

The point of method choice, therefore, is not only to enable the client to make a method choice that is most effective for them, in terms of having a good fit with their worldview and immediate circumstances. The aim is to facilitate a moment of reflection, or a series of moments of reflection, around broader issues concerned with self-efficacy, personal power, agency, learning how to learn, and similar themes. The successful use of a method opens up important possibilities for the client and therapist. It creates the shared memory of a joint accomplishment that can be called on if times get hard at some future point in the therapy. It can also lead to the client possessing the confidence, beyond and outside therapy, that they possess a skill that can be applied when further problems in living arise.

Note, also, that the three method options being suggested by this therapist are drawn from a much more extensive list of *possible* options. They happen to be the methods with which this particular therapist feels comfortable and competent, or that the therapist senses might make most sense to this individual client. Another therapist, or the same therapist with a different client, might introduce different suggestions, such as learning relaxation or mindfulness skills, working through a self-help book, doing some social skills/assertiveness practice, using paint and drawing to explore the issue, two-chair work, and so on.

Box 6.5: The ethics of method choice

One of the basic principles of ethical good practice in any area of health care is that the client or patient should give *informed consent* in respect of any treatment that they receive. Patrick O'Neill (1998) interviewed a number of psychotherapists and clients about their experience of giving and receiving consent. He found that there was wide variation among therapists around consent-seeking. While some therapists carefully explained and explored the options to their clients, others just assumed that their clients would go along with the treatment plans that the therapist had decided for them. The clients who were interviewed overwhelmingly wanted more choice, more information, and a greater degree of involvement in the process of deciding on what kind of therapy was best for them. When consent issues were not explicitly discussed, many clients reported either that they were dissatisfied with the therapy they received, or that they had dropped out of therapy altogether.

Disagreements over methods

What happens if, as with goals or tasks, a therapist does not think that a client is opting for the most appropriate methods? It may appear to a therapist, for example, that a client wants to use a method that has not worked for them in the past, lacks any kind of rationale, goes against the research evidence, or is a means of avoiding unwanted – but perhaps necessary – anxiety. For instance, a client with a fear of dogs may say that they want to address this by looking at their relationship with their mother rather than going through some kind of 'exposure' method, even though the evidence for the latter method is much stronger (Emmelkemp, 2004). Again, then, what is important to emphasise here is that working collaboratively with a client involves much more than simply ceding to whatever they believe or want. Rather, it involves developing an honest and transparent dialogue in which the therapist, like the client, brings in their expertise, understandings and perceptions.

For example, the following dialogue comes from a first session of therapy that Mick had with a client, Saskia (see Chapter 3). Mick had asked Saskia what she thought might be helpful to her in the therapy and what she had found helpful or unhelpful with previous therapists, and Saskia had replied that she had found it unhelpful when there is 'just a man sitting behind you' not giving you any feedback. She said that she wanted lots of input and guidance. Mick was fairly happy to work in this way. However, he had also sensed that Saskia had a relatively 'externalised locus of evaluation' (i.e., she tended to look towards others to tell her what to do) and he had some concerns about simply reinforcing this.

Mick: So it sounds like feedback will be useful?

Saskia: Yeah, Yeah.

Mick: OK.

Saskia: Yes, definitely, because ... no matter who we are in the world, wherever we are in life, there is always going to be something that we've missed, either because we don't want to see it, or because we just didn't see it. Even if someone is 90% 'actualised' ... they're not going to see everything. [So] you [can] turn around and say: 'You could have said this, you could have done that.' And they're: 'Oh, really, thanks Mick, I never – I never saw that.'

Mick: I guess the important thing for me, in giving feedback, is that you can say 'That's not right' [*Saskia*: Sure.] And you can say, 'No, that doesn't fit,' or 'That's not helpful' [*Saskia*: Sure, sure.]. I mean, one of the ways that I like to work is – is very much with feedback ... and that needs you to say to me, 'No, don't like that...' 'That's good...'

Collaboration, then, is not about the uncritical acceptance of the client's viewpoint; but it is also not about its uncritical negation (Borrell-Carrio, et al., 2004, see Chapter 2). And, in our experience, the suggestions that clients make are almost always useful. For instance, Jessica had struggled since her childhood with obsessive-compulsive patterns that included constantly checking and rechecking anything that she read or wrote, and rituals that were intended to ward off harm to family members. These behaviours stood in the way of living life to the full, and Jessica readily identified them as goals for change in therapy. Over the course of a few weeks, it proved difficult for Jessica and her therapist to find an effective method of altering her obsessive-compulsive lifestyle. Reflecting on this situation, Jessica acknowledged that she did not believe that any of the strategies suggested by her therapist were going to work, because she knew, inside herself, that the only way to change was through the application of 'will-power'. Her therapist was sceptical about the potency of will-power because, she pointed out, the use of will-power over many years had not helped Jessica in relation to this difficulty. The subsequent discussion of what will-power meant to each of them, however, opened up a conversation around the importance of being able to trust and rely on other people (experiences that had been largely absent from Jessica's early life), as a basis for living a satisfying life, as well as the importance of being ready to take responsibility for oneself. What emerged from this conversation was a capacity of being able to move on together in relation to the OCD issue, by talking about it in ways that tacked back and forward between exploration of the relational meaning of these behaviours, and the moment-by-moment choices that Jessica was making or 'willing'. A key moment in this process was an improvised method, where Jessica taught her therapist how to perform some of her rituals, thereby transforming the OCD into a shared experience.

As in our chapter on goals (Chapter 4), however, a core pluralistic competence is the willingness and ability to refer on a client (see Box 4.3 on see page 76) – whether to a psychological or non-psychological therapist – if a therapist does not feel, following discussion and negotiation, that they can work in a way that a client wants or that is most able to help a client achieve their goals. Lazarus (1981: 89–91) gives the example of a 42-year-old woman who was experiencing chronic restlessness and shakiness. After an initial exploration, Lazarus came to the conclusion that this was probably more linked to a recent change in the client's medication than any psychological factors. He referred her back to her doctor, and the problem was cleared up in a matter of days.

Developing a shared understanding of the rationale for a method

The use of change methods in therapy is not merely a matter of selecting the right 'tool' for the job, and then putting it to use. The aim is to open up conversational spaces for reflection and exploration of important questions around the person's practical understanding as they take care of the hopes, emotions and relationships around which their life is organised. In order to facilitate such a conversation, it is helpful for a therapist to have some kind of framework for explaining how and why certain ways of talking and behaving can have particular consequences. If a therapist and client are to engage in an open discussion about which method to use to accomplish a specific task, then it is necessary for the therapist to be able to offer a rationale for any methods that they suggest, and help the client to articulate the rationale for any method that they might put forward. Establishing a shared rationale makes it much easier to collaborate around the 'fine-tuning' of the method that often occurs as a method is being implemented.

There are two key principles that are useful to keep in mind when discussing the rationale for a method. The first principle is to try to keep the conversation grounded in 'action language' (Schafer, 1976). This is based on the use of the words 'I', 'we' and 'you', and reflects an underlying assumption that each person (client and therapist) intends, and takes responsibility, for what they are doing. This is an obvious point, but is nevertheless worthy of emphasis. For example, if a therapist and client have agreed to use a relaxation technique, it is generally most effective to discuss the proposed method using action language: 'If you tense and then relax your muscles, you can learn how to make yourself calm. This can also be useful by giving you a way of paying attention to how you feel in a situation, rather than listening to the worries going round your head.' By contrast, a more distanced or impersonal use of language does not convey a sense of mutual involvement: 'The CD will take you through the instructions – relaxation is a skill that is really important in anxiety management.'

A further principle that is helpful in relation to exploring the advantages and disadvantages of different methods is to think about them in terms of *opportunities* or 'offers' (Moore, 2005). Using a particular method does not lead to a specific result in a straightforward cause-and-effect way. For example, it does not make sense to say to a client that dream analysis will lead to insight, or that walking in the countryside necessarily leads to enhanced wellbeing. Instead, it is better to say that these activities provide opportunities for particular types of experience. Walking in the countryside is an *opportunity* to get tired and hungry, to remember the importance of nature in one's life, to do something good for oneself, to take time out of the demands of work and domestic life, to invest in relationships with fellow-walkers, and so on; but none of these things are *certain* to happen. Getting tired and hungry, for instance, depends on making the decision and commitment to walk far or fast enough to induce that kind of physical state.

An example of approaching methods as opportunities can be seen in John's work with Haruki, discussed earlier in this chapter. At one point in the counselling, John took this client through some instructions on relaxation skills. However, this activity was not framed as something that would necessarily eliminate Haruki's performance anxiety. Instead, it was introduced as something that 'maybe you could try out and we can see whether it makes a difference'. The idea that methods comprise bundles of opportunities positions the client in relation to the activity in a particular way. By constructing a method in terms of a set of opportunities, there is a reduced risk of the client 'failing' – within any method that has been agreed, there will almost always be some opportunities that were taken, even if many others were not. Haruki may not have been able to enter a state of relaxation, or he may have felt relaxed in a seminar but still unable to talk. If either of these outcomes had been reported, it would have been open to John to describe what had happened as an opportunity to learn something further about Haruki's problem: 'maybe we need to find out how you stop yourself from relaxing', or 'there's more to your difficulties in seminars than just whether or not you are relaxed or tense – would it be helpful to look at what that might be?'

The idea of 'opportunity' implies movement towards a future desired state, which creates a basis for talking about the sequence of activity and decision-making that leads from the current method, to the accomplishment of a therapeutic task, and then to the achievement of a therapy goal. Finally, the concept of opportunity fits well with a pluralistic perspective. If one particular activity can represent an opportunity to do something, then surely there will be other activities that generate similar opportunities – there are always different ways to achieve the same ends.

Monitoring the Helpfulness of a Method

Methods are merely ways in which therapeutic tasks can be accomplished. The helpfulness of a method is assessed not by whether a technique or intervention is administered elegantly, or in accordance with a protocol, but in terms of whether it makes a difference to the client's life. It is important to monitor task completion, for example, by asking the client and by observing changes in relevant aspects of the client's behaviour. It is hard to predict how long it will take for a method to have some effect. It makes sense to work on the basis that some therapy methods will take time to have an impact, and will require a considerable amount of practice. For example, someone who is fearful of developing relationships with other people, and has become socially isolated, may need to practise social skills over a period of many weeks or months, and gradually build up a repertoire of relationship-building competences. On the other hand, there is evidence from psychotherapy research that 'sudden gains' occur in at least 25% of cases (Present, et al., 2008; Stiles, et al., 2003). A sudden gain is defined as a significant reduction in a person's problem, or pattern of symptoms, between one therapy session and the next. The implication of this phenomenon is that clearly there are some occasions where a method can have an instant effect, as though the client suddenly 'sees' what they need to do differently, or makes a decision to change. At the present state of knowledge, it is not possible to anticipate whether a method will trigger a sudden gain, or a more incremental pattern of benefit over a longer time.

Exercise 6.4: Carrying learning forward

The way of working described in this chapter ideally leaves the client, on completion of therapy, with an explicit understanding of 'what works for me' in terms of future re-occurrence of problems in living. Working on your own or with a partner, take 15 minutes or so to reflect on the 'methods' that you may have encountered in therapy (or in other personal development contexts), and consider the extent to which you have been able to use these methods to enable you to deal with difficulties at other points in your life. As a therapist, what might you do to assist your clients to carry forward their learning?

Another area in which monitoring is required concerns the *intensity* with which a method is being implemented by client and therapist. It may be that the way that a therapist and client have agreed to work together is appropriate, but that it is either not being pursued with sufficient energy, or is being implemented in a manner that is overwhelming for the client. For example, an agreement to explore an issue by talking it through, with the therapist's role being that of 'helping you to get a hold of what this means to you', implies that the therapist would make use of empathic reflection to tune into implicit meanings in the client's discourse. However, empathic reflection can range from a simple mirroring or restating of what the client has said, through to more 'additive' responses that seek to capture underlying strands of meaning and emotion (Hammond, Hammond & Smith, 1997). It may be that, for a particular client, low-intensity empathy is just not enough. For other clients, high-intensity empathy may be experienced as too threatening and intrusive. The issue of method intensity arises with all therapy methods. For example, how much homework is right for a client, how much exposure to fear-inducing situations, how much two-chair work?

The effective use of therapy methods depends on the establishment of a 'culture of feedback' (see Box 3.5 on page 49), through which the client is invited to let the therapist know about whether the agreed approach is producing the desired effects, and if not, then what might be done to get the process back on track. The Therapy Personalisation Form, presented in Appendix B on page 186, is one means by which this might be achieved.

Basic Method Competences for Pluralistic Practice

The therapeutic principles and practices that have been introduced in this chapter hold a number of important implications for the training and supervision of counsellors and psychotherapists. These issues are discussed more fully in Chapter 8. At this point, it is perhaps sufficient to note five main areas where a pluralistic way of working makes specific demands on practitioners. First, a therapist practising in this way needs to be willing and able to dismantle or deconstruct therapy theories in order to be able to identify concrete methods that can be suggested to clients. Second, it is necessary to develop a repertoire of methods that can be offered to clients. These methods probably need to include, at a minimum, the options of approaching a task using conversation, structured problem-solving/behaviour change, and strengths-based strategies. This repertoire can never be inclusive of all possible therapy methods that might be relevant because no individual practitioner could ever be sufficiently trained within one lifetime to make this possible. However, the practitioner does need to be able to draw on enough options to stimulate a process of reflection on the part of the client. Third, to work in this way with clients requires an ability to facilitate collaborative discussions around method choice. Fourth, practising pluralistically means that a therapist needs to be willing, and able, to be flexible in their way of working: adopting new methods or dropping previous methods in tune with the emerging dialogue. Finally, all therapy methods rely on the possession of generic counselling skills. There are many excellent books and training programmes that demonstrate and explain what is involved in effectively using 'micro-skills' such as listening, appropriate non-verbal communication, observing, reflecting back, questioning, challenging and so on (Hill, 1999; Ivey & Ivey, 1999). Typically, skills training programmes provide opportunities for trainees to practise these skills in a safe environment, and receive feedback. These micro-skills form the basis of any therapeutic intervention. Complex interventions, such as two-chair work or systematic desensitisation, can be viewed merely as sequences of micro-skills that are designed to achieve a particular result. Most of the time, a client and therapist working collaboratively can work out for themselves what they need to do to achieve these results, as long as the therapist has sufficient basic skill to enable this process to take place.

Summary

Methods are the actual procedures or actions that a therapist and client jointly perform in order to make a difference. It is likely that many different methods can be used to accomplish the same task. Methods always require the active involvement of clients, and are likely to be most helpful if agreed on by therapist and client. Methods can be drawn on from many sources: the established therapeutic literature, everyday cultural resources, and the client's and therapist's own personal knowledge about what works for them. Methods should be negotiated with clients in a time-conscious manner, with an emphasis on helping clients to develop a sense of efficacy – and personal responsibility – in making change happen. The effectiveness of chosen methods should be monitored on an ongoing basis.

Questions for reflection and discussion

1. Do you agree or disagree with the hypothesis that there are many different ways of completing the same task? Do you think that there are some therapeutic tasks, or some problems, for which there is just one effective method?
2. 'Sometimes the most helpful therapeutic methods for clients are the ones that take place outside therapy.' Discuss.
3. What do you think are the best ways of telling whether a therapeutic method is helpful or not? How might you check this in your own work?

7 Research: Developing Pluralistic Counselling and Psychotherapy

This chapter discusses:

- The implications for counselling and psychotherapy research of adopting a pluralistic outlook.
- A pluralistic approach to counselling and psychotherapy research, in which:
  - potential pathways of change are identified, rather than universal laws of change;
  - a research-informed approach is adopted;
  - there is a focus on 'micro-change' processes.
- The ways in which this approach can overcome some of the problems inherent in traditional psychotherapy research.
- Strategies for using research to contribute to the further development of a pluralistic approach.

In recent years, the profession of counselling and psychotherapy has seen an unprecedented rise in the importance attributed to research findings. In the UK, for instance, government funding is increasingly being directed towards those therapies that have been shown, through experimental study, to be effective (see, for instance, the Improving Access to Psychological Therapies programme, Clark, et al., 2009). Research competences are also taking an increasingly prominent role in the training requirements of such organisation as the British Association of Counselling and Psychotherapy (BACP).

For many counsellors and therapists, this move towards a research-driven profession is highly problematic (e.g., Rowan, 2001), and the concerns expressed are very consistent with a pluralistic outlook. Nevertheless, in this chapter, we hope to show that research can play a valuable role in the development of pluralistic counselling and psychotherapy. For this to happen, however, we need to revise the way in which we generate, and make use of, research findings. This chapter seeks to re-vision counselling and psychotherapy research in two ways. First, some general principles are offered in relation to a pluralistic framework for counselling and psychotherapy research as a whole. Second, there are some suggestions for ways in which research can be used to contribute to the development of pluralistic approach.

A Pluralistic Approach to Counselling and Psychotherapy Research

Pluralism provides a philosophical and socio-political perspective from which it is possible to take a fresh look at contemporary research in counselling and psychotherapy. We believe that a pluralistic stance has important implications for research policy and practice.

Research as an invaluable, but not privileged, source of guidance for practice

One of the reasons why counsellors and psychotherapists may be concerned about the recent moves towards an evidence-based culture is that, in many respects, empirical knowledge is becoming privileged over all other forms of understanding. National Institute for Health and Clinical Excellence (NICE) Guidelines in the UK (e.g., National Institute for Health and Clinical Excellence, 2009), for instance, draw almost exclusively from the empirical research to make recommendations for practice – and from a very narrow band of research methods at that. Here, then, factors such as a client's preferences, the therapist's experience, intuitive understandings, the client's case history, supervisory guidance, and personal reflections are all considered very much secondary sources of guidance as compared with what has been observed to take place in clinical trials. However, as even advocates of an evidence-based approach state, such guidelines are no substitute for the therapist's clinical judgements (e.g., Chambless, Sanderson, Shoham, Bennett Johnson & Pope, 1996). Indeed, the American Psychological Association has recently defined evidence-based psychological practice as 'the integration of the best available research *with clinical expertise in the context of patient characteristics, culture, and preferences*' (APA, 2006: 273, italics added). This means that, if research findings are relied upon over all other sources of knowledge, there is a very real danger that information critical to a case may be overlooked. It is one thing, for instance, for a therapist to know that non-directive therapy is of proven short-term benefit for depression in clinical trials (King, et al., 2000), but if they ignore the fact that an individual client is asking for a more directive approach, or their clinical judgement tells them that their approach is wrong with this particular client, then there is a very real danger that a client might be disadvantaged.

By contrast, a pluralistic approach, which holds that there is no 'royal road' to the truth, starts from the assumption that research evidence is one, but only one, very valuable source of guidance on how to practise counselling and psychotherapy. This means that it is seen as standing alongside other factors such as client choice, therapist experience and theoretical understandings, but not above them. This is a 'research-informed' approach to counselling and psychotherapy, rather than a 'research-directed' one (Westen, Novotny, & Thompson-Brenner, 2004). So, for instance, in working with a client, it may be very useful to know that, in general, higher levels of empathy are associated with more favourable outcomes (Bohart, Elliott, Greenberg & Watson, 2002). But, in thinking about how to work with this client, there are many other things that need to be taken into account: for instance, the therapist's personal reaction to the client, guidance from supervisors, theories of why the client may be experiencing their problems and intuitive feelings about what may be most helpful to the client.

Having said that, it is worth noting that research evidence is one of the areas in which counsellors and psychotherapist, despite the recent developments, are often least informed (e.g., Boisvert & Faust, 2006). And, indeed, many counselling and psychotherapy training courses continue to teach theory, encourage self-reflection, and offer supervision long before they invite clients to engage with the research evidence – if at all. On these grounds, then, from a pluralistic perspective, it could be argued that acquiring an understanding of the research evidence *is* a key priority for many therapists. This is not, however, on the basis that it is a superior form of knowledge to all others, but because it is so entirely absent in so many therapists' knowledge bases.

Recommended reading

Cooper, M. (2008). *Essential Research Findings in Counselling and Psychotherapy: The Facts are Friendly.* London: Sage. Mick's book provides an accessible and comprehensive review of the client, therapist, relational, technique and orientation factors that are associated with positive outcomes. See also Ladislav Timulak's excellent *Research in Psychotherapy and Counselling* (London: Sage, 2008) and, for a definitive overview of the research findings, see Michael Lambert (Ed.). (2004). *Handbook of Psychotherapy and Behavior Change.* New York: John Wiley.

Actively encouraging the development of research that is grounded in user perspectives

A pluralistic outlook on therapy research acts as a reminder that there are different stakeholders who have different perspectives and interests in relation to the production of research knowledge. At the present time, almost all of the research that is published in the field of counselling and psychotherapy is conceived and carried out from within the professional community. As a result, this research privileges the point of view of therapists and therapy academics. By contrast, a pluralistic stance invites consideration of the fact that therapy clients and service users may well have different research questions that they would like to explore, and different criteria around the kind of research knowledge that is available to them. Within the broader world of consumer affairs, there are many organisations that carry out research solely on behalf of those who purchase and make use of products. For example in the UK, the Consumer Association (which publishes the magazine *Which?*) carried out independent tests on a wide range of goods and services. The results of their research serve as a challenge and a stimulus to manufacturers and service providers, to achieve higher standards, eliminate defective products, and in general to give people what they want. A truly pluralistic research sector within the field of counselling and psychotherapy would include a vastly expanded body of consumer-based research, which was engaged in ongoing dialogue and debate with counselling and psychotherapy professional groups.

Embracing methodological pluralism

As might be expected, from a pluralistic standpoint, no one method is considered best for researching counselling and psychotherapy, nor is there a given 'hierarchy of evidence'. Rather, a diversity of strategies – qualitative (word-based) and quantitative (number-based), case studies, process–outcome studies, outcomes studies, surveys, experimental designs – are all seen as having the potential to contribute to the development of knowledge in this field. More than that, knowledge from these different sources is seen as having the potential to be mutually enhancing: corroborating, triangulating and elaborating each other, with the possibility of an active, continual process of interpretation and re-interpretation (Goss & Mearns, 1997).

Identifying possibilities, not universalities

Many therapists are cautious, or uninterested, in drawing on the research literature because of its desire to establish general or universal 'laws' – when what therapists are primarily interested in is what is helpful to an individual client. Most research today, for instance, asks questions like: 'Which therapy is effective for people with a particular psychological diagnosis?' or 'Which factors relate to positive therapeutic outcomes?' But what most therapists experience, and what we have argued in this book, is that actual clients are very different, and it is relatively meaningless to try to establish laws that are universal for all clients. Worse than that, if we end up concluding that 'motivational interviewing *is* effective for clients with substance abuse' or 'cognitive analytic therapy *works* for clients with anorexia nervosa', we may end up imposing on a client a method that is not right for them individually, or may actively harm them.

And, indeed, while claims are often made in the research literature along the lines of 'X has been shown to lead to Y', no therapy or therapeutic factor has ever been shown to be helpful to *all* people *all* of the time. Even relational qualities such as high levels of empathy, which Carl Rogers (1957) believed to be necessary and sufficient for therapeutic personality change to take place, have been found to be counterproductive for certain clients (Bohart, et al., 2002). Similarly, when outcome studies claim to have shown that a therapy is effective, what they will have actually shown is something far more heterogeneous. For instance, an evaluation that Mick conducted of a schools' counselling service found a 'significant reduction in levels of psychological difficulties from pre- to post-counselling' (Cooper, 2006a: 49). This is true, but what this states is only something at the level of average changes. When one looks at individual changes, on the other hand, what the evidence shows is that 40% of those who started counselling at 'abnormal' levels of psychological difficulties got better, while 10% of those who started at 'normal' levels got worse. Typically, such individual differences have been treated in the research literature as 'random variance' (Shoham-Salomon & Hannah, 1991), that is, peripheral factors that get in the way of us seeing what effect an intervention actually has. But if we reject the 'patient uniformity myth' (i.e., that clients are a homogeneous group, Kiesler, 1966), and instead see such individual differences as critical to the subjects of our inquiry, then a finding of average effects across individuals becomes much more difficult to interpret, and even more difficult to apply to practice.

In contrast to this way of making sense of research findings, a pluralistic approach starts from the assumption that there are never any definitive, universal givens: only possibilities. From this standpoint, then, research evidence can never provide certainties about how people change. Rather, what it can do is to help us map out the *potential* 'pathways' (Doss, 2004) by which people might change. In particular, and linking this in to the pluralistic framework, what research can tell us about is:

- the particular therapist activities that might facilitate particular client activities;
- the particular client activities that might lead to the successful fulfilment of particular tasks;
- the particular tasks that might lead to the achievement of particular goals.

In this way, the pluralistic framework allows us to draw on, and incorporate into practice, research findings, without requiring us to claim universal truthhood for our beliefs. For instance, from the research, it is clear that many clients who experience panic benefit enormously from cognitive therapy (e.g., Clark, et al., 1999). Some may claim that this shows that cognitive therapy – in correcting dysfunctional cognitions – *is* beneficial in the treatment of panic. However, if we view this as a potential change pathway, then we can see it as one method that might be very helpful for some clients, but is not guaranteed to be helpful to all. Such a standpoint, as discussed above, can then help to ensure that we do not go about trying to apply such a treatment to clients who may not benefit from it. It helps us stay open to a wide variety of possibilities, and to knowledge and understandings from a broad range of sources.

Of course, as in the example above, it may be that some change pathways are more 'well-trodden' than others, and research evidence – both quantitative and qualitative – can be very useful in helping us to establish that fact. For instance, if we conducted a comparative study of relaxation therapy and existential therapy for generalised anxiety, we might find out that 80% of clients improved in the former condition, while only 20% of clients improved in the latter. On this basis of this, we might then be more inclined to adopt relaxation methods into our work with anxious people, particularly in the early stages or in the absence of other knowledge. But such an inclination would not preclude us from being aware of the possibility that, for some clients, the less well-trodden path – existential methods – may be most helpful. Similarly, the finding that clients tend to rate 'listening' as a more helpful therapist activity than 'asking questions' (Williams, 2002) might guide us towards the former, while at the same time leaving open the possibility that, for some clients some of the time, asking questions may be of enormous value.

Along somewhat similar lines, it may also be very valuable to learn from the research that certain therapist activities, to a greater or lesser extent, are actually associated with negative experiences. A considerable body of research evidence, for instance, indicates that a high frequency of transference interpretations tends to be associated with poorer outcomes (Piper, Azim, Joyce & McCallum, 1991). Translated into a universal law of cause-and-effect, one may conclude from this that 'High levels of transference interpretations should be avoided' (Crits-Christoph & Gibbons, 2002: 298). However, from a pluralistic standpoint, it may be more appropriate to conclude that, in the absence of other information, it may be wise to avoid high levels of transference interpretations, but with the right client at the right time they have the potential to be extremely helpful.

Of course, if research is considered an invaluable, but not privileged, source of information, then many other forms of knowledge can also be drawn on to map out potential client change pathway. One of the unique values of research knowledge, however, is that it can provide a very valuable insight into change processes *from the clients' perspective.* That is, it articulates something of what clients experience in therapy without being mediated or interpreted by therapists. This is a particularly important feature given how frequently therapists misjudge clients' experiences. 'In this respect, the value of empirical research findings may not be so much in what they *teach* therapists, but more the way in which they can *challenge* therapists to reconsider their implicit assumptions and expectations: shaking them out of rigid belief systems such that they can be more responsive to the actual clients in front of them' (Cooper, 2008: 3, 2010). As argued above, therapists' experiences, intuitive feelings and clinical insights all have their place in determining therapeutic programmes. But it is also important for therapists to be aware that their deeply, intuitive felt-senses of what clients want or need can sometimes be totally and utterly wrong, and attending to the research evidence can help therapists develop a less therapist-centric understanding of potential pathways of change.

Finally, there are two further advantages of understanding research findings in terms of potential pathway of change. First, it means that an appreciation of clients as agentic, freely-choosing beings can be retained. In more traditional understandings, research findings are used to establish causal laws of change – that input X leads to output Y – as if the clients themselves had nothing to do with it. But, seen as potential pathways of change that clients *could* go down, there is nothing that we need construe as *determined* to happen. Second, and closely related to this, the notion of change pathways allows us to conceptualise processes that are reciprocal and circular in nature – such as positive and negative feedback loops – rather than solely linear relationships. Doss (2004: 373) gives the example, for instance, that 'successfully completing exposures may increase the client's self-efficacy, which may in turn help the client to subsequently tackle more threatening exposures'. Here, to simply conclude that exposure techniques cause a reduction in anxiety would be to overlook much of the process that is actually taking place. Rather, there is a positive feedback loop between undergoing exposure and increasing self-efficacy that can be mapped out in terms of reciprocal relationships between methods and tasks, leading to the achievement of clinical goals.

A focus on micro-processes

A further limitation within much contemporary psychotherapy research, closely linked to the above, is that it tends to focus on very broad-scale, macro-level relationships between different factors. Typically, for instance, psychotherapy outcome research asks about the relationship between particular therapist activities and the achievement of particular goals. For example, does non-directive practice lead to greater or lesser levels of depression than CBT (King, et al., 2000)? Viewed through the lens of the pluralistic framework, however, such a question overlooks the many pathways and stages by which specific therapist activities may lead to specific goals. It does not look, for instance, at the kinds of client activities that non-directive therapist activities facilitates, or the kinds of tasks that such client activities can then support, or the kinds of very specific goals and outcomes that then emerge through the achievements of these tasks. Consequently, such research provides only a very blurry image of what happens in therapy – like looking at a picture from a very long way away – and one that is difficult to translate into specific practices with specific clients at specific points in time.

Box 7.1: What works for *me*?

More than 40 years ago, Gordon Paul (1967: 111), a psychologist at the University of Illinois, wrote a highly influential paper entitled 'Strategy of outcome research in psychotherapy'. Challenging the psychotherapeutic research establishment, he argued that the question 'Does psychotherapy work?' was virtually meaningless because the term 'psychotherapy' encompassed so many heterogeneous practices. For him, narrowing the question down to specific schools of therapy was little better because of the vast array of methods within each school. He also argued that it was meaningless to ask about the efficacy of therapies for particular 'kinds' of clients, as 'the range of individual differences within standard diagnostic categories remains so diversified as to render meaningless any questions or statements about individuals who become so labelled'. Famously, he concluded that the appropriate question to be asked of all outcome research was '*what* treatment, by *whom*, is the most effective for *this* individual with *that* specific problem, and under *which* set of circumstances?' From a pluralistic standpoint, it is exactly this sort of specificity that is still needed from counselling and psychotherapy research, rather than the much more general 'What works for whom?' (Roth & Fonagy, 2005). However, the formulation suggested by Paul can be augmented by the phrase 'for this individual *on this specific occasion*', in recognition of the possibility that the person may find meaning in pursuing a multiplicity of methods, each of which may be foregrounded at different therapy sessions. In the context of everyday practice, the question under consideration is not the somewhat distanced 'What works for whom?' but the more concrete and immediate 'What works for me?'

As a consequence of such limitations, Doss (2004: 368) has argued that we need to change the way in which we study change in psychotherapy, focusing on the actual mechanisms and process of therapeutic change rather than the more macro 'what works' agenda. In support of this position, Donald Kiesler (2004: 392) has written, 'Psychotherapy researchers must shift focus away from primary concern with "ultimate" patient outcomes (*Big Os*) to the proximate (*Little Os*) patient outcomes, which are conceptually and empirically connected to each other as they antedate the more distal Big Os found at therapy termination and at follow-up periods.'

The pluralistic framework provides one means by which this programme of research can be achieved. Rather than focusing on distal associations between therapist activities and outcomes, the approach provides a conceptual framework in which this relationship can be broken down into proximal, micro-change processes. Hence, for instance, research might look at the particular client activities that are facilitated by such therapist activities as supportive listening, advice, or the teaching of relaxation exercises. Or researchers might look at the various pathways by which clients might achieve a goal of an increased sense of self-esteem. Such studies will inevitably lead to the construction of complex, intricate maps. But by focusing on the concrete realities of what has the potential to lead to what, and what that might lead to, it has the possibility of being of far greater use for practitioners in proposing to clients, and trying out, particular methods.

Box 7.2: Using research to generate an understanding of therapeutic principles

From 2002 to 2004, two of the key international figures in current psychotherapy research, Louis Castonguay and Larry Beutler, chaired a task force charged by the American Psychological Association and the North American Society for Psychotherapy Research with the task of identifying the effective 'principles' of psychotherapeutic change. As with the pluralistic framework, the concept of 'principles of therapeutic change' was an attempt to articulate middle levels of abstraction, filling the gulf between methods and outcomes. These principles were defined as 'general statements that identify participant characteristics, relational conditions, therapist behaviors, and classes of interventions that are likely to lead to change in psychotherapy' (Castonguay & Beutler, 2006c: 5). Examples of principles of change that the Task Force arrived at were that: 'The most effective treatments are those that do not induce patient resistance' (Castonguay & Beutler, 2006a: 357); 'Therapy is likely to be beneficial if a therapist facilitates change in clients' cognitions' (Castonguay & Beutler, 2006a: 363); and that, for clients with anxiety disorders, 'Providing feedback is likely to be useful' (Castonguay & Beutler, 2006a: 360). In total, over 50 principles were arrived at, encompassing and supporting a wide and diverse range of practices. The Task Force report was published as *Principles of Therapeutic Change that Work* (New York: Oxford University Press, 2006), and remains one of the most forward-thinking texts in the counselling and psychotherapy research field. A leading psychotherapy researcher based at the University of Memphis, Heidi Levitt, has taken this agenda forward through a programme of research that has invited clients and therapists to identify the principles that have been most significant for them in their experience of therapy (Levitt, Butler, & Hill, 2006; Levitt, Neimeyer & Williams, 2005).

A Pluralistic Research Programme

In the remaining sections of this chapter, we offer an outline of the kind of research that we believe has the potential to facilitate and enhance the further development of a pluralistic approach to counselling and psychotherapy. In making these suggestions, we are mindful of the fact that the most significant turning points in the history of psychotherapy have occurred when theory, practice, research and training have been brought together into a mutually influencing whole. We are thinking here in particular of the example that has had a major impact on our own ideas about how useful knowledge about therapy can be assembled: the emergence of client-centred therapy from the work of a small group of practitioner-researchers, led by Carl Rogers at the University of Chicago in the early 1950s (McLeod, 2002). Meaningful advances in therapy occur when new ideas can be tested and refined through practice *and* research, in the context of a like-minded group of individuals. Of course, unlike the situation in Rogers' era, nowadays it is not necessary for a group of this type to all reside in the same place – the internet and international travel mean that effective research teams can function on a world-wide basis.

Identifying change pathways

As discussed above, the pluralistic framework provides a basis by which we can move away from macro therapist activity – outcome relationships, and instead look at the pathways by which therapist activities can stimulate client activities, client activities can lead to the accomplishment of tasks, and the accomplishment of tasks can help clients achieve their goals. An excellent means of undertaking such research is through in-depth qualitative interviewing (Kvale, 1996): dialoguing with clients about what was helping in their therapeutic work, and what outcomes it led to.

An example of this comes from a study of young people's experiences of counselling in a secondary school setting (see full analysis in Cooper, 2004). Nineteen former clients were interviewed about their experiences and with respect to what they had found helpful in the work. These interviews were then transcribed and analysed to create categories and sub-categories, which could be placed within the domains of client activities, therapist activities and tasks. Frequencies of respondents are given as per Rodgers and Cooper's (2006) scoring scheme for qualitative thematic analysis.

In terms of what the counsellor did that was helpful, most of the participants talked about the value of the counsellor simply *listening* to them. Closely related to this, some of the participants talked about the way in which the counsellor seemed to *understand* them: to see things from their perspective and empathise with what they were going through. In addition, some of the participants also talked about the value of talking to someone who was *not critical or judgemental.*

While many of the participants, as seen above, valued the counsellor's non-directivity and encouragement to talk, around half of them also said that they valued the *questions* that the counsellor asked them. Most of the participants indicated that one of the main reasons that counselling had helped them was because of the *suggestions or advice* that the counsellor had provided. Some of these pupils specifically talked about the value of being given advice on how to behave: for instance, standing up to bullies or telling adults about their problems. Closely related to being given advice on how to behave, some of the pupils said that they particularly valued the *relaxation techniques* that they were taught during the counselling, such as breathing exercises, guided visualisation and progressive muscular relaxation.

In terms of *client* activities, nearly all of the pupils indicated that they valued having *an opportunity to talk*. More specifically, some of the participants said that they really valued the opportunity to 'get things off their chest', to 'just talk about whatever was stressing you or whatever', to 'let it all out'. For around half of the participants, what had been helpful to them was *reflecting* on why they felt, thought and behaved in the way that they did: exploring aspects of their being that they had been hitherto unaware of. For some of the participants, it was the chance to *explore alternative – and potentially more constructive – ways of behaving* and responding to situations that was particularly of value to them.

What were the specific benefits of participating in counselling? The most frequent answer here, given by around half of the participants, was that it led to *positive changes*

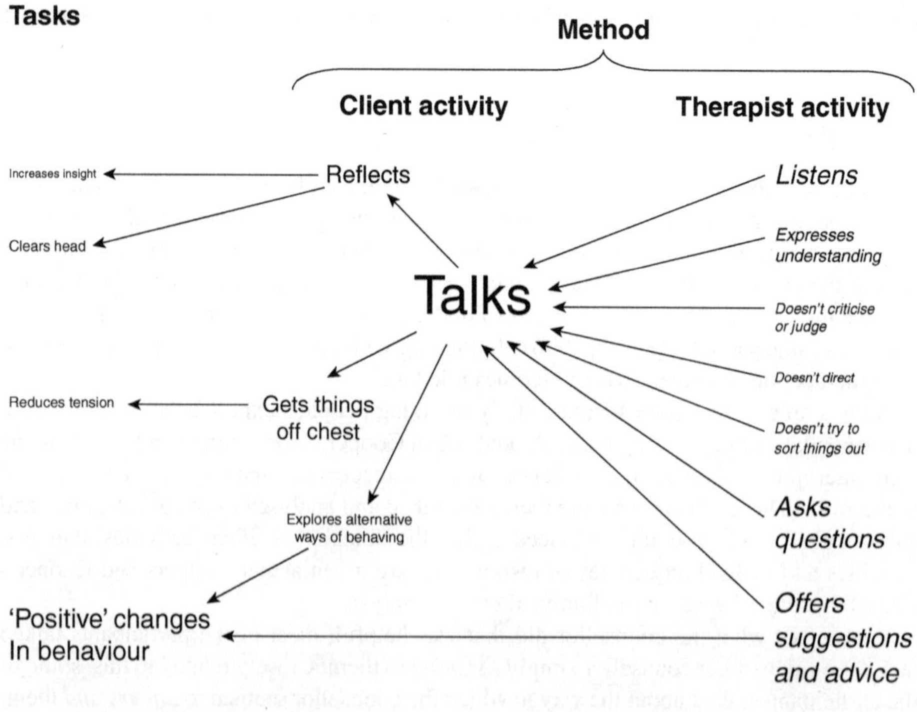

Figure 7.1: Process map of children and young people's experiences of counselling in schools
Note: Larger fonts indicate greater numbers of children and young people giving a response.

in the way they behaved. Some of the participants, for instance, described acting in more assertive ways following counselling: they were more willing to tell other people how they were feeling, ask for help, and face up to bullies. Another couple said that, after counselling, they were less reactive: they were more able to walk away from situations when they felt angry, or to stop and think before 'blurting' things out. Some of the participants said that, as a consequence of the counselling, they felt less burdened by their thoughts and feelings – a reduced sense of inner tension and pressure. Some of the participants described how, as a consequence of the counselling, they developed a *greater insight* into their feelings and behaviours. Closely related to this, some of the participants said that, as a consequence of the counselling, their minds became *clearer*: less confused and tangled up.

Figure 7.1 presents a 'process map' giving an overview of the different findings. To convey the relative prevalence of different categories, font sizes have been used that are in proportion to the number of people giving each answer. Such a map illustrates how the pluralistic framework can articulate a wide range of potential change processes, which may be of value for practitioners in this setting when considering the most appropriate methods to adopt. Further research using this paradigm might seek to develop a more comprehensive description of client and therapist activities associated with successful 'talking' (for example, the use of questioning strategies), or might seek to expand the range of possible methods that contributed to the completion of a task such as 'reducing tension'.

Creating an open-access library of goal–task–method narratives

One particularly useful means of developing an understanding of these pathways of change would be by building up a library of goal–task–method narratives. A 'task–method narrative' can be understood as a personal account of what a person did in order to accomplish a particular type of task. For example, a fairly common task that arises for many people in therapy is that of 'doing something to shift a painful feeling or emotion'. What could be offered by carefully-written narrative accounts would be stories that described the circumstances under which a person attempted to make use of a specific method or methods, what they did, what worked, what didn't work, their understanding of what contributed to the effectiveness or otherwise of a method, and possibly the long-term sustainability of what they learned.

It would be very exciting if such a library of task–method narratives, written by both clients and therapists, could accumulate on an open-access 'wiki' site. Over time, such a resource would generate a highly differentiated body of practical knowledge around a vast range of methods, and also the *possibilities* associated with these methods. For example, it could emerge that relaxation skills are potentially useful in leading to certain types of beneficial outcome, but have been of limited value in some specified circumstances for some people. This information would be of interest to clients, potential clients, ordinary members of the public and therapists because it would represent a treasure-house of hopefulness in terms of ways of dealing with everyday problems in living.

Evaluating the outcomes of pluralistic therapy

There are ever-increasing expectations, from policy-makers and service users, that any form of therapy that is on offer will be backed up by research evidence of its effectiveness. If pluralistic therapy is to flourish, it will need to be supported by the results of well-conducted outcome studies. From a pluralistic perspective, it is important that this evidence does not rely on information from just one method of investigation, such as randomised clinical trials, but draws on multiple methods. There are several different ways of conducting therapy outcome studies:

- practice-based or naturalistic studies that evaluate the outcomes of therapy in everyday practice;
- randomised trials where clients are randomly allocated to different therapies to compare their effectiveness;
- outcome-focused case studies, such as 'n=1' studies and Hermeneutic Single Case Efficacy Design studies;
- case-series, in which a set of case studies are analysed together;
- qualitative follow-up interviews with clients;
- client satisfaction studies;
- research carried out by service user groups.

Each of these methodologies can make a distinctive contribution to building up a picture of the strengths and limitations of pluralistic therapy with different client groups. From a pluralistic perspective, none of these methodologies represents a 'gold standard' of outcome evidence. Instead, any of these methods has the potential to generate information that can have an impact on policy and practice.

In order to carry out convincing outcome studies, it is necessary to be able to specify the therapy that is being delivered. For example, in randomised trials therapy is carried out in accordance to a practice manual or protocol that defines what the therapist should be doing, and adherence to the manual is assessed by independent judges who listen to tapes of the therapy session and rate whether the therapist is acting in accordance with the principles outlined in the manual. In relation to future studies of pluralistic therapy, we propose that this book could be used as a basic manual. At the present time, procedures for rating adherence have not been developed. The key observable characteristics of pluralistic therapy that would need to be assessed in an adherence rating scale would include evidence that:

- pre-therapy preparation had been given for an 'active client' role;
- therapy was being conducted with reference to agreed goals;
- regular episodes of therapist-initiated metacommunication could be observed, consisting of conversations around goals, tasks and methods;
- clients talked about their preferences for therapy procedures;
- a culture of feedback was being implemented, in which the client's views were sought and acted upon;
- links between client preferences and the therapy tasks and methods were being pursued.

In outcome studies that do not require full-blown adherence checks to be implemented (e.g., practice-based studies, case studies), therapists could be asked to indicate through a self-report questionnaire whether their practice was informed by the principles listed above.

The version of therapy that is described in this book advocates the routine use of process, outcome and client preference scales in therapy as a means of providing clients with channels of communication to give feedback to their therapist and influence the therapist's way of working. When this kind of approach is taken, an enormous amount of outcome data is quickly accumulated. There should therefore be plentiful opportunities to carry out outcome studies on pluralistic therapy merely by devising systems to capture and analyse these routine data.

Box 7.3: The role of case study research in the development of pluralistic therapy

A key element of pluralistic therapy is *flexibility*, the capacity for the client and therapist to accommodate each other to make the best use of the strengths and resources that are available to each of them. One of the implications of this characteristic of pluralistic practice is that it is possible that many different patterns of therapy process and activity can be generated. This phenomenon presents a problem for research approaches that seek to observe pre-defined factors across a large sample of clients. However case study methods are ideally suited to explore the processes and outcomes of counselling and psychotherapy that follow pluralistic principles. In recent years, a variety of methodological strategies have been devised to ensure that single case studies produce knowledge that is rigorous and generalisable (see McLeod, 2010). Alongside the other methods described in this chapter, systematic case studies have a vital role to play in documenting, analysing and evaluating the outcomes and processes of pluralistic ways of working in counselling and psychotherapy.

Developing tools and procedures to support a 'culture of feedback'

Establishing a culture of feedback (Box 3.5 on page 49), in which the client is able to engage in dialogue with the therapist around whether therapy is or is not being helpful, is a central strand of a pluralistic approach. There are many ways in which a culture of feedback can be established and maintained. In this book, we have placed a particular emphasis on the routine use of brief questionnaires that are designed to make it easy for a client to convey their views to their therapist around the outcomes of therapy, the quality of the collaborative relationship between them, and their preferences for different ways of working. In recent years, a great deal of research has been carried out that demonstrates that providing this kind of information to therapists can have a significance positive impact on the effectiveness of therapy, mainly by acting as a signal of when things are going wrong (see Chapter 3). In addition, there is a growing body of knowledge around how clients and therapists make use of this kind of information – what it means to them. Sundet (2009b) has described these techniques as functioning as 'conversational tools'.

The research into ways of developing a 'feedback culture' in counselling and psychotherapy has done a great deal to demonstrate the potential value of this aspect of practice. We believe that what is now needed is to build on existing research by involving clients and therapists in looking at how feedback tools and procedures can be further developed. For example, one of our colleagues in Scotland, Brian Rodgers (2006, 2010), has found that clients who were invited to draw 'life space maps' (i.e., using non-verbal means to express their experience of therapy), reported that this activity was highly valuable in giving them an understanding of how they had changed over the course of therapy, and in ways that were not captured in paper-and-pencil questionnaires that they also completed. This study suggests that we have only just began to tap the many feedback possibilities that could be introduced into therapy. A pluralistic stance suggests that different clients will have their own personal preferences of the type of feedback that is most useful to them. There are also important questions to be explored concerning therapist skill and sensitivity in eliciting feedback, and responsiveness to feedback once it has been offered.

Exploring strategies for maximising effective therapist–client collaboration

One of the 'givens' of contemporary research in counselling and psychotherapy is that the quality of the therapeutic relationship or 'alliance' plays a key role in effective therapy (see Cooper, 2008, for a review of this literature). Most of this research has defined the therapeutic relationship in terms of three alliance factors that were first identified by Bordin (1979): the existence of an emotional *bond* between therapist and client, and therapist–client agreement around *goals* and *tasks*. Research has shown that when the client *perceives* that they have a bond with the therapist, and *believes* that they are in agreement around goals and tasks, then good outcomes will follow. What is missing from this research, up to now, is an exploration of what it is that therapists can actually do, in practice, to achieve these relationship attributes. As a result, it is hard for practitioners to know, on the basis of research, what they might do to improve their relationship competence. Some research by Bedi, Davis and Williams (2005) suggests that, at least from the point of view of the client, there are many things that therapists can do to enhance the quality of their collaboration. For example, the clients interviewed by Bedi said that it was important for them that their therapist conveyed a sense of *caring* about them.

There is an absence of research that has directly observed the actions of therapists who are effective in negotiating agreement around goals, tasks and methods, and those who are less effective. As Thoma and Cicero (2009: 406) write, 'Understanding more about this flexible process of tailoring psychotherapy to clients' needs may be a valuable contribution towards the goal of understanding what works for whom and when.'

There are many other aspects of collaborative activity that might be studied by therapy researchers. For example: What intensity of collaborative 'checking-out' is optimal (several times in each therapy session, or every few weeks)? What are the implications of introducing collaborative 'checking-out' into the structure of therapy sessions (for instance, at the start and end of sessions)? The intention with this research is not to seek to establish a fixed set of rules around 'good practice in collaboration', but rather to map out possibilities that can be selected and adapted in response to particular circumstances.

Enabling people to be 'better' clients

Formal research into counselling and psychotherapy began with the work of Carl Rogers and his colleagues in the 1940s. There now exists a cumulative store of 70 years of research knowledge into all aspects of therapy practice. Virtually all of this research has focused on the question of how to make better therapists. Very little research has considered the question of how to make better clients. A collaborative pluralistic perspective emphasises the central importance of the client and therapist working together to find what works for them. From this perspective, the more that the client knows and understands about therapy, the better. Research into strategies for preparing clients for therapy (for example, by asking them to read a leaflet or watch a video) have generally shown a small, but positive effect on therapy outcome (Cooper, 2008; Orlinsky, Grawe & Parks, 1994). However, much of this work can be criticised on the basis that the client preparation approaches that were used tended to focus on providing information to clients so that they would know what to expect once therapy commenced. From a pluralistic stance, client preparation needs to involve much more than passive assimilation of information.

In pluralistic terms, 'good' clients are those who are actively involved in therapy, who ask for what they want and are not afraid to give feedback to their therapists. Further research on this topic might examine how client active participation in therapy is affected by reading the pluralistically-orientated pre-therapy information leaflet provided in Appendix A (see page 182), and evaluating improved versions of this leaflet. Beyond the provision of information to clients at the point at which they seek therapy, it would also be very interesting to explore what might be possible at a broader cultural level to make people better clients. For example, John is old enough to be able to remember when few people in Britain drank wine, or knew anything about different types of wine. Over the last 40 years in Britain, many people have learned to be 'better' wine drinkers, or even to develop a degree of connoisseurship around one's choice and appreciation. This shift has come about through dissemination of knowledge and skills through a wide range of sources: newspaper and magazine articles, TV programmes, local wine clubs, and so on. Maybe some of these activities can be adapted in the goal of enabling more people to become better therapy clients, in the sense of being able to make informed choices, achieve best value and get maximum satisfaction.

Pluralistic exploration of different types of client problem

From a pluralistic orientation, people live in worlds that encompass multiple contexts, multiple relationships, and multiple meaning-systems. When a person develops a problem for which they then seek assistance from a counsellor or psychotherapist, it is certain that multiple realities will be relevant. Conversely, adopting a narrow stance, and defining the problem solely in psychological or psychiatric terms, can lead to loss of potentially valuable insights and resources. One of the areas in which this issue is of particular importance relates to therapist appreciation of the nature of client problems. Occasionally, therapists may possess personal knowledge from their own life experience, or may have seen several clients with the same kind of problem, and so may have had an opportunity to build a richly detailed, nuanced understanding of what it is like to suffer from a particular kind of life difficulty. Much of the time, however, therapists need to rely on what the client tells them, about the ways in which a problem has affected their life. In these situations, therapists often have a sense of not really 'getting it' – they know that they are missing important issues and areas of experience. Reading mainstream research, in the form of statistical information based on large samples, is generally not very helpful because it does not allow a therapist to get close enough to the lived experience of their client. What is much more useful is to read qualitative research studies that have sought to capture the complex, multifaceted reality of what life is like for people with particular problems. An example can be found in relation to the experience of living with dementia or Alzheimer's disease. Anyone who is doing therapy with a client suffering from dementia will find enormous meaning in the research carried out by Steven Sabat (2001), based on carefully documented observation of the ways in which this disease reconstructs the communicative world of the person with dementia. The implications for therapy practice of this research (and other qualitative studies of dementia) have been outlined by Weaks, McLeod, and Wilkinson (2006).

Adjusting to dementia is just one among many types of problem that are brought to therapy. For the majority of these problems there exists qualitative research that is potentially highly informative for therapists. More needs to be done to make these studies accessible to therapy practitioners. This kind of research is vitally important to the development of pluralistic approaches to counselling and psychotherapy because it represents an evidence base that directly feeds into practice. It is also an evidence base that will be relevant to some clients who are interested in finding ways of talking about their own experience.

Effective training and supervision: testing the limits of therapist flexibility

The advancement of pluralistic therapy over the next few years will depend on the development of effective training programmes that will enable practitioners to acquire competence and confidence in relation to the adoption of a pluralistic approach. Some suggestions about the structure of pluralistic training are provided in Chapter 8. Research has an important part to play in the development of training courses, through being able to identify the type and extent of training that is required to become a safe pluralistic practitioner.

Underlying the model of pluralistic therapy that is outlined in this book are two basic assumptions about the nature of therapist competence. The first assumption is that competence is fundamentally grounded in a set of personal qualities and attitudes, and generic skills. The second assumption is that practitioners or trainees who possess these underlying qualities and attitudes can learn to deliver specific methods to a satisfactory level of competence with minimal additional training. Evidence for this assumption can be found in a number of studies. For example, Lappalainen et al. (2007) took a group of psychology students who had completed basic training in interview skills, and gave them an additional six hours of training in the specific techniques of Action and Commitment Therapy (ACT – Hayes, Strosahl & Wilson, 2003), a third-generation variant of cognitive-behavioural therapy. The effectiveness of these students was then evaluated in relation to the first two clients they were allocated, in a university-based community psychotherapy clinic. Students received regular clinical supervision. Clients were people with a range of problems, including anxiety, depression and interpersonal difficulties, and outcomes were assessed using standard symptom measures administered before therapy and at termination. The effectiveness rates achieved by these trainees was equivalent to those reported by experienced therapists. In another study, Cottraux et al. (2008) took some trained CBT therapists and asked them to deliver client-centred therapy to clients with long-term post-traumatic stress disorder (PTSD), on the basis of 10 hours of training supported by regular supervision. Again, high rates of effectiveness were reported. These studies suggest that, at least in principle, it is possible to take people who already possess good generic skills and teach them how to deliver specific interventions within a limited space of time. The role of supervision appears to be important in this process, in relation to consolidating and reinforcing what has been learned.

What is being suggested here is that it is possible, under the appropriate conditions and with suitable support and opportunity to practice, for competent counsellors and psychotherapists to develop competence in certain methods/interventions on the basis of about 10 hours of formal training. This statement can be regarded as a *hypothesis of therapist flexibility*, which requires rigorous testing through further research.

Summary

Many counsellors and psychotherapists are sceptical about the moves towards an evidence-based culture. The pluralistic framework provides a means of translating research into practice that maintains a dignified and individualised view of its 'subjects'. The basis of a pluralistic approach to research is that it adopts a research-informed, rather than research-driven, perspective; embraces a range of methods; strives to establish potential pathways of change rather than universal laws; and focuses on micro-processes rather than global relationships. Developing a pluralistic approach to therapy requires research in which potential relationships between goals, tasks and methods are mapped out. Other suggestions for a pluralistic research agenda include evaluating the effectiveness of pluralistic therapy; looking at different ways of enhancing a culture of feedback and client–therapist collaboration; helping clients to become more effective service users; examining different client problems from a pluralistic standpoint; and looking at the limits of therapist flexibility.

Questions for reflection and discussion

1. What role do you think research findings should have in determining or influencing concrete practice? Do you agree or disagree with a 'research-informed' perspective?
2. If you were going to carry out a research project within the pluralistic framework, what would you study?
3. What are the implications for research and practice of seeking to identify therapeutic 'principles'? What are the key principles that you use in guiding your own work with clients? What kind of research evidence would it take to convince you to add to this set of principles?
4. Pluralistic therapy is grounded in a commitment to meaningful and effective *collaboration* between clients and therapists. How important is it that the core value of collaborative dialogue is also reflected in research into pluralistic therapy? If it is important, then how can collaboration become part of the design and conduct of research studies?

8 Supervision, Training, CPD and Service Delivery: Pluralistic Perspectives

This chapter discusses:

- A pluralistic approach to therapeutic supervision.
- A pluralistic approach to training in therapy.
- Pluralistic perspectives on continuing professional development (CPD) for those who have not undertaken an initial pluralistic training.
- A pluralistic perspective on the delivery of therapeutic services.

Previous chapters in this book have explored the ways in which pluralism can be applied within therapy, through the work that clients and therapists do together. Basic principles that have emerged can be summarised as follows:

- there is no one right way of doing things: different people need different things at different points in time;
- if we want to know what is most likely to be helpful to people, it is generally a good idea to ask them about it;
- in helping people get what they want, it is often best to start with their goals, and then work back from there to the particular methods that might be helpful in achieving this.

The present chapter stands back from the immediate therapy process and relationship, and looks at how such pluralistic principles might be applied to various aspects of the 'support system' that exists in order to ensure that high-quality therapy is provided to clients on a consistent basis. The activities of counsellors and psychotherapists are underpinned by structures of clinical supervision, training, continuing professional development (CPD), and integrated into various types of service delivery network. The following sections of this chapter provide an overview of the implications of adopting a pluralistic outlook within these domains.

Supervision: A Pluralistic Perspective

There is an extensive literature that supports the relevance of regular, career-long clinical supervision as a means of ensuring quality of service delivery and therapist wellbeing (e.g., Lambert & Ogles, 1997; Wheeler & Richards, 2007). A pluralistic perspective underscores the crucial role of supervision as a way of allowing counsellors and psychotherapists to bring multiple perspectives to bear on their work with clients. The characteristics of effective supervision have been discussed in detail in a number of publications (e.g., Neufeldt, Beutler & Banchero, 1997; Weaks, 2002) and a pluralistic approach need not diverge from these established principles in any substantial way. Indeed, leading writers in the field of integrative supervision have already emphasised the importance of such pluralistic practices as flexibility and tailoring in the supervisory work (Norcross & Halgin, 2005; Wosket, 2000). Nevertheless, a pluralistic perspective on supervision does bring with it some novel challenges, possibilities and emphases. This is in two, closely interconnected, respects: first, in terms of supervising in a pluralistic way and, second, in terms of the key tasks of pluralistic supervision.

Supervising in a pluralistic way

When considering how supervision might be conducted from a pluralistic standpoint, nearly all the points made in this book about the client–therapist relationship can be transposed to the supervisor–supervisee domain. Specifically:

- The supervisor should start from the assumption that there is no one right way to offer supervision: different supervisees are likely to need different things at different points in time.
- Supervision is construed as a collaborative endeavour: the supervisor strives to respect, trust and value the supervisee's perspective, while also respecting and expressing their own.
- There is an emphasis on helping supervisees to identify and cultivate their strengths: the areas of practice in which they feel they are most proficient.
- The supervisor endeavours to facilitate a 'culture of feedback' in the supervisory relationship, in which the supervisee and supervisor feel able to be honest with the other about what they like, want and do not want.
- Supervisees are encouraged, particularly at the start of the supervisory relationship, to look at what their overall goals are for this work, and to use this as the orientating point for subsequent activities. Although, in contrast to the therapeutic relationship, the range of possibilities is more limited (because the supervisory relationship has clearer external demands, such as the need to ensure good practice), supervisees can still raise, discuss and negotiate with their supervisors around specific personalised goals.
- Supervisors should be aware of the limits of their practice, and be willing to refer on to another supervisor if they do not feel that they can help a particular supervisee.
- To help supervisees achieve their goals, it may be useful for supervisors and supervisees to discuss and agree particular tasks, or foci (Wosket, 2000), for the therapeutic work. This could be at the beginning of the supervisory relationship, as it proceeds, or at the beginning of each session. Wosket identifies a number of potential issues that a supervisee might want to focus on, such as a boundary problem, a difficulty with ending, lack of motivation, a personal issue affecting the client work, or a sense of achievement or success.
- Supervisors and supervisees might also find it useful to discuss and agree on the particular methods that a supervisee may be most likely to find helpful. For instance, one supervisee may find it useful to role-play their work with clients; another may find it particularly helpful to listen to recordings of their sessions.

- As a corollary of this, pluralistic supervisors may be most helpful if they are skilled in a range of supervision methods and techniques.

Wosket (2000) adds to this that matching between supervisor and supervisee may be important for an effective supervisory collaboration on such factors as worldview and cultural framework.

Exercise 8.1: What you have found helpful and unhelpful in supervision

If you are a therapist, take 20 minutes or so to think back, or talk with a partner, about the following questions:

- What have you found helpful in your own supervision (if anything)?
- What have you found unhelpful in your own supervision (if anything)?

You may also want to think, or talk, about whether or not you are getting the things that you want from your *current* supervisory work. If not, how might you try to change this?

As with helping clients to identify goals, tasks and methods, there are a range of prompts that supervisors might use to help their supervisees identify what they want from supervision and how they might achieve it. For instance:

Goals (most likely to be asked at the beginning of the supervisory relationship)

- 'What do you want to get out of our work together?'
- 'Are there particular areas of your practice that you would like to develop?'
- 'Where would you like to be by the end of our supervisory relationship?'

Tasks (these might be asked at the beginning of each supervision session)

- 'What would you like to work on today?'
- 'What is your dilemma with your client?' (Wosket, 2000: 283)
- 'Could you try putting your issues in one sentence?' (Wosket, 2000: 283)
- 'What do you need help with to work more effectively with your client?' (Wosket, 2000: 283)

Methods (explored at the beginning and on an ongoing basis)

- 'What way(s) of working would be most helpful for you in our supervision sessions?' (e.g., role-plays, advice, listening to recordings, case formulation, exploring personal blocks and difficulties, discussing theory, looking at 'parallel processes', exploring broader professional issues)

- 'What have you found most helpful in previous supervision work?'
- 'What haven't you found helpful, previously, in supervision?'
- 'What *style* of supervision do you find most productive?' (e.g., formal, informal, structured, unstructured, supportive, nurturing, authoritarian)
- 'How are you finding this supervision? Are there ways in which it could be more helpful to you?'

The task of supervision: A pluralistic perspective

As indicated above, pluralistic supervision is likely to be highly diverse: drawing from a wide variety of possible methods and understandings. At the same time, given that an underlying aim of all supervision is to help therapists be more effective in their practice, and given that the pluralistic approach has a particular view on how this can be achieved (i.e., through increased collaboration, flexibility and responsiveness), a pluralistic perspective brings something relatively unique to the pantheon of potentially helpful supervisory tasks. More specifically, from a pluralistic perspective, where difficulties or ruptures are emerging in a particular piece of therapeutic work, it may be very useful to encourage a supervisee to reflect on the quality of their alliance with the client, and to look at ways in which the degree of agreement over the goals, tasks and methods might be enhanced. For instance, a supervisee might be asked:

- 'What does your client seem to want from their work with you?' 'Is this consistent with what you want for them?' 'How might you more effectively help them reach their goals?' (goals)
- 'What aspect(s) of their lives is the client trying to focus on?' 'Is this the same as what you want them to focus on?' 'How could you go about agreeing with them a shared focus in the work?' (tasks)
- 'What ways of working does your client prefer?' 'Are these the ways of working that you are most comfortable with?' 'How might you relate to your client in a way that feels most helpful to them?' (methods)

In many instances, such a line of exploration may reveal to supervisees that they are really not clear about what their client wants from therapy or their preferred means of achieving it; or they may come to see that their own assumptions about what their client wants and prefers are almost entirely conjecture. A good outcome from this may be that the supervisee then decides to go back to the client and talk to them about this, and see if a greater clarity and consensus can be reached. For instance, Rami was a student on a diploma course in person-centred therapy. He was working with a client called Pete at a drugs and alcohol counselling service and, after seven sessions, was feeling increasingly exasperated and lost in the work. Pete was in his late 40s, had been drinking heavily since his teens, and had been referred to counselling by his doctor, who thought that it might help him cut down on his alcohol intake and improve his relationship with his estranged wife and sons. Initially, Rami had found the work with Pete fine, and had listened to him talk about his family, his problems, and how much he thought he should stop drinking. After about session four, though, Pete had started missing sessions; in session five Pete seemed to have turned up drunk; and in sessions six and seven, Pete had turned up 20 minutes late and, although apologetic, did not seem to be particularly interested in the therapeutic work. When Rami explored this in supervision, the question was raised as to what Pete might actually want from therapy. 'Er… I guess he wants to give up drinking,' said Rami, 'I don't know, I've never actually asked him.' The supervision group discussed this further, and Rami came to the conclusion that this was something he really needed to take back to his work with Pete.

Pete missed the next two appointments, but turned up the following week. 'It's really good to see you here,' said Rami, 'And I'm also really aware of how many sessions you've missed recently. Would it be ok if we spent a bit of time looking at what we are doing here, and how you want to use your time with me?'

At this point, Pete admitted that he wasn't really sure: it was his doctor who had told him to go, and he had just done it because he thought it would help. 'Help in what way?' Asked Rami.

'I don't really know,' said Pete , 'Maybe cut down on my drinking, improve things with my ex-.'

'Are those things that you want to change?' asked Rami.

Pete was quiet for a few seconds. 'I don't really know,' he said, 'I definitely want to get on better with my boys – but I'm not really sure if I ever want to see my ex- again.'

Rami invited Pete to talk more about his relationship with his boys, the first time they had really focused on this topic. At the end of the session, they agreed that they would spend the next few meetings talking about how Pete could try to re-establish a good relationship with his sons. Pete missed the next session, but turned up at the following one, and said that he had made some contact with his boys and that things had improved there a bit. Rami and Pete explored what else he could do.

In this example, the supervisory impetus towards goal- and methods-dialogue did not bring about dramatic changes in the effectiveness of the therapy. It did, however, help Pete use the time in a way that was more helpful to him, and also helped Rami to feel much less frustrated in the therapeutic work. Now, he no longer had a sense that he was pulling in an opposite direction from Pete: trying to get him to work on giving up drinking and resolve things with his ex- when he did not seem particularly bothered about either of them. Rather, he now knew what Pete wanted and had a sense that he was being of help.

Recommended reading

Wosket, V. (2000). Integration and eclecticism in supervision. In S. Palmer & R. Woolfe (Eds.), *Integrative and Eclectic Counselling and Psychotherapy* (pp. 271–290). London: Sage. A useful starting point for thinking about issues and practices in pluralistic supervision.

Norcross, J. C., & Halgin, R. P. (2005). Training in psychotherapy integration. In J. C. Norcross & M. R. Goldfried (Eds.), *Handbook of Psychotherapy Integration* (pp. 439–458). New York: Oxford University Press. Brief, but very useful, set of principles for integrative supervision, highly relevant to pluralistic practice.

Training in Counselling and Psychotherapy: A Pluralistic Approach

In this book, we have distinguished between pluralism as a general sensibility that can be adopted by a wide variety of practitioners (including single orientation and integrative specialists) and as a specific form of therapeutic practice. It is possible, therefore, to consider the implications of a pluralistic outlook for both specialised programmes and for a specifically pluralistic training curriculum.

Implications for specialised training programmes

At its most basic, a pluralistic outlook calls on trainers in single orientation and specialised training programmes to avoid 'critically disparaging alternative interventions' (Orlinsky & Rønnestad, 2005d: 186) and to ensure that students are taught to respect and value other ways of working. Students should be taught about the strengths of other orientations (as well as their limits), and the times and context in which they may be more helpful to a client than the trainee's own approach. Concomitantly, students should be encouraged to reflect critically on the therapeutic orientation they are being taught, and to see its limits as well as its strengths. Developing the skills to be able to communicate this to prospective clients – that is, what the trainee feels they can offer them and what they cannot – may also be very helpful. Given the lack of evidence for any one particular psychological theory (see Chapter 2), it may also be important to encourage students to see their orientations' particular models or hypotheses are exactly that – and not given, confirmed truths about the human condition. Note, the implication here is not that trainees should be taught to be diffident or unconfident about their own therapeutic orientation. Clearly, a certain degree of confidence is essential to help trainees work effectively. But, from a pluralistic perspective, trainees can be encouraged to feel confident and proud about the work that they do while *also* seeing the value in alternative practices.

In practical terms, one very important competence leading on from the above is that trainees should, from a pluralistic standpoint, develop the capacity to make informed referral decisions – ideally in collaboration with their clients (see Box 4.3 on page 76). In other words, specialised practitioners need to have the ethics, knowledge and skills to be able to 'relinquish patients for whom another approach is better' (Norcross & Halgin, 2005: 440).

Trainees in specialised practices can also be encouraged, more explicitly, to see their work as sitting within a larger pluralistic frame, and this is something that might be stated in a course handbook or taught at the beginning of a programme. For instance, on the Doctorate in Counselling Psychology jointly delivered by Glasgow Caledonian University and the University of Strathclyde, students spend the first year learning about person-centred ways of working, but this is preceded by a brief lecture on the pluralistic approach. The idea, here, is that this input will help students to locate their person-centred practice within a general pluralistic stance of open-mindedness and respect towards other orientations, 'inoculating' them against a more doctrinarian worldview.

Moving further towards a specifically pluralistic way of working, students on specialised training programmes may also be encouraged to consider how they might help clients identify their goals – particularly at the commencement of therapy (see Chapter 4).

Another pluralistic method that may be of help to single orientation trainees is to develop the skills to metacommunicate and negotiate with clients around the most helpful ways of working (see Chapters 5 and 6) within, of course, the parameters set by the therapist's particular orientation.

Pluralistic training

In recent years, there has emerged a broad consensus around the shape of therapist training. It is widely agreed that training programmes need to encompass theory, research, professional issues, work on self, development of therapeutic skills, and supervised practice. There is no reason to believe that pluralistic training needs to diverge from this template in any fundamental ways. However, a specifically pluralistic training programme is likely to have a number of relatively unique features and emphases, and these are discussed below.

Selection

There are some therapists who prefer to identify themselves with clearly-defined, single models of therapy, and who are able to develop productive careers on this basis. Such people are likely to become frustrated with therapy training that is orientated towards a pluralistic way of working. It is essential, therefore, to select people for pluralistic training who find meaning in a pluralistic worldview.

Encouraging a 'critical/affirmative' perspective on therapy theory

Within a specifically pluralistic training, theories and concepts need to be taught in a way that construes them as resources or as tools for understanding, and not as fixed truths. Pragmatically, a concept or theory is of value in a particular situation if it can be used to achieve a valued outcome. In terms of the teaching and learning of theory within such a programme, a balance needs to be achieved between two competing demands:

- *affirmation of the value of theory*: attaining a sufficient intellectual and experiential depth of understanding of theories and concepts in order to appreciate their practical utility and explanatory power;
- *developing critical distance*: being able to accept that a theory only provides one way of looking at an issue, limited in scope and explanatory power, and that other perspectives will always be available.

The successful accomplishment of this balance between affirmation and critique is central to the learning culture that is established on a pluralistic programme. The challenge can be viewed as that of assisting trainees to tolerate the co-existence of knowing and not-knowing, or belief and scepticism. With any client, a therapist is engaged in a collaborative search to construct a way of knowing that permits the person to arrive at a satisfactory sense of understanding, or coherent narrative, around the issues that have troubled them. At the same time, to be able to do this work effectively, a good therapist needs to be able to suspend their assumptions and preconceptions around how to understand the client's problem, to allow the client's own personal 'truth' to emerge, and to avoid imposing a therapist-defined or societally-defined 'false truth'. This dilemma is central to training because most students are anxious about their capacity to help clients, and are likely to equate 'not knowing' with incompetence. There needs to be a sufficient level of supportive connection within a course culture for students to stay with the discomfort of moments of not knowing.

There are some strategies that can contribute to the development of a critical/affirmative approach to theory on the part of therapy trainees. These include:

- reflection on the nature of theory, how theories are structured, and the social role of theory – these issues are discussed in McLeod (2009b: Chapter 3);
- discussion of the social, historical and personal factors that have influenced the ideas of key theorists and theoretical approaches in therapy;
- exposure to therapeutic concepts that are used by people living in non-Western cultural groups;
- exploration of underlying philosophical perspectives that inform all therapy theories – for example, human agency, the nature of explanation, postmodernism;
- enabling students to meet and interact with experienced single orientation therapists who can provide them with a sense of the power and flexibility of particular theories that go beyond textbook accounts;
- participation in experiential activities (for instance, workshops, learning journal tasks) in which students are invited to make use of different theoretical perspectives in respect of issues in their own lives;
- case discussions in which alternative theoretical frameworks are applied to case material.

The ultimate aim, in relation to learning about theory, is that students will become 'connoisseurs of ideas': aware of their own preferences, but open to a wide variety of understandings and possibilities.

Cultivating a deep respect for users of therapy

The model of pluralistic counselling and psychotherapy espoused in this book places a strong emphasis on the active involvement of the client in therapy, in terms of maximising the client's personal strengths and resources for change. To be able to work effectively in this way requires a willingness to be genuinely interested in services users as people who are actively seeking to resolve the difficulties in their lives and who are the experts on their own condition. There are many ways in which therapy trainees can be helped to embrace the image of the 'heroic client' (Duncan, et al., 2004). Individual clients, or service user groups, can be brought in as consultants to a training programme, or as tutors. Students can be required to read and review the literature on the client's experience of therapy (e.g., Levitt, Butler & Hill, 2006; Rennie, 2002) and to reflect on how these accounts typically present a picture of the therapeutic process that is quite different from the assumptions of established theories of therapy. Writings from within the mental health 'recovery movement' similarly delineate the multiple ways in which people can deal with overwhelmingly difficult life experiences, using a combination of 'official' therapy and their own resources (see Davidson, Harding & Spaniol, 2005, 2006). Finally, students can also be invited – or required – to participate in therapy themselves, such that they develop an in-depth, embodied sense of what it is like to be in the 'client's chair'.

Skilfulness in collaborative ways of working

Existing training programmes and learning materials offer a wide range of strategies for helping trainees to develop both generic counselling skills (e.g., listening, questioning, challenging) and specific therapeutic interventions. What is typically given less attention, probably because it is assumed to happen anyway, is the central pluralistic skill of *collaboration.* Being able to work collaboratively requires an appreciation of barriers to effective collaboration, such as the intrinsic power imbalance in professional therapist–client relationships and the lack of information available to most clients about the therapeutic options that are open to them. Collaborative work also requires skill and experience in agreeing goals and tasks, appreciation of the client's readiness for collaboration, providing relevant information, using metacommunication to check out and explore both client and therapists assumptions, intentions and reactions around what is happening in therapy, and the establishment of a 'culture of feedback' built around the use of specific client feedback instruments. Within a training programme, space needs to be provided for each of these areas of collaborative competence to be acquired, and to be assessed through application in practice and discussion in case reports.

Developing task-based competences

Approaches to therapist training that are grounded in specific schools of therapy tend to produce practitioners who are specialists in perhaps one or two tasks. For example, CBT therapists are comfortable around behaviour change tasks and emotion-regulation tasks; psychodynamic therapists are comfortable around meaning-making tasks and life-stage transition tasks. From a pluralistic perspective, while these areas of competence represent a valuable starting point, they are not always sufficient for the wide range of client preferences, wants and needs. The implication is that it would be helpful to organise pluralistic training in such a way that trainees are exposed to the following activities:

- learning to identify the signals or markers, in the client's story, that suggest that certain tasks require to be addressed;
- time to reflect on the meaning and significance of different types of task, for example by undertaking personal reflection and personal development work in these areas;
- acquisition of a basic sense of competence and confidence across a spectrum of tasks (even if the training and the practitioner's personal proclivities lead in the direction of a higher level of interest and investment in some tasks rather than others);
- readiness and skill in holding conversations with clients around the process of task agreement;
- a capacity to read and analyse the research literature as a means of becoming sensitised to the possible therapeutic tasks associated with particular areas of client difficulty.

These activities are recommended as part of introductory and basic counsellor and psychotherapist training. There are further training activities that may arise as therapists develop interests in specialist areas of practice. For example, counsellors working in some health care settings, such as infertility clinics, AIDS clinics and genetic counselling services, may find it useful to undergo focused and more advanced training around *finding, analysing and acting on information* tasks. Counsellors in universities and colleges may benefit from training experiences that explore *negotiating a life transition or developmental crisis* tasks.

Levels of pluralistic training

At the heart of pluralistic therapy is an assumption that people are helped best through change processes that correspond to their preferences, life experience, and general sense of what will be most useful for them in the specific circumstances within which they find themselves. In order to engage flexibly and responsively to these preferences, therapists working in a pluralistic way need to be able to make effective use of a range of therapy methods. This requirement presents a significant challenge within basic training programmes. Because of time limitations, it is seldom possible to offer intensive training in any one method. The result can be that students may feel that they lack competence and confidence, and therefore cling on to the one or two methods that constitute their therapeutic 'comfort zone'. A strategy for dealing with this problem is to view method training as consisting of three levels:

Level 1: Development of generic counselling skills and identification of pre-existing capacity to facilitate change. It should be the case that the majority of people who enter training to become counsellors or psychotherapists already possess an ability to help other people who have problems in living. Trainees are typically selected, at least in part, on their demonstrated ability to be good listeners, to be aware of their inner emotional world, to possess a secure sense of their own boundaries, and so on. A key focus of the initial stages of pluralistic training can be to enable students to identify these personal strengths in relation to their capacity to establish facilitative relationships. This learning can be reinforced and augmented by participation in counselling skills training practicums, where students work together to develop their awareness and competence around micro-skills such as reflection of feeling, use of silence, sensitivity to non-verbal cues, use of different types of question, etc. It can be useful at this stage to introduce students to theory and research into non-specific/common factors (see Chapter 2), so that they appreciate that therapeutic change does not rely on mastery of sophisticated intervention techniques, but instead is grounded in a capacity to provide a set of general learning experiences that they are already able to offer. It can also be useful at this stage to invite students to reflect on their experience of 'therapeutic moments' in their own life (Exercise 8.2), and to see that these episodes may have been made possible by the willingness of other people to listen to them, to respond in a non-judgemental fashion, to be caring, and to be genuine. The outcome of this stage of training should be that the student develops a fundamental sense of confidence in their own capacity to be helpful, while realising that they still have a lot to learn.

Exercise 8.2: Therapeutic moments in your life

On your own, or with a partner, take 15 minutes or so to think about moments in your own life where another person has been of therapeutic help to you (this may, or may not, have been a professional counsellor or psychotherapist). What was it that that person did that was of help? Is this something that you can offer to others?

Level 2: Differentiation of specific methods. The next stage of methods training involves beginning to engage with alternative strategies for facilitating learning and change that exist within contemporary therapeutic practice. Students may need to be reminded at this point in their training, or on a regular basis, that the goal is not to become omni-competent, but merely to become able to offer choices to clients around the ways that therapeutic tasks might be tackled. It seems reasonable to identify three broad categories of method that reflect mainstream therapy practice: (a) exploratory/meaning-making methods; (b) structured approaches to problem-solving and behaviour change; (c) methods that activate the client's strengths and resources. These method categories are described in more detail in Chapter 6. Within each category, there exists a wealth of therapy models and techniques that are potentially of value. For example, a wide range of methods for exploring the meaning of a problem can be found within person-centred therapy, psychodynamic therapies, existential therapy, constructivist therapy, expressive arts therapies, Socratic questioning in CBT, and elsewhere. Current CBT practice includes a large number of suggestions around how to identify dysfunctional patterns of behaviour, and implement change in a structured manner. Strengths-based and resource-based methods are available in the domains of narrative therapy and solution-focused therapy, and in the literature on self-help approaches. It probably does not matter which exploratory, structured and strengths-based methods are taught to students, as long as they are able to develop a secure appreciation of what they doing within each category. The specific methods that are taught within each category will usually depend on the staff that are available – students need to be able to observe methods being used effectively in order to gain confidence in their utility.

Level 3: Advanced training in specific methods. Levels 1 and 2 methods training can be covered within basic counsellor or psychotherapist training. There is then a more advanced level of methods training that takes place post-qualification, as part of the continuing professional development in which accredited practitioners are expected to engage. For example, all approaches to exploring meaning involve sensitivity to feelings and emotional content, and helping the client to become aware of what they are feeling, name the feeling, and so on. However, there are also some very highly developed therapeutic methods for assisting clients to work with their feelings. Emotion-focused therapy (EFT) is a therapeutic approach that has brought together a range of effective, empirically validated methods for exploring emotional meaning and resolving emotional difficulties (Greenberg, Rice & Elliott, 1993). It may be that a therapist who has completed an initial pluralistic training may wish at a later stage to undertake some, or all, of the EFT training programme. This decision may be motivated by the therapist's realisation that they are lacking skill in working with client emotions, or because they practice in a setting that presents particularly challenging emotional issues (e.g., depression). There are many excellent advanced training workshops and programmes that are open to therapists who have completed initial training, for example in the use of CBT with different disorders. Practitioners who have initially trained within a pluralistic programme are in a good position to make decisions about which advanced courses are most relevant to them, and are readily able to integrate this new learning into their existing repertoire of ideas and methods.

Box 8.1: Training in a pluralistic way

As with supervision, a pluralistic approach to training brings with it more than just content. It also brings a certain way of doing things. In particular, there is likely to be the development of a culture of feedback on a pluralistic course, in which students feel that they can respond to, and alter, aspects of the programme, in dialogue with the trainers and in relation to external constraints. In this respect, formal and informal evaluation is likely to play an important role in any pluralistically-informed training, with trainers attending to, and being willing to adjust their courses in the light of, student feedback. Closely connected to this, trainees within a pluralistic programme are likely to be engaged with as informed and able individuals, who have a wealth of strengths and resources that they can bring to the training environment. Personalisation is likely to be another key feature of a pluralistic training programme, with a focus on helping students identify their personal learning goals and preferred methods of study, and there is a commitment to tailoring the programme accordingly. Here, scope for personalisation may be more limited than in one-to-one therapeutic or supervisory relationships – given the existence of multiple goals and preferences across multiple trainees as well as the presence of numerous external demands – but some degree of flexibility, adaptation and responsiveness is always likely to be possible.

Conclusions: overview of the pluralistic training curriculum

The aim of this section has been to identify the skills and knowledge that contribute to competence as a pluralistic counsellor and psychotherapist, and to identify some of the training activities and structures that might contribute to the development of these competences. It is probably unhelpful to attempt to over-specify the counselling and psychotherapy training curriculum. Almost certainly, there are many pathways to becoming a competent pluralistic therapist, and many different types of learning structures that can evolve within different training institutions. A central debate regarding integrative training, for instance, is 'whether it should occur after trainees have acquired a solid foundation in pure-form therapies, or whether individuals should be trained integratively from the start' (Eubanks-Carter, Burckell & Goldfried, 2005: 514), and the same question can be asked of a pluralistic training programme. That is, while the model outlined here suggests that trainees should be introduced to a range of orientation-based methods from the beginning of their programme, an alternative approach might be to commence with orientation-specific method and ideas, and only subsequently go on to alternative methods.

Despite these variations, it is possible to identify four key principles that are likely to be associated with any kind of pluralistic training. First, students need to be offered a critical *overview* of the therapy field, drawing on historical, cultural and philosophical perspectives. Second, it needs to be explained to students that what they are being trained for is a process of *lifelong learning* that supports a position of curiosity and inclusiveness. Third, pluralistic training places an emphasis on the identification and appreciation of personal and cultural *strengths and resources* in both therapists and clients. Finally, pluralistic working relies on a practical appreciation of the nature of *collaboration*, which is understood as a principled, ethical commitment to the valuing of human connectedness and community.

Recommended reading

The following texts on eclectic and integrative training provide valuable starting points for considering the development of a specifically pluralistic programme:

Hollanders, H. (1999). Eclecticism and integration in counselling: Implications for training. *British Journal of Guidance & Counselling, 27*(4), 483–500.

Norcross, J. C., & Halgin, R. P. (2005). Training in psychotherapy integration. In J. C. Norcross & M. R. Goldfried (Eds.), *Handbook of Psychotherapy Integration* (pp. 439–458). New York: Oxford University Press.

Box 8.2: Challenges for pluralistic training

Hollanders (1999), in a valuable paper on integrative and eclectic training (see recommended reading), identifies several key challenges to such programmes, many of which are equally relevant to a pluralistic training. These are presented below, with suggestions for how they might be met.

'An eclectic/integrative training must address the issue of the incommensurability of paradigms' (1999: 487).

– A pluralistic training programme needs to help trainees understand that, beneath the heterogeneity of paradigms, goals and methods, lies a coherent, underlying principle: a commitment to welcoming diversity, differences and otherness.

'Eclectic/integrative training needs to provide a focal point for trainees to be able to gain a sense of identity and commitment' (1999: 488).

– The focal point for therapeutic work within a pluralistic practice is a client's goals, and this commitment to helping clients achieve their individual goals in a collaborative, open-minded and empowering way provides a potential identity for pluralistic trainees. The fact that this identity is based on a commitment not to a set of techniques, but to a set of values and ethics, may make it all that much more meaningful.

'Eclectic/integrative training needs to make a particular effort to provide criteria for good practice' (1999: 490).

– Key criteria for good pluralistic practice might be: 1. The ability to discuss, and agree, with clients appropriate goals, tasks and methods; 2. The ability to work collaboratively with clients throughout the therapy; 3. The ability to implement effectively a range of therapeutic methods; 4. The ability to help clients draw on their strengths and resources to achieve their goals.

Eclectic/integrative training takes time (1999: 491).

– Norcross (2005: 441), too, makes the point that trainees need to have the time – as well as the talent – to acquire competence in multiple methods. It will therefore be important to emphasise to trainees that development as a pluralistic therapist is ongoing and incremental (*see* Levels of pluralistic training, on page 143) and is likely to continue way past the completion of an initial training programme.

'Trainers involved in eclectic/integrative trainings need themselves to be engaged in the process of integration' (1999: 493).

– With respect to pluralistic trainings, another way of putting this would be to say that pluralistic trainers need to have a clear sense of where they sit within a pluralistic worldview. They would not necessarily have to practise in a pluralistic way (indeed, specialist practitioners can be of great value to a pluralistic programme), but they would have to have an overall commitment to a pluralistic sensibility.

'Integrative training requires the provision of an integrative/eclectic form of supervision' (1999: 494).

– The corollary of this is that pluralistic training requires pluralistic supervision, and the nature of this is discussed above.

Another potential challenge for students on a pluralistic training programme is the lack of adequate literature and resources on which to base their practice. However, accessible and relevant literature can be found within the body of writing on the topic of therapy integration. An overview of strategies that have been developed to enable integration of therapy concepts and methods can be found in McLeod (2009b: Chapter 13), and detailed accounts of how clinicians have sought to embrace an integrative or pluralistic vision of therapy can be found in the *Handbook of Psychotherapy Integration* (edited by Norcross and Goldfried, 2005), *Casebook of Psychotherapy Integration* (Stricker & Gold, 2006), the *Journal of Psychotherapy Integration*, and in Polkinghorne (1992). The key learning that can be facilitated through this kind of reading is an appreciation that, certainly at the present stage of the evolution of psychological therapies, there is no simple answer to the challenge of pluralism, but that at least there are some promising pathways through this territory that have been established by the pioneers of the psychotherapy integration movement.

A final challenge for pluralistic training courses is that, while it is hoped that trainees develop a passion for, and sense of identity around, the approach, they should not become 'card-carrying, flag-waving "eclectic" or "integrative" psychotherapists' (Norcross & Halgin, 2005: 454). In other words, if pluralism becomes one more dogmatic creed in the pantheon of therapeutic doctrines, it would defeat the very purpose for which it was developed. As Orlinsky & Rønnestad (2005d: 186) write, open-minded learning is key: trainees will need to develop a critical attitude towards a pluralistic stance itself, and also be able to appreciate the value of more specialised therapeutic practices.

Continuing Professional Development For Therapists Trained In A Specialist Orientation

In the previous section, some of the elements of basic training in pluralistic counselling and psychotherapy were described, along with some suggestions about how pluralistic practice implies a willingness to engage in ongoing learning that will extend the repertoire of methods and understanding that are available for use with clients. However, it is probable that the majority of readers of this book will be practitioners who have already completed their initial training, probably within a specific therapy orientation such as psychodynamic, person-centred, existential, CBT, solution-focused, transactional analysis, gestalt, or narrative therapy. Therapists in this position who are interested in developing a more pluralistic way of working are unlikely to want to re-train in pluralistic therapy. What is more relevant for trained therapists moving in the direction of pluralism is to look for supervision and continuing professional development (CPD) opportunities in methods and theories that are outside their original orientation. For instance, a counsellor with an original person-centred training may take a short course in CBT, or a psychodynamic counsellor may take additional training in systemic theory and practice.

Exercise 8.3: Your CPD

If you are a practitioner who has been trained in a single or specialist orientation, what do you see as the next step in your development as a therapist? What methods would you like to acquire, and why? Take 10 minutes or so to reflect on this or to discuss this with a partner.

Such CPD trainings offer therapists an excellent opportunity to develop a more pluralistic orientation within their existing approach. However, for therapists who have been trained in a specific orientation, and whose practice is organised around ways of understanding and methods associated with that approach, it can be hard to make effective use of new ideas and methods. For example, someone who is trained in CBT might well be interested in psychodynamic ways of working with dreams, and attend a psychodynamically-orientated workshop on using dream analysis in therapy. This therapist might gain a great deal at a personal level from the workshop, but be left without any capacity to make use of this knowledge with their own clients because the workshop did not provide them with any strategies for making the link between CBT activities and dream analysis activities. It can be frustrating, therefore, for therapists trained in a single approach to attend workshops on different approaches. What is missing from this kind of CPD is any kind of integrative 'bridge' that will enable new ideas to be implemented alongside existing ideas.

One of the values of adopting a pluralistic sensibility may be that it can provide such a bridge. Because the orientating point of the therapeutic work is the client's goals, rather than any particular theoretical hypothesis or method, it allows therapists to hold, alongside one another, a range of methods from diverse sources and trainings. Moreover, the pluralistic emphasis on client–therapist collaboration may provide a particularly valuable integrating construct. Through opening up conversation with the client around alternative possibilities for how to work together, all kinds of combinations of therapy methods can be employed. For example, combining CBT techniques for identifying and modifying negative or irrational thoughts, and psychodynamic procedures for exploring the meaning of dreams, does not require a therapist to have devised a 'meta-theory' of cognitive-behavioural-psychodynamic therapy. Instead, what counts is whether this particular mix of ideas and methods makes sense to the client, and pragmatically contributes to the attainment of the client's tasks and goals.

A crucial step for single-orientation therapists who are drawn to pluralistic ideas, therefore, may be systematic reflection on the way that they collaborate with clients, and on the degree to which they are able to be *responsive* to the client's preferences and ideas about what will work (Stiles, Honos-Webb & Sturko, 1998). Responsiveness, as discussed in Chapter 3, encompasses listening and asking in relation to the client's preferences, then exploring and implementing different possibilities that emerge from these conversations, and monitoring/reviewing the helpfulness of all aspects of this process. Becoming a pluralistic therapist can be viewed as a kind of personal and professional development 'project' that involves allocating time to reflecting on how one engages in these kinds of collaborative activities, and then trying out ways of extending one's 'collaborative repertoire' – all this within whatever therapy approach is already being used. What tends to happen when an experienced practitioner engages in this kind of self-exploration is that they realise (a) how little time they allow within sessions for collaborative conversations, and (b) how many possibilities there are within their existing approach for flexibly responding to client preferences. This kind of personal project can be assisted by participation in workshops on pluralistic collaboration, involvements in peer learning or supervision groups, or working with a supervisor who uses a pluralistic approach.

Service Delivery From A Pluralistic Perspective

The concept of *service delivery* refers to the way that therapy is arranged in terms of organisational structures and procedures. A pluralistic stance presents a number of challenges to the kinds of service delivery models that currently operate in the world of counselling and psychotherapy. This is partly because, on the whole, the taken-for-granted traditions that dominate therapy practice have tended to specify fixed and inflexible ways of working (e.g., weekly one-hour sessions with the same therapist). This rigidity has been reinforced by evidence-based practice guidelines that have been interpreted as indicating that certain therapy models should be favoured, and by the creation of therapy bureaucracies within health services. In contrast to the somewhat inflexible arrangements that currently prevail within therapeutic services, a pluralistic perspective suggests that different people have different needs, wants and learning styles, with the implication that it is important to build flexible services that are tailored to the requirements of individuals.

Some of the dimensions of flexibility that it might be desirable to factor into the organisation of therapy services include the provision of choice around:

- frequency of sessions (daily, weekly, irregular intervals);
- length of sessions (20 minutes, one hour, a whole day…);
- access to the therapist other than in face-to-face meetings (e.g., telephone consultation, email, letter);
- choice of therapist (gender, age, ethnicity, sexual orientation, religion, personality style);
- capacity to change therapist, or to see more than one therapist at the same time;
- availability of couple, family and group work;
- availability of self-help resources;
- access to specialist treatments;
- location of therapy (office, own home, outdoors).

It is obvious that a willingness to offer maximum flexibility and responsiveness around all of these dimensions has the potential to increase administrative costs, and create situations where some clients might make unreasonable demands on the system. However, it is also obvious that, for some people seeking help, the knowledge that these choices are open to them might make the difference between being able to make use of therapeutic help and either not making contact or prematurely dropping out of therapy.

Box 8.3: Allowing clients to decide how long, how often and how much assistance is needed

Two studies published by the clinical psychologist Tim Carey (Carey, 2005; Carey & Mullan, 2007) have explored the effectiveness of allowing clients to schedule their own appointments. Clients referred for psychotherapy in NHS primary care settings were told that they could contact the receptionist to book appointments at any day or time when there was an available slot. They could also make an appointment with any therapist who was available and could specify the length of the session. When asked at the end of therapy about how they felt about these arrangements, the majority of clients reported that they appreciated the flexibility of the service. Clients exhibited a wide range of attendance patterns, including multiple appointments in one week, weekly and bi-weekly appointments, with the majority of clients varying the frequency of appointments that they scheduled. The length of sessions varied from between 15 and 80 minutes, and the proportion of missed appointments was significantly reduced. Carey (2005: 332) concluded that there were benefits to the therapeutic process arising from the introduction of client control of the appointment schedule: 'the scheduling of appointments by the therapist disturbs the way the patient intends to experience the world. … Perhaps many of the "problems" that occur during the process of psychotherapy [e.g., missed appointments, ruptures in the therapeutic alliance] are patients seeking to remove the disturbing effect of decisions they have not made.'

The pluralistic approach to therapy that is described in this book is mainly intended for 'front-line' practitioners who are working with clients with a range of presenting problems and preferences for what they believe will be most helpful for them. The image is that of the therapist as 'primary care general practitioner'. This form of service delivery is consistent with the existence of secondary care specialist services that provide specific forms of therapy for specific problems. For example, a front-line counsellor or psychotherapist working in a pluralistic way may be able to provide effective therapy for the majority of clients that they come across who exhibit obsessive patterns of behaviour, and whose lives are restricted by their need to carry out repetitive safety rituals. However, a few of these clients may have longstanding obsessive-compulsive disorder (OCD) problems that are so serious or chronic that they would be better served by consulting a therapist or clinic that specialised in working with this kind of client, and had much more experience in this specific area. In an ideal world, where there were no financial or professional barriers, pluralistic therapy services would consist of a combination of pluralistic front-line therapists and specialist centres for unusual, severe or complex problems. Also, in this ideal scenario, referrals and consultations could be made in any direction. For example, people seeking help do not necessarily need to be 'screened' or assessed by a front-line worker in order to be appropriately referred to a specialist centre. There are many people struggling to live with OCD, alcohol problems or eating disorders, and their family members, who know perfectly well that what is required is intensive specialist help.

The concept of 'stepped care' refers to a model of service delivery in which people seeking help are first offered a 'low intensity' service, for example support and encouragement to work through a self-help manual or online programme, and are only referred to 'high intensity' services (e.g., individual therapy or inpatient treatment) if the initial 'step' proves to be ineffective. Typically, the decision to 'step up' treatment intensity is made by a case worker, based on mentoring of the symptoms exhibited by the client. This model of service delivery reflects a pluralistic stance in its recognition that different people require different types of help. However, if referral decisions are essentially being made by mental health professionals, with little scope for client preference or choice, then stepped care can be regarded largely as a framework for rationing scarce (i.e., high intensity) services, rather than as a means of implementing a flexible and personalised approach to the provision of services.

Another strategy that can be used to introduce a pluralistic ethos into service delivery can be to organise the provision of therapy around teams or networks of therapists. For example, if a group of psychotherapists are working together on a team basis, then a client who is working with one therapist around exploring and making sense of an issue may find it helpful to consult with another member of the team who has had more training in CBT, at the point when they wish to implement behaviour change in respect of their problem. This kind of team working can involve therapists from other professional backgrounds. A client engaged in therapy for an eating problem, for instance, may benefit from sessions with a sport and exercise therapist, or a nutritionist. There are many patterns of conjoint working that can be envisaged, involving couple and group therapy, creative arts therapies, psychoeducational programmes, spiritual practices, and many other types of resource.

It can be seen, therefore, that there exist a range of possibilities for the organisation of delivery of counselling and psychotherapy services in order to maximise the benefits of a pluralistic, multi-perspective approach to helping people to overcome problems in living. These different patterns of therapeutic activity represent a challenge to prevailing policies around 'evidence-based' practice, which specify (through NICE guidelines and other protocols) one or two approved or validated interventions for each 'disorder'. From a pluralistic perspective, service delivery systems should be designed to allow people sufficient choice to find the type of therapeutic experience that makes most sense to them.

Summary

The pluralistic approach to therapy developed in this book can be extended to the full range of systems that support the delivery of effective counselling and psychotherapy. Pluralistic supervision involves a collaborative, flexible relationship between supervisor and supervisee, and has a particular focus on developing the level of client–therapist collaboration over the goals, tasks and methods of therapy. Where pluralistic principles are incorporated into single orientation training programmes, students will be encouraged to respect and value other orientations, develop a critical awareness of their own limitations, and have the skills and knowledge to make onward referrals. Programmes which train therapists in a specifically pluralistic way of working will need to focus on facilitating an attitude of openness to new skills and therapeutic methods. Trainees should become 'connoisseurs of ideas': skilled and knowledgeable in a range of concepts, but able to keep a critical distance from them. They will also need to develop a deep respect for users and a willingness to collaborate with them. Pluralistic training can be conceptualised in terms of three levels: development of generic counselling skills, differentiation of specific methods, and advanced training. For therapists whose initial training is in a specific therapeutic orientation, pluralistic CPD can involve the acquisition of a wide variety of additional methods, but developing skills in collaborative working, responsiveness and goal-orientation can act as an integrative bridge for this programme of development. In terms of service delivery, it is proposed that the most efficient and successful structure may involve front-line pluralistic workers, with single orientation therapists offering more specialised psychotherapeutic interventions.

Questions for reflection and discussion

1. What would you see as some of the strengths and weaknesses of a pluralistic approach to supervision?
2. If trainees are to develop as pluralistic practitioners, do you think it is better that they learn one way of working well, first, or learn a wider range of methods consecutively?
3. How do you think organisations offering psychological therapies, ideally, should be organised? Do you agree or disagree with the suggestion in this chapter that there should be front-line practitioners working in a pluralistic way, backed up by single orientation specialists?

9 Discussion: Towards a New Paradigm

This chapter discusses:

- The key themes of the book.
- Some commonly asked questions about and criticisms of the pluralistic approach and pluralistic practice.
- Challenges and developments for the future.

A Summary of The Book

The pluralistic approach to therapy holds that different clients are likely to benefit from different things at different points in time, and that therapists should work collaboratively with clients to help them identify what they want from therapy and how they might achieve it. This overarching pluralistic outlook can be translated in to a pluralistic therapeutic practice, where therapists draw on a range of methods to help clients work towards their goals. The pluralistic approach emerges from a desire to transcend schoolism and binary thinking in the counselling and psychotherapy world, advocating an attitude of prizing to the wide array of methods and concepts that different orientations have to offer. The approach is supported by a pluralistic philosophical outlook, and is rooted in the humanistic commitment to deeply valuing the Other in all their otherness. Support for the approach also comes from psychological research, which shows that human functioning is multifaceted, multidetermined and multilayered; and from psychotherapy research, which shows that no one therapy is most effective, and that clients tend to do better when they get a therapy that matches their characteristics and preferences. It is also consistent with a contemporary health and social care policy agenda. At the heart of this pluralistic approach is a commitment to a collaborative relationship between therapist and client. There are many ways in which therapists can help to build this, and the pluralistic approach particularly emphasises the use of negotiation and metacommunication around the goals, tasks and methods of therapy.

In terms of actual practice, pluralistic therapy, or therapy that is informed by a pluralistic perspective, will start by working with clients to help them identify their goals for therapy. Whether the client can clearly articulate these, or whether they only have a vague glimpse of them, this conversation will serve as the orientating point for the ongoing therapeutic work. Early on in the therapy, the therapist is also likely to invite the client to explore the particular foci that they may want for the work, and the methods and ways of working that they may find most helpful. Once the therapeutic activity gets under way, the therapist is likely to draw from a range of methods and skills, depending on their training and the client's particular wants and preferences, but they will continue to try to provide clients with opportunities to feed back on, discuss, and decide the best ways forward in the therapeutic work.

This pluralistic approach to therapy has the potential to change the way that we think about, and conduct, research, focusing on specific micro-change processes rather than large-scale cause–effect relationships. It also has implications for the supervision and training of therapists, with an emphasis on collaborative client–therapist activity and an openness to a diversity of methods.

Frequently Asked Questions

As the pluralistic approach has evolved, so a number of common questions and criticisms have been put to us. These have been very useful in helping us reflect on, and refine, the approach, and also in seeing some of its limitations. Many of the answers are already presented earlier in the book, but we hope that it will be useful to reiterate some of these key points.

Does a pluralistic approach mean that I have to be skilled in every therapeutic method going?

No. As we discuss in Chapter 1, it is quite possible to adopt a pluralistic perspective on therapy and still practice within a single orientation. What makes someone pluralistic in their outlook is an appreciation of the many different ways that therapy can be helpful (and unhelpful) for different clients, an awareness of their own limitations, and a willingness to refer on if a client's wants do not match their own resources. Even for therapists who are working in a specifically pluralistic way, there is no expectation that they will be able to do everything. No one can learn all 450+ types of therapeutic practice. Again, what is important is that they are aware of what they can and cannot offer clients, and are able to discuss and negotiate this with the people with whom they work.

Most of my clients can't say what they want from therapy, so what is the point of asking them?

Discussion and negotiation around the goals of therapy does not simply involve asking a client, in a first session, what they want, and expecting an immediate and definitive answer. In general, it takes time for people to identify their goals for therapy (and for life), so it is probably more useful to think about this as an invitation to clients to start thinking about, and talking about, what they want, and as part of creating a culture of feedback. As it is, though, clients may begin to get a much better clarity about their goals just by talking about them and feeling safe enough to communicate them.

What happens if a client does not want a pluralistic approach – if they just want the therapist to decide what to do and to take the lead?

It is a paradox of a pluralistic approach that, sometimes, a pluralistic perspective on therapy means delivering therapy in a non-pluralistic way! There is no doubt that, for some clients, metacommunication and discussion over the goals, tasks and methods of therapy are the last thing they will want. As Elizabeth Freire, one of Mick's person-centred colleagues put it, 'If you are down a hole, the last thing you might find useful is someone saying to you, "Now… How can I help you? Would you like a ladder… or some rope… or shall we talk more about what might help you get out?" Rather, you just want someone to haul you out.' So working pluralistically means being sensitive to the appropriateness and helpfulness of pluralistic therapist activity itself, and adjusting accordingly.

It is also important to note that, for some clients, the offer of choices and alternatives and metacommunication around the processes of therapy may be interpreted as a sign that the therapist 'does not know what they are doing'. Given the importance of hope, expectation and confidence in the therapist to positive outcomes (Cooper, 2008), this has the potential to have quite detrimental effects. In working pluralistically with clients, therefore, it is important that therapists find a balance between flexibility and conveying a confidence in their ability to help (if that is what they feel). This means that statements like, 'I've got some good ideas about what might be useful for you, but let's see what you think…' is likely to be much more helpful than, 'I really don't know what is going to help you… can you decide?'

Does working pluralistically mean that I have to do whatever a client wants?

No. Clients, like all of us, get things wrong some of the time, or want things that, ultimately, will not be of help to them. And, as individuals with an in-depth understanding of human psychological functioning, therapists may have much to offer in terms of helping clients identify what will be of benefit in the long run. So a pluralistic approach does not require therapists to put their own understandings, perceptions or expertise to one side – these may be a very valuable part of the collaborative therapeutic dialogue. What it does do, though, is to ask therapists to treat clients' wants with respect and understanding, and to put these at the heart of the therapeutic work.

The pluralistic framework feels very task-orientated, with its focus on goals and outcomes – whatever happened to just 'being with' a client?

From a pluralistic standpoint, it is undoubtedly the case that some clients will want a therapist who just strives to be 'alongside them', without any expectations of achieving particular goals. So terms in the pluralistic framework like 'goals', 'tasks' and 'methods' should not be taken too literally, or as meaning to imply that clients should be pressurised to achieve particular outcomes. Rather, the terms are used in the loosest sense to simply refer to what clients want, how they hope to get there, and what they might do to make that happen. In this sense, 'just being with a client' can be seen as one type of therapeutic task, which might be undertaken to achieve a range of therapeutic goals, such as 'feeling more comfortable about being myself'. Hence, although the terms 'method', 'task' and 'goal' tend to imply something that is consciously and deliberately chosen, they do not need to be. Rather, they are intended to be inclusive of much more subtle, non-conscious and organismic processes.

What difference will adopting a pluralistic approach actually make to my practice?

For therapists who work within a single orientation, thinking pluralistically, at least initially, may not make an enormous difference to practice. But it should lead to an increased amount of discussion and metacommunication with clients about what they want from therapy, and how they might achieve it. For those of us who have gone down this route, one consequence of this is a greater sense of confidence and a feeling of 'I know what I am doing now', rather than a sometimes vague sensation of 'I'm not quite sure what I'm doing with this client and it doesn't seem to be making much difference'. Our experience has also been of an increased sense of engagement and enjoyment in the therapeutic practice: of working alongside the client, and feeling more free to start drawing on other therapeutic knowledge and skills. For therapists who go down the route of developing a fully pluralistic practice, there will be more noticeable changes in the work: in particular, the use of an increasing range of therapeutic methods.

Does a pluralistic approach mean that any therapeutic method goes?

No. A pluralistic approach means appreciating the *potential* value that any therapeutic method may have, but it is also open to the possibility that some methods, for some clients (and maybe for most clients), for some of the time (and perhaps for much of the time), can be harmful, and that it is very important to find out when this might be the case. Unfortunately, at present, we know very little about which 'therapeutic' methods may be unhelpful, above and beyond the macro-level question marks that hang over particular therapies (e.g., single session debriefing for psychological trauma – Bisson, Jenkins, Alexander, & Bannister, 1997). This is why the research agenda outlined in Chapter 7 may be so important in helping to establish the particular contexts in which particular methods might be actively harmful.

Isn't pluralistic therapy just a bit superficial, a mish-mash of lots of different techniques without any underlying coherence?

Although pluralistic therapy draws on a range of different ideas and methods, it is orientated around one very clear focal point: clients' goals. So while it does incorporate a great deal of diversity, it is a diversity in the service of a focused and coherent objective.

Moreover, we hope to have shown, in Chapter 2, that a pluralistic approach to therapy is rooted in a coherent – albeit complex – set of philosophical and ethical principles.

Surely all the different therapeutic orientations are based on different philosophical and psychological assumptions, so how can you just clump them together?

It only becomes problematic to combine different worldviews when they are held as fixed and mutually exclusive truths, rather than as offerings that may or may not be of use to a client. In other words, for instance, a person-centred belief that people *are* actualising beings is difficult to integrate with a cognitive-behavioural belief that people *do* think in dysfunctional ways. But if both of these viewpoints are 'held lightly' – in other words, that it can *sometimes* be useful to see people as moving towards growth, and that people can *sometimes* be seen as making errors in their thinking – then there is no problem in holding them concurrently. Furthermore, until there is really good evidence to suggest that any one set of these underlying assumptions is more 'true' than another, we think that holding them in this light way is the most ethical stance to take (see Chapter 2).

Aren't many of us pluralistic therapists anyway, so what's the big deal?

As the research indicates (see Chapter 1 and Box 6.1 on page 99), it is undoubtedly true that many therapists already think, and practise, in a way that is consistent with the pluralistic approach described here. However, we think this text is the first book to try to really articulate this perspective and practice. It is also true that some of the established integrative and eclectic approaches, particularly multimodal therapy (Lazarus, 2005), approximate pluralistic practice, but we think there are certain features of this pluralistic approach that make it uniquely inclusive and collaborative (see Chapter 1). What we also really hope is that this book sets down a framework and a research agenda by which this way of working with clients – flexible, responsive and collaborative – can be understood much more deeply and developed.

It is one thing to say that we should value all the different therapeutic orientations, but is it really that easy to be so open-minded?

If our own experiences are anything to go by, it almost certainly is not. Mick, for instance, has variously aligned himself with existential, person-centred and relational approaches to therapy, and more than once has been accused of being dismissive or overly critical towards other schools of thought. Given the powerful psychological forces that pull us towards schoolism and in-group favouritism (see Box 1.1 on page 3), however, such biases should come as no surprise, and might be best thought of as the rule rather than the exception. From this perspective, then, an 'us and them' attitude towards methods from other counselling and psychotherapy fields is something that we will always need to watch out for. However, just as professional training, for many of us, involved acknowledging our biases and prejudices and learning to put them to one side, so we can learn to acknowledge, and bracket, our biases and prejudices towards other methods and practices. As Connolly (2005: 81) puts it, it may require a great deal of courage to bear the 'agony of diversity' in the interests of promoting freedom.

Interestingly, Connolly (2005) also suggests that one of the best strategies for opening ourselves up to diversity *across* groups is by acknowledging the diversity *within*. That is, the more we can see that our own orientation is heterogeneous, fluid and with amorphously defined internal boundaries, the less rigid our boundaries to the 'outside' world are likely to feel. This could certainly be argued to be the case, for instance, in the person-centred field, where a growing acknowledgement of different 'tribes' (Sanders, 2004) has coincided with the development of more integrative person-centred perspectives (Keys, 2003; Worsley, 2004). Also, in terms of overcoming in-group/out-group barriers, Connolly emphasises that this is not just about thinking things through at an intellectual level, but about working on the gut feelings sedimented within. It is, as discussed in Chapter 1, about noticing those times when our shoulders start to hunch, our lips start to purse, and our skin starts to tighten in response to alternative perspectives, and finding a way of standing back and retaining an open mind.

Isn't pluralism, itself, a monism, in that it holds a core set of values (e.g., acceptance of diversity is a good thing) and says, effectively, that there is a better way of doing therapy (i.e., a pluralistic practice)?

Yes and no – it is a paradox of all pluralistic and relativistic thinking that, in many respects, it presents another set of truths, and these always have the potential to congeal into yet one more fixed and dogmatic -ism. That is why, in the pluralistic perspective outlined in this book, we have tried very hard to develop it in a way that is inclusive of non-pluralistic, single orientation practices. We have also not argued that a pluralistic way of working is necessarily more effective than a single orientation specialism. It also means that, for us, it is essential to hold the theory of pluralism lightly, and not to assume that it is a given or unquestionable truth. It may turn out that pluralism is not the best way of taking the counselling and psychotherapy field forward, and this is something we would want to stay open to.

Having said that, in Chapter 2, we did put forward a set of core underlying values for the pluralistic approach – a humanistic appreciation of Others and of difference – that is unapologetically monist. Is this a contradiction? One answer to this is that pluralism can exist at different levels, and the *Stanford Encyclopaedia of Philosophy* (2006) distinguishes between the most radical 'foundational pluralism', which holds that there are no given values whatsoever, and a more moderate 'normative pluralism', which roots a pluralistic perspective in a monist set of assumptions and values. In this respect, the pluralistic approach outlined in this book can be seen as an example of the latter: a prizing of diversity and difference which emerges from a set of fairly specific humanistic values and assumptions which, to a large extent, are not considered negotiable.

Closely related to this, if pluralism is about accepting the full range of perspectives and overcoming binary thinking, how can it take such a strong stand against schoolism? Surely that is a valid viewpoint too? This is an issue that has taxed pluralists in all fields: How do you accept an Other that does not accept others? Connolly (2005: 67) is particularly clear on this. He argues that, while modesty, negotiation and adjustment are all cardinal virtues of pluralism, 'The limit point is reached when pluralism itself is threatened by powerful unitarian forces that demand the end of pluralism.' Here, he argues, there is a need for a 'militant assemblage of pluralists', that can resist the onslaught of monist repression and its drive for uniformity. In other words, from a pluralistic standpoint, it is quite legitimate to resist those who seek to annihilate otherness and difference – though this is not to say that they cannot still be understood, empathised with and valued – whether in the field of politics or psychological therapies.

OK – I'm convinced that pluralism is a good idea. But what do I do now?

This book includes many suggestions for further reading and study. In addition to these sources, it may be useful to develop a sense of what pluralistic therapy is like in practice by reading case studies such as those published by Bohart (2006), Duncan, Sparks & Miller (2006) and Gold (2006). At some point, it is necessary for anyone who is seeking to work in a pluralistic way to sit down and review their own practice in terms of the extent to which it reflects an openness to different ideas and methods, an ability to elicit and act on information about client preferences, and a capacity to establish a culture of feedback. This kind of personal audit will usually generate an action plan around further training, private study, personal therapy and supervision that may be necessary.

Challenges for The Future

From its very inception, our hope has been that the pluralistic approach to therapy will be a way of thinking about, and practising, counselling and psychotherapy that others will come to modify, develop and own. As discussed in Chapter 2, we see it along the lines of an open source software program or an internet resource like Wikipedia that emerges from a community of interested parties, rather than any one or two individuals.

In terms of its development, perhaps the most important task is for therapists who are interested in this perspective, or who already hold this perspective, to start talking more about what it is like to think and work in this pluralistic way. Writing about the experience of pluralistic practising, and about its strengths and limitations, would be a great way of developing a dialogue around this approach and its potential contribution to the field.

As discussed in Chapter 7, there is also a need for much more research in this area, and the pluralistic research agenda set out in that chapter is something that practitioners can engage in, as well as students and academics. Most basically, what we need to find out about is the particular client activities, therapist activities and tasks that are helpful in achieving particular goals. Case studies or qualitative research projects are an ideal way of undertaking such inquiry; or therapists could simply keep a record of this in their client notes: What did clients seem to do that was helpful? What did they, as therapists, do to facilitate this? What seemed to be the outcomes? Developing a list of therapeutic tasks, and perhaps a taxonomy (see Chapter 5), would also be very valuable. At a more academic level, there is also the need for controlled research that can assess the efficacy of pluralistic practice and methods.

In terms of developing the approach, it might also be useful to look at whether there are ways of developing, reconfiguring or re-terming the overall framework with its domains of 'goals', 'tasks' and 'methods'. Are there other domains, for instance, that can be considered, like 'cultural resources', or can the framework be simplified by combining different domains?

Another challenge for the future is to develop tools, techniques and strategies that can help to develop pluralistic practice. In Chapter 3, for instance, we discussed the development of the Therapy Personalisation Form (Appendix B see page 186), but what about a measure that can help clients to identify their particular strengths and resources? And metacommunication, as an activity at the heart of therapeutic practice, is something that can be much more fully examined and developed: What kinds of metacommunications are most helpful for clients? How can we improve our ability to metacommunicate? How can we know when it is appropriate, and not appropriate, to metacommunicate? There may also be other strategies to help facilitate client–therapist collaboration that have yet to be discovered, as well as strategies that can more fully help clients build on their resources and their willingness to participate in the therapeutic work.

Developing an ability to train and supervise people in pluralistic practice is also important if the approach is going to move forward. As discussed in Chapter 8, there are many questions and issues concerning this area. For instance, what are the basic tasks and methods that students should be trained in? Is it better to train people in single orientation methods first and then help them integrate other ways of working, or is it better to teach pluralism from the start? And how do you help students keep an open mind towards a range of methods without feeling overwhelmed by them?

A final, and perhaps over-arching, challenge is in the political domain. On the one hand, it might be argued that pluralism is very much in the ascendancy. McLellan (1995: 99) writes:

> We are all pluralists now. If the monism-pluralism encounter is about as close as you get to an eternal configuration of human dialogue, a glacial shift away from monism, towards pluralism, has occurred over time. Where once the onus was on pluralists to bounce off, and to try to dismantle, the grand monistic edifices, today any credible 'big picture' will have to be very careful not to appear to obliterate or devalue perceived plurality.

In the therapeutic field, too, there are those who believe the era of 'both/and' thinking is upon us. Kenneth Gergen (2000: 368), for instance, writes that: 'Therapists will feel increasingly free to create unique confluences, practices that will combine and integrate elements that have traditionally been separate. Competition among traditionally competing schools or practices will melt away in favour of unique and robust combinations.'

In the foreseeable future, however, it seems highly likely that the push towards evidence-based monist treatments, randomised controlled trials, and structured and manualised therapy will continue.

As discussed above, there are grounds for suggesting that pluralistic therapists should be at the forefront of resisting such unitarian forces, but how can this be done in a way that does not end up polarising the field or demonising those who, almost certainly, are offering very helpful interventions and are also primarily concerned with creating the best care for clients? Perhaps one way forward is for pluralistic therapists to work closely with user groups and campaigning organisations such as the Mental Health Foundation (www.mentalhealth.org.uk/), Depression Alliance (www.depressionalliance.org/) and MIND (www.mind.org.uk/), whose position on the politics of counselling and psychotherapy tends to much less based on any particular dogma or creed (including pluralism), and much more on the specific needs of service users. Here, one tends to find a very fertile middle ground, which both acknowledges the different needs that different clients have, but also the enormous value of evidence-based practices such as CBT.

Box 9.1: Pluralism: A way of being?

It is said of some therapies, in particular the person-centred approach, that it is more than just a way of doing therapy – it is a way of being. To some extent, the pluralistic approach, as a value-based standpoint, has a similar potentiality. Of course, this is not to suggest that there is one type of 'pluralistic personality', but that a pluralistically-orientated individual, in their way of being:

- strives to be open to, and interested in, feedback from others;
- is responsive, flexible, and adaptive to feedback received, and looks at what they can learn from it;
- tries to find out from others what they want and need, rather than making assumptions about what might be best for them;
- tries to be clear with others about what they want, and strives to articulate this in a negotiative, collaborative way;
- values difference and diversity, and consequently has a commitment to social justice;
- believes that there are no single, right answers to life's most fundamental questions, and hence values alternative opinions and is keen to engage in dialogue.

Conclusion

Is pluralism a 'philosophy for wimps', for those 'whose beliefs are too saturated with uncertainty and ambivalence to take definitive action?' (Connolly, 2005: 3) Connolly concludes not, and ranks among those committed to pluralism people with 'a sensitive soul' but 'a strong will'. The same might be said of those who adopt a pluralistic approach towards counselling and psychotherapy. As discussed above, it is by no means easy to stand back from one's biases and assumptions and hold a position of openness, while at the same time not falling into an anything-goes relativism. But it is our belief that the pluralistic project captures something of what many of us in the counselling and psychotherapy field see as essential to good mental well-being: an openness to diversity, difference and challenge; a wariness towards black-and-white thinking; and the capacity to acknowledge, accept and bracket our prejudices and assumptions.

Our hope is that the pluralistic approach outlined here can provide a starting point for a new paradigm in thinking about, and practising, psychological therapies. Perhaps, finally, we can move on from the era of schoolism and inter-orientation rivalry towards a constructive and mutually-regarding relationship across the approaches, and towards a more collaborative relationship between practitioners and service users. We will never all agree on what makes therapy effective – indeed, a lack of consensus is at the heart of a pluralistic philosophy – but we can agree to respect, and learn from, our differences, and if not for ourselves, then for our clients. This book is intended to function as an invitation to further dialogue and debate around the implications of a pluralistic perspective on counselling and psychotherapy theory, research, practice, training and supervision. We look forward to learning about the experiences of others who find meaning in this way of thinking and working.

Summary

This chapter summarises the pluralistic approach and answers a range of frequently asked questions and challenges. A pluralistic approach does not mean having to be skilled in every therapy going, doing whatever a client wants, being mechanistically task-orientated, practising in a radically different way, or assuming that each and every therapeutic method is going to be helpful. Rather, it is most likely to be helpful when applied sensitively and tailored to the individual client. The biggest challenge for the future is to bring together the experiences of those who work in pluralistic ways to find out what is helpful in therapy and how therapists can improve their practice. Adopting and developing a pluralistic approach is by no means an easy option for therapists, and requires a commitment to open-mindedness, flexibility and a willingness to resist all-or-nothing thinking. Our hope, however, is that it has the potential to usher in a new paradigm within the counselling and psychotherapy field, characterised by mutual respect and a willingness to work together with each other and our clients to deliver the best therapies we can.

Questions for reflection

1. Having completed this book, what is your gut response now to the pluralistic approach?
2. What other questions or criticisms do you have of the pluralistic approach or pluralistic practice that you feel have not been answered here? (Please do email them to us via Sage.)
3. 'Pluralism provides the most humane and promising agenda to pursue, even as we encounter strong pressure against it'? (Connolly, 2005: 10). Discuss.

References

Addis, M. E., & Jacobson, N. S. (1996). Reasons for depression and the process and outcome of cognitive-behavioral psychotherapies. *Journal of Consulting and Clinical Psychology*, *64*(6), 1417–1424.

Ahn, H. N., & Wampold, B. E. (2001). Where oh where are the specific ingredients? A meta-analysis of component studies in counseling and psychotherapy. *Journal of Counseling Psychology*, *48*(3), 251–257.

Alexander, F., & French, T. M. (1946) *Psychoanalytic Therapy: Principles and Applications*. New York: Ronald Press.

Andersen, T. (1987) The reflecting team: Dialogue and meta-dialogue in clinical work. *Family Process*, *26*, 415–428.

Anderson, R., & Cissna, K. N. (1997). *The Martin-Buber–Carl Rogers Dialogue: A New Transcript with Commentary*. Albany, NY: State University of New York Press.

APA (American Psychological Association). (2006). Evidence-based practice in psychology. *American Psychologist*, *61*(4), 271–285.

Appleby, L. (2009). Key themes. In Department of Health (Ed.), *New Horizons: Towards a Shared Vision for Mental Health (Consultation Document)*. London: Department of Health.

Ashworth, M., Shepherd, M., Christey, J. et al. (2004) A client-generated psychometric instrument: The development of 'PSYCHLOPS'. *Counselling and Psychotherapy Research*, *4*: 27–31.

Bachelor, A. (1995). Clients' perception of the therapeutic alliance: A qualitative analysis. *Journal of Counseling Psychology*, *42*(3), 323–337.

Baker, D., & Fortune, S. (2008) Understanding self-harm and suicide websites: A qualitative interview study of young adult website users. *Crisis*, *29*(3), 118–122.

Bakhtin, M. (1973). *Problems of Doestoevsky's Poetics* (R. W. Rostel, Trans., 2nd edn). Ann Arbor, MI: Ardis.

Bakhtin, M. (1975) *Speech Genres and other Late Essays*. Austin, TX: University of Texas Press.

Baumeister, R. F. (1991). *Meanings of Life*. New York: Guilford Press.

Berne, E. (1961). *Transactional Analysis in Psychotherapy*. New York: Grove Press.

Beck, A. T., John, R. A., Shaw, B. F., & Emery, G. (1979). *Cognitive Therapy of Depression*. New York: Guilford Press.

Bedi, R. P., Davis, M. D., & Williams, M. (2005). Critical incidents in the formation of the therapeutic alliance from the client's perspective. *Psychotherapy: Theory, Research, Practice, Training*, *42*(3), 311–323.

Beitman, B. D., Soth, A. M., & Bomby, N. A. (2005). The future as an integrating force through the schools of psychotherapy. In J. C. Norcross & M. R. Goldfried (Eds.), *Handbook of Psychotherapy Integration*. New York: Oxford University.

Berg, A. L., Sandahl, C., & Clinton, D. (2008). The relationship of treatment preferences and experiences to outcome in generalized anxiety disorder (GAD). *Psychology and Psychotherapy: Theory, Research and Practice*, *81*, 247–259.

Berking, M., Holtforth, M. G., Jacobi, C., & Kroner-Herwig, B. (2005). Empirically based guidelines for goal-finding procedures in psychotherapy: Are some goals easier to attain than others? *Psychotherapy Research*, *15*(3), 316–324.

Berlin, I. (1958). Two concepts of liberty. In H. Hardy (Ed.), *Liberty*. Oxford: Oxford University.

Berlin, I. (2003). The pursuit of the ideal. In H. Hardy (Ed.), *The Crooked Timber of Humanity: Chapters in the History of Ideas*. London: Random House.

Beutler, L. E., Blatt, S. J., Alimohamed, S., Levy, K. N., & Angtuaco, L. (2006). Participant factors in treating dysphoric disorders. In L. G. Castonguay & L. E. Beutler (Eds.), *Principles of Therapeutic Change that Work*. Oxford: Oxford University Press.

Beutler, L. E., Engle, D., Mohr, D., et al. (1991). Predictors of differential response to cognitive, experiential, and self-directed psychotherapeutic procedures. *Journal of Consulting and Clinical Psychology*, *59*(2), 333–340.

Beutler, L. E., Machado, P. P. P., Engle, D., & Mohr, D. (1993). Differential patient x treatment maintenance among cognitive, experiential, and self-directed psychotherapies. *Journal of Psychotherapy Integration*, *3*(1), 15–31.

Beutler, L. E., Mohr, D. C., Grawe, K., Engle, D., & MacDonald, R. (1991). Looking for differential treatment effects: Cross-cultural predictors of differential psychotherapy efficacy. *Journal of Psychotherapy Integration*, *1*(2), 121–141.

Binder, P.-E., Holgersen, H., & Nielsen, G. H. S. (2009). Why did I change when I went to therapy? A qualitative analysis of former patients' conceptions of successful psychotherapy. *Counselling and Psychotherapy Research: Linking Research with Practice*, *9*(4), 250–256.

Bird, A. (2009). Thomas Kuhn. In E. N. Zalta (Eds.), *The Stanford Encyclopedia of Philosophy* (Fall 2009 Edition). Available from: plato.stanford.edu/archives/fall2009/entries/thomas-kuhn/ (retrieved 1 December 2009).

Bisson, J. I., Jenkins, P. L., Alexander, J., & Bannister, C. (1997). Randomised controlled trial of psychological debriefing for victims of acute burn trauma. *British Journal of Psychiatry*, *171*(1), 78–81.

Bohart, A. C. (2001). Emphasising the future in empathy responses. In S. Haugh & T. Merry (Eds.), *Empathy*. Ross-on-Wye: PCCS Books.

Bohart, A. C., & Tallman, K. (1999). *How Clients Make Therapy Work: The Process of Active Self-Healing*. Washington, DC: American Psychological Association.

Bohart, A. C., Elliott, R., Greenberg, L. S., & Watson, J. C. (2002). Empathy. In J. C. Norcross (Ed.), *Psychotherapy Relationships that Work: Therapist Contributions and Responsiveness to Patients*. New York: Oxford University Press.

Bohart, A. C. (2006). The client as active self-healer. In G. Stricker & J. Gold (Eds.), *A Casebook of Psychotherapy Integration*. Washington, DC: American Psychological Association.

Boisvert, C. M., & Faust, D. (2006). Practicing psychologists' knowledge of general psychotherapy research findings: Implications for science–practice relations. *Professional Psychology: Research and Practice*, *37*(6), 708–716.

Bordin, E. S. (1979). The generalizability of the psychoanalytic concept of the working alliance. *Psychotherapy Theory, Research Practice, Training*, *16*(3), 252–260.

Borrell-Carrio, F., Suchman, A. L., & Epstein, R. M. (2004). The biopsychosocial model 25 years later: Principles, practice, and scientific inquiry. *Annals of Family Medicine*, *2*(6), 576–582.

Braaten, L. F. (1989). The self-development project list-90: A new instrument to measure positive life attainment. *Small Group Behavior*, *20*, 3–23.

Bragesjo, M., Clinton, D., & Sandell, R. (2004). The credibility of psychodynamic, cognitive and cognitive-behavioural psychotherapy in a randomly selected sample of the general public. *Psychology and Psychotherapy: Theory Research and Practice*, *77*, 297–307.

Buber, M. (1947a). *Between Man and Man* (R. G. Smith, Trans.). London: Fontana.

Buber, M. (1947b). Dialogue. In *Between Man and Man* (R. G. Smith, Trans.). London: Fontana.

Buber, M. (1958). *I and Thou* (R. G. Smith, Trans., 2nd edn). Edinburgh: T. & T. Clark Ltd.

Cain, D. J., & Seeman, J. (Eds.). (2002). *Humanistic Psychotherapies: Handbook of Research and Practice*. Washington, DC: American Psychological Association.

Care Service Improvement Partnership. (2009). *Our Choices in Mental Health*. Available from: www.mentalhealthnurse.co.uk/images/Other%20Guidance/Choices%20Doc.pdf (retrieved 26 June 2009).

Carey, T. A. (2005). Can patients specify treatment parameters? A preliminary investigation. *Clinical Psychology and Psychotherapy*, *12*, 326–335.

Carey, T. A., & Mullan, R. J. (2007). Patients taking the lead: A naturalistic investigation of a patient-led approach to treatment in primary care. *Counselling Psychology Quarterly*, *20*(1): 27–40.

Carr, S. (2008). *Personalisation: A Rough Guide* (Adults' Services Report No. 20). London: Social Care Institute for Excellence.

Carrell, S. E. (2001). *The Therapist's Toolbox*. Thousand Oaks, CA: Sage.

Carver, C. S., & Scheier, M. F. (1990). Principles of self-regulation: Action and emotion. In E. T. Higgins & R. M. Sorrentino (Eds.), *Handbook of Motivation and Cognition: Foundations of Social Behaviour*. New York: Guilford Press.

Castonguay, L. G., & Beutler, L. E. (2006a). Common and unique principles of therapeutic change: What do we know and what do we need to know? In L. G. Castonguay & L. E. Beutler (Eds.), *Principles of Therapeutic Change that Work*. Oxford: Oxford University Press.

Castonguay, L. G., & Beutler, L. E. (2006b). Preface. In L. G. Castonguay & L. E. Beutler (Eds.), *Principles of Therapeutic Change that Work*. Oxford: Oxford University Press.

Castonguay, L. G., & Beutler, L. E. (Eds.). (2006c). *Principles of Therapeutic Change that Work*. New York: Oxford University Press.

Castonguay, L. G., Goldfried, M. R., Wiser, S., Raue, P. J., & Hayes, A. M. (1996). Predicting the effect of cognitive therapy for depression: A study of unique and common factors. *Journal of Consulting and Clinical Psychology*, *64*(3), 497–504.

Chambless, D. L., Sanderson, W. C., Shoham, V., Bennett Johnson, S., & Pope, K. S. (1996). An update on empirically validated therapies. *The Clinical Psychologist*, *49*(4), 5–18.

Chu, B. C., & Kendall, P. C. (2009). Therapist responsiveness to child engagement: Flexibility within manual-based CBT for anxious youth. *Journal of Clinical Psychology*, *65*(7), 736–754.

Clark, D. M., Layard, R., Smithies, R., Richards, D. A., Suckling, R., & Wright, B. (2009). Improving access to psychological therapy: Initial evaluation of two UK demonstration sites. Behaviour Research and Therapy, *47*(11), 910–920.

Clark, D. M., Salkovskis, P. M., Hackmann, A., Wells, A., Ludgate, J., & Gelder, M. (1999). Brief cognitive therapy for panic disorder: A randomized controlled trial. *Journal of Consulting and Clinical Psychology*, *67*(4), 583–589.

Clarke, H., Rees, A., & Hardy, G. E. (2004). The big idea: Clients' perspectives of change processes in cognitive therapy. *Psychology and Psychotherapy: Theory Research and Practice*, *77*(1), 67–89.

Clarkson, P. (1990). A multiplicity of psychotherapeutic relationships. *British Journal of Psychotherapy*, *7*(2), 148–163.

Clarkson, P. (1995). *The Therapeutic Relationship*. London: Whurr.

Cochrane-Brink, K. A., Lofchy, J. S., & Sakinofsky, I. (2000). Clinical rating scales in suicide risk assessment. *General Hospital Psychiatry*, *22*(6), 445–451.

Comer, R. J. (1998). *Abnormal Psychology* (3rd edn). New York: W. H. Freeman.

Comtois, K. A., & Linehan, M. M. (2006). Psychosocial treatments of suicidal behaviors: A practice-friendly review. *Journal of Clinical Psychology*, *62*, 161–170.

Connolly, W. E. (2005). *Pluralism*. Durham, NC: Duke University Press.

Constantino, M. J., Marnell, M. E., Haile, A. J., et al. (2008). Integrative cognitive therapy for depression: A randomized pilot comparison. *Psychotherapy Theory, Research, Practice, Training*, *45*(2), 122–134.

Cooper, C. (1996). Psychodynamic therapy: The Kleinian approach. In W. Dryden (Ed.), *Handbook of Individual Therapy* (4th edn). London: Sage.

Cooper, M. (2003). *Existential Therapies*. London: Sage.

Cooper, M. (2004). *Counselling in Schools Project: Evaluation Report*. Glasgow: Counselling Unit, University of Strathclyde. Available from: www.strath.ac.uk/Departments/counsunit/research/cis.html (retrieved 1 December 2009).

Cooper, M. (2005). Working at relational depth. *Therapy Today*, *16*(8), 16–20.

Cooper, M. (2006a). Analysis of the evaluation data *East Renfrewshire Youth Counselling Service (ERYCS): Development and evaluation of a full-time secondary school and community based youth counselling service in Scotland 2005*. East Renfrewshire: East Renfrewshire Council.

Cooper, M. (2006b). Socialist humanism: A progressive politics for the twenty-first century. In G. Proctor, M. Cooper, P. Sanders, & B. Malcolm (Eds.), *Politicising the Person-Centred Approach: An Agenda for Social Change*. Ross-on-Wye: PCCS Books.

Cooper, M. (2007). Humanizing psychotherapy. *Journal of Contemporary Psychotherapy*, *37*(1), 11–16.

Cooper, M. (2008). *Essential Research Findings in Counselling and Psychotherapy: The Facts are Friendly*. London: Sage.

Cooper, M. (2009). Welcoming the Other: Actualising the humanistic ethic at the core of counselling psychology practice. *Counselling Psychology Review*, *24*(3&4), 119–129.

Cooper, M. (2010). The challenge of counselling and psychotherapy research. *Counselling and Psychotherapy Research, 10*(3).

Cooper, M., & McLeod, J. (2007). A pluralistic framework for counselling and psychotherapy: Implications for research. *Counselling and Psychotherapy Research*, *7*(3), 135–143.

Cooper, M., & Spinelli, E. (in press). A dialogue on dialogue. In L. Barnett & G. Madison (Eds.), *Existential Psychotherapy: Legacy, Vibrancy and Dialogue*. London: Routledge.

Cottraux, J., Note, I., Yao, S. N., de Mey-Guillard, C., Bonasse, F., Djamoussian, D., Mollard, E., Note, B., & Chen, Y. (2008). Randomized controlled comparison of

Cognitive Behavior Therapy with Rogerian supportive therapy in chronic post-traumatic stress disorder: A 2-year follow-up. *Psychotherapy and Psychosomatics*, *77*, 101–110.
Cox, W. M., & Klinger, E. (2002). Motivational structure: Relationships with substance use and processes of change. *Addictive Behaviors*, *27*(6), 925–940.
Crepaz-Keay, D. (2007). *What will patient-led services look like?* Available from: ipnosis.postle.net/pages/SavoyCrepaz-LeahTranscript.htm (retrieved 1 December 2009).
Crits-Christoph, P., & Gibbons, M. B. C. (2002). Relational interpretations. In J. C. Norcross (Ed.), *Psychotherapy Relationships that Work: Therapist Contributions and Responsiveness to Patients*. New York: Oxford University Press.
Cytrynbaum, S., Ginath, Y., Birdwell, J., & Brandt, L. (1979). Goal attainment scaling: A critical review. *Evaluation Quarterly*, *3*(1), 5–40.
Davidson, L, Harding, C., & Spaniol, L. (Eds.). (2005). *Recovery from Severe Mental Illnesses: Research Evidence and Implications for Practice, Volume 1*. Boston: Boston University Center for Psychiatric Rehabilitation.
Davidson, L., Harding, C., & Spaniol, L. (Eds.). (2006). *Recovery from Severe Mental Illnesses: Research Evidence and Implications for Practice, Volume 2*. Boston: Boston University Center for Psychiatric Rehabilitation.
Davis, F. A. (2010). Can we sustain the 'magic'? *The Psychologist*, *23*(1), 32–33.
Deane, F. P., Spicer, J., & Todd, D. M. (1997). Validity of a simplified target complaints measure. *Psychological Assessment*, *4*, 119–130.
den Boer, P., Wiersma, D., & van den Bosch, R. J. (2004). Why is self-help neglected in the treatment of emotional disorders? A meta-analysis. *Psychological Medicine*, *34*(6), 959–971.
Department of Health. (2001). *Treatment Choices in Psychological Therapies and Counselling*. London: Department of Health.
Department of Health. (2009). *New Horizons: Towards a Shared Vision for Mental Health (Consultation Document)*. London: Department of Health.
Derrida, J. (1974). *Of Grammatology* (G. C. Spivak, Trans.). Baltimore, MD: Johns Hopkins University Press.
Devine, D. A., & Fernald, P. S. (1973). Outcome effects of receiving a preferred, randomly assigned, or nonpreferred therapy. *Journal of Consulting and Clinical Psychology*, *41*(1), 104–107.
Dimsdale, J. E., Klerman, G. L., & Shershow, J. C. (1979). Conflict in treatment goals between patient and staff. *Social Psychiatry*, *14*(1), 1–4.
Doidge, N. (2007). *The Brain that Changes Itself: Stories of Personal Triumph from the Frontiers of Brain Science*. London: Penguin.
Doss, B. D. (2004). Changing the way we study change in psychotherapy. *Clinical Psychology: Science and Practice*, *11*(4), 368–386.
Downing, J. N. (2004). Psychotherapy practice in a pluralistic world: Philosophical and moral dilemmas. *Journal of Psychotherapy Integration*, *14*(2), 123–148.
Dreier, O. (2008). *Psychotherapy in Everyday Life*. New York: Cambridge University.
Duncan, B. L., & Miller, S. D. (2008). 'When I'm good, I'm very good, but when I'm bad I'm better': A new mantra for psychotherapists. Available from: www.psychotherapy.net/article/Scott_Miller_When_Im_Good (retrieved 27 January 2010).
Duncan, B. L., Miller, S. D., & Sparks, J. A. (2004). *The Heroic Client: A Revolutionary Way to Improve Effectiveness through Client-directed, Outcome-informed Therapy*. San Fransisco: Jossey-Bass.

Duncan, B. D., Sparks, J. A., & Miller, S. D. (2006). Client, not theory, directed: Integrating approaches one client at a time. In G. Stricker & J. Gold (Eds.), *A Casebook of Psychotherapy Integration.* Washington, DC: American Psychological Association.

Eells, T. (Ed.). (2007). *Handbook of Psychotherapy Case Formulation* (2nd edn). New York: Guilford Press.

Egan, G. (1994). *The Skilled Helper: A Problem-Management Approach to Helping.* Belmont, CA: Brooks/Cole.

Elkin, I., Yamaguchi, J. L., Arnkoff, D. B., Glass, C. R., Sotsky, S. M., & Krupnick, J. L. (1999). 'Patient–treatment fit' and early engagement in therapy. *Psychotherapy Research, 9*(4), 437–451.

Elliot, A. J., & Church, M. A. (2002). Client-articulated avoidance goals in the therapy context. *Journal of Counseling Psychology, 49*, 243–254.

Elliott, R., Shapiro, D. A., & Mack, C. (1999). *Simplified personal questionnaire procedure. Network for Research on Experiential Therapies.* Available from: www.experiential-researchers.org/instruments/elliott/pqprocedure.html (retrieved 21 December 2008).

Emmelkemp, P. M. G. (2004). Behavior therapy with adults. In M. J. Lambert (Ed.), *Bergin and Garfield's Handbook of Psychotherapy and Behavior Change* (5th edn). Chicago: John Wiley & Sons.

Engel, G. L. (1977). The need for a new medical model: A challenge for biomedicine. *Science, 196*(4286), 129–136.

Eubanks-Carter, C., Burckell, L. A., & Goldfried, M. R. (2005). Future directions in psychotherapy integration. In J. C. Norcross & M. R. Goldfried (Eds.), *Handbook of Psychotherapy Integration.* New York: Oxford University Press.

Feltham, C. (Ed.). (1999). *Understanding the Counselling Relationship.* London: Sage.

Festinger, L. (1957). *A Theory of Cognitive Dissonance.* Evanston, IL: Row, Peterson.

Firestone, R. W. (1986). The 'inner voice' and suicide. *Psychotherapy, 23*, 439–447.

Firestone, R. W. (1997). *Suicide and the Inner Voice: Risk Assessment, Treatment, and Case Management.* Thousand Oaks, CA: Sage.

Flückiger, C., & Holtforth, M. G. (2008). Focusing the therapist's attention on the patient's strengths: A preliminary study to foster a mechanism of change in outpatient psychotherapy. *Journal of Clinical Psychology, 64*, 876–890.

Flückiger, C., Wüsten, G., Zinbarg, R. E., & Wampold, B. E. (2010). *Resource Activation: Using Clients' Own Strengths in Psychotherapy and Counseling.* Cambridge, MA: Hogrefe & Huber.

Ford, S., Schofield, T., & Hope, T. (2003). What are the ingredients for a successful evidence-based patient choice consultation? A qualitative study. *Social Science & Medicine, 56*(3), 589–602.

Foresight Mental Capital and Wellbeing Project. (2008). *Final Project report – Executive summary.* London: The Government Office for Science.

Frankl, V. E. (1986). *The Doctor and the Soul: From Psychotherapy to Logotherapy* (R. Winston & C. Winston, Trans., 3rd edn). New York: Vintage Books.

Friedman, M. (1985). *The Healing Dialogue in Psychotherapy.* New York: Jason Aronson.

Frovenholt, J., Bragesjo, M., Clinton, D., & Sandell, R. (2007). How do experiences of psychiatric care affect the perceived credibility of different forms of psychotherapy? *Psychology and Psychotherapy: Theory Research and Practice, 80*, 205–215.

Gergen, K. J. (2000). The coming of creative confluence in therapeutic practice. *Psychotherapy*, *37*(4), 364–369.

Ghaderi, A. (2006). Does individualization matter? A randomized trial of standardized (focused) versus individualized (broad) cognitive behavior therapy for bulimia nervosa. *Behaviour Research and Therapy*, *44*(2), 273–288.

Gielen, U. P., Fish, G. M., & Draguns, J. G. (Eds.). (2004). *Handbook of Psychotherapy, Culture and Healing*. New York: Routledge.

Gold, J. (2006). Patient-initiated integration. In G. Stricker & J. Gold (Eds.), *A Casebook of Psychotherapy Integration*. Washington, DC: American Psychological Association.

Goldfried, M. R., Pachanakis, J. E., & Bell, A. C. (2005). A history of psychotherapy integration. In J. C. Norcross & M. R. Goldfried (Eds.), *Handbook of Psychotherapy Integration*. New York: Oxford University Press.

Goss, S., & Mearns, D. (1997). A call for a pluralist epistemological understanding in the assessment and evaluation of counselling. *British Journal of Guidance and Counselling*, *25*(2), 189–198.

Greenberg, L. (2002). *Emotion-Focused Therapy: Coaching Clients to Work Through Feelings*. Washington, DC: American Psychological Association.

Greenberg, L. S., Rice, L. N., & Elliott, R. (1993). *Facilitating Emotional Change: The Moment-by-Moment Process*. New York: Guilford Press.

Greenfield, S., Kaplan, S., & Ware, J. E. (1985). Expanding patient involvement in care. *Annals of Internal Medicine*, *102*(4), 520–528.

Guajardo, J. M. F., & Anderson, T. (2007). An investigation of psychoeducational interventions about therapy. *Psychotherapy Research*, *17*(1), 120–127.

Hammond, D. C., Hammond, D. H., & Smith, V. G. (1997). *Improving Therapeutic Communication: A Guide for Developing Effective Techniques*. San Francisco: Jossey-Bass.

Handelzalts, J. E., & Keinan, G. (2010). The effect of choice between test anxiety treatment options on treatment outcomes. *Psychotherapy Research*, *20*(1), 100–112.

Hatcher, R. L., & Gillaspy, J. A. (2006). Development and validation of a revised short form of the Working Alliance Inventory. *Psychotherapy Research*, *16*, 12–25.

Hayes, S. C., Luoma, J. B., Bond, F. W., Masuda, A., & Lillis, J. (2006). Acceptance and commitment therapy: Model, processes and outcomes. *Behaviour Research and Therapy*, *44*(1), 1–25.

Hayes, S., Strosahl, K., & Wilson, K. (2003). *Acceptance and Commitment Therapy: An Experiential Approach to Behavior Change*. New York: Guilford Press.

Heidegger, M. (1962). *Being and Time* (J. Macquarrie & E. Robinson, Trans.). Oxford: Blackwell.

Henry, W. P., Strupp, H. H., Butler, S. F., Schacht, T. E., & Binder, J. L. (1993). Effects of training in time-limited dynamic psychotherapy: Changes in therapist behavior. *Journal of Consulting and Clinical Psychology*, *61*(3), 434–440.

Higginson, S., & Mansell, W. (2008). What is the mechanism of psychological change? A qualitative analysis of six individuals who experienced personal change and recovery. *Psychology and Psychotherapy: Theory, Research and Practice*, *81*, 309–328.

Hill, C. E. (1999). *Helping Skills: Facilitating Exploration, Insight and Action* (2nd edn). Washington, DC: American Psychological Association.

Hill, C. E., Sim, W. E., Spangler, P., Stahl, J., Sullivan, T., & Teyber, E. (2008). Therapist immediacy in brief psychotherapy: Case Study 2. *Psychotherapy: Theory, Research, Practice and Training*, *45*(3), 298–315.

Hill, C. E., Thompson, B. J., Cogar, M. C., & Denman, D. W. (1993). Beneath the surface of long-term therapy: Therapist and client report of their own and each other's covert processes. *Journal of Counseling Psychology*, *40*(3), 278–287.

HM Government. (2007). *Putting People first: A Shared Vision and Commitment to the Transformation of Adult Social Care*. London: HM Government.

Hoehn-Saric, R., Frank, J. D., Imber, S. D., Nash, E. H., Stone, A. R., & Battle, C. C. (1964). Systematic preparation of patients for psychotherapy – I. Effects on therapy behavior and outcome. *Journal of Psychiatric Research*, *2*, 267–281.

Hollanders, H. (1999). Eclecticism and integration in counselling: Implications for training. *British Journal of Guidance & Counselling*, *27*(4), 483–500.

Hollanders, H. (2003). The eclectic and integrative approach. In R. Woolfe, W. Dryden, & S. Strawbridge (Eds.), *Handbook of Counselling Psychology*. London: Sage.

Holtforth, M. G., & Grawe, K. (2002). Bern inventory of treatment goals: Part 1. Development and first application of a taxonomy of treatment goal themes. *Psychotherapy Research*, *12*(1), 79–99.

Holtforth, M. G., Reubi, I., Ruckstuhl, L., Berking, M., & Grawe, K. (2004). The value of treatment-goal themes for treatment planning and outcome evaluation of psychiatric inpatients. *International Journal of Social Psychiatry*, *50*(1), 80–91.

Horvath, A. O., & Bedi, R. P. (2002). The alliance. In J. C. Norcross (Ed.), *Psychotherapy Relationships that Work: Therapist Contributions and Responsiveness to Patients*. New York: Oxford University Press.

Hougaard, E., Madsen, S. S., Hansen, L. M., Jensen, M., Katborg, G. S., Morsaa, L., Pedersen, M., Pedersen, S. M., & Piet, J. (2008). A novel group therapeutic format in cognitive behavioral treatment for clients with social phobia in a training setting: A case study of one treatment group with nine clients. *Pragmatic Case Studies in Psychotherapy*, *4*(4), 1–52.

House, R., & Totton, N. (Eds.). (1997). *Implausible Professions: Arguments for Pluralism and Autonomy in Counselling and Psychotherapy*. Ross-on-Wye: PCCS Books.

Howard, G. S., Nance, D. W., & Myers, P. (1987). *Adaptive Counseling and Therapy: A Systematic Approach to Selecting Effective Treatments*. San Francisco: Jossey-Bass.

Hubble, M., Duncan, B. L., & Miller, S. D. (1999). *The Heart and Soul of Change: What Works in Therapy*. Washington, DC: American Psychological Association.

Hunsley, J., & Di Giulio, G. (2002). Dodo bird, phoenix, or urban legend? *The Scientific Review of Mental Health Practices*, *1*(1), 11–22.

Hycner, R. (1991). *Between Person and Person: Towards a Dialogical Psychotherapy*. Highland, NY: Gestalt Journal Press.

Hycner, R., & Jacobs, L. (1995). *The Healing Relationship in Gestalt Therapy*. Highland, NY: Gestalt Journal Publications.

Ivey, A. E., & Ivey, M. B. (1999). *Intentional Interviewing and Counseling: Facilitating Client Development in a Multicultural Society* (4th edn). Pacific Grove, CA: Brooks/Cole.

Jacobson, N. S., Schmaling, K. B., Holtzworth-Munroe, A., Katt, J. L., Wood, L. F., & Follette, V. M. (1989). Research-structured vs clinically flexible versions of social learning-based marital therapy. *Behaviour Research and Therapy*, *27*(2), 173–180.

James, W. (1996). *A Pluralistic Universe*. Lincoln, NB: University of Nebraska Press.

Jamison, K. R. (1999). *Night Falls Fast: Understanding Suicide*. New York: Vintage.

Johnstone, L., & Dallos, R. (Eds.). (2006). *Formulation in Psychology and Psychotherapy: Making Sense of People's Problems*. London: Routledge.

Jorm, A. F., Medway, J., Christensen, H., Korten, A. E., Jacomb, P. A., & Rodgers, B. (2000). Public beliefs about the helpfulness of interventions for depression: Effects on actions taken when experiencing anxiety and depression symptoms. *Australian and New Zealand Journal of Psychiatry, 34*, 619–626.

Joseph, D. I. (2000). The practical art of suicide assessment: A guide for mental health professionals and substance abuse counselors. *Journal of Clinical Psychiatry, 61*(9), 683–684.

Josselson, R. (1996). *The Space between Us: Exploring the Dimensions of Human Relationships*. Thousand Oaks, CA: Sage.

Kahn, M. (1997). *Between Therapist and Client: The New Relationship* (2nd edn). New York: W. H. Freeman.

Kaplan, S. H., Sheldon, G., & Ware, J. E., Jr. (1989). Assessing the effects of physician–patient interactions on the outcomes of chronic disease. *Medical Care, 27*(3), S110–S127.

Karon, B. P. (2008). An 'incurable' schizophrenic: The case of Mr. X. *Pragmatic Case Studies in Psychotherapy, 4*(1), 1–24.

Kasper, L. B., Hill, C. E., & Kivlighan, D. E. (2008). Therapist immediacy in brief psychotherapy: Case Study 1. *Psychotherapy: Theory, Research, Practice and Training, 45*(3), 281–297.

Kazantzis, N., Deane, F. P., Ronan, K. R., & L'Abate, L. (Eds.). (2005). *Using Homework Assignments in Cognitive Behaviour Therapy*. London: Routledge.

Keys, S. (Ed.). (2003). *Idiosyncratic Person-Centred Therapy*. Ross-on-Wye: PCCS Books.

Kiesler, D. (1988). *Therapeutic Metacommunication: Therapist Impact Disclosure as Feedback in Psychotherapy*. Palo Alto, CA: Consulting Psychologists Press.

Kiesler, D. B. (1966). Some myths of psychotherapy research and the search for a paradigm. *Psychological Bulletin, 65*(2), 110–136.

Kiesler, D. J. (2004). Intrepid pursuit of the essential ingredients of psychotherapy. *Clinical Psychology: Science and Practice, 11*(4), 391–395.

King, M., Sibbald, B., Ward, E., et al. (2000). Randomised controlled trial of non-directive counselling, cognitive-behaviour therapy and usual general practitioner care in the management of depression as well as mixed anxiety and depression in primary care. *Health Technology Assessment, 4*(19), 1–83.

Kiresuk, T. J., & Sherman, R. E. (1968). Goal attainment scaling: A general method for evaluating comprehensive community mental health programs. *Community Mental Health Journal, 4*(6), 443–453.

Kiresuk, T. J., Smith, A., & Cardillo, J. E. (1994). *Goal Attainment Scaling: Applications Theory, and Measurement.* Hillsdale, NJ: Lawrence Erlbaum.

Knox, R. (2008). Clients' experiences of relational depth in person-centred counselling. *Counselling and Psychotherapy Research, 8*(3), 118–124.

Koestner, R., Lekes, N., Powers, T. A., & Chicoine, E. (2002). Attaining personal goals: Self-concordance plus implementation intentions equals success. *Journal of Personality and Social Psychology, 83*(1), 231–244.

Kramer, U. (2009). Individualizing exposure therapy for PTSD: The case of Caroline. *Pragmatic Case Studies in Psychotherapy*, *5*(2), 1–24.
Kuhn, T. (1970). *The Structure of Scientific Revolutions* (2nd edn). Chicago: University of Chicago.
Kvale, S. (1996). *InterViews*. London: Sage.
Lambert, M. J. (1992). Implications of outcome research for psychotherapy integration. In J. C. Norcross & M. R. Goldstein (Eds.), *Handbook of Psychotherapy Integration*. New York: Basic Books.
Lambert, M. J. (2007). Presidential address: What we have learned from a decade of research aimed at improving psychotherapy outcome in routine care. *Psychotherapy Research*, *17*(1), 1–14.
Lambert, M. J., & Ogles, B. M. (1997). The effectiveness of psychotherapy supervision. In C. E. Watkins (Ed.), *Handbook of Psychotherapy Supervision*. Chichester: Wiley.
Lambert, M. J., Bergin, A. E., & Garfield, S. L. (2004). Overview, trends and future issues. In M. J. Lambert (Ed.), *Bergin and Garfield's Handbook of Psychotherapy and Behavior Change* (5th edn). Chicago: John Wiley & Sons.
Lappalainen, R., Lehtonen, T., Skarp, E., Taubert, E., Ojanen, M., & Hayes, S. C. (2007). The impact of CBT and ACT models using psychology trainee therapists: a preliminary controlled effectiveness trial. *Behavior Modification*, *31*, 488–511.
Larsen, R. J., & Buss, D. M. (2002). *Personality Psychology: Domains of Knowledge about Human Nature*. Boston: McGraw-Hill.
Layard, R. (2006). *Happiness: Lessons from a New Science*. London: Penguin.
Lazarus, A. A. (1981). *The Practice of Multimodal Therapy*. Baltimore, MD: Johns Hopkins University Press.
Lazarus, A. A. (1993). Tailoring the therapeutic relationship: On being an authentic chameleon. *Psychotherapy*, *30*(3), 404–407.
Lazarus, A. A. (2005). Multimodal therapy. In J. C. Norcross & M. R. Goldfried (Eds.), *Handbook of Psychotherapy Integration*. New York: Oxford University Press.
Lazarus, A. A., & Lazarus, C. N. (1991). *Multimodal Life History Inventory*. Champaign, IL: Research Press.
Lee, A. (2009). *Person-Centred Therapy & Cognitive-Behavioural Therapy: A study of Preferences & Moderating Factors*. Unpublished dissertation University of Strathclyde/Glasgow Caledonian University, Glasgow.
Leigh, A. (1998). *Referral and Termination Issues for Counsellors*. London: Sage.
Levinas, E. (1969). *Totality and Infinity: An Essay on Exteriority* (A. Lingis, Trans.). Pittsburgh, PA: Duquesne University Press.
Levinas, E. (2003). *Humanism of the Other* (N. Poller, Trans.). Chicago: University of Illinois Press.
Levitt, H., Butler, M., & Hill, T. (2006). What clients find helpful in psychotherapy: Developing principles for facilitating moment-to-moment change. *Journal of Counseling Psychology*, *53*, 314–324.
Levitt, H. M., Neimeyer, R. A., & Williams, D. C. (2005). Rules versus principles in psychotherapy: Implications of the quest for universal guidelines in the movement for empirically supported treatments. *Journal of Contemporary Psychotherapy*, *35(1)*, 117–130.
Lindner, R., Fiedler, G., Altenhofer, A., Goetze, P., & Happach, C. (2006). Psychodynamic ideal types of elderly suicidal persons based on countertransference. *Journal of Social Work Practice*, *20*(3), 347–365.

Linehan, M. M., Goodstyen, J. L., Nielsen, S. L., & Chiles, J. A. (1983). Reasons for staying alive when you are thinking of killing yourself: The Reasons for Living questionnaire. *Journal of Consulting and Clinical Psychology*, *51*, 276–286.

Locke, E. A., & Latham, G. P. (2002). Building a practically useful theory of goal setting and task motivation: A 35-year odyssey. *American Psychologist*, *57*(9), 705–717.

Lopez, S. J., & Kerr, B. A. (2006). An open source approach to creating positive psychological practice: A comment on Wong's strengths-centered therapy. *Psychotherapy*, *43*(2), 147–150.

Luborsky, L., Rosenthal, R., Diguer, L., et al. (2002). The Dodo bird verdict is alive and well – mostly. *Clinical Psychology: Science and Practice*, *9*(1), 2–12.

Luborsky, L., Singer, B., & Luborsky, L. (1975). Comparative studies of psychotherapies: Is it true that 'Everyone has won and all must have prizes'? *Archive of General Psychiatry*, *32*, 995–1008.

Mace, C. (Ed.). (1995). *The Art and Science of Assessment in Psychotherapy*. London: Routledge.

Mackrill, T. (2010). Goal consensus and collaboration in psychotherapy: An existential rationale. *Journal of Humanistic Psychology*, *50*(1), 96–107.

Mackrill, T. (in press). Differentiating life goals and therapeutic goals. *British Journal of Guidance & Counselling*.

Madigan, S. (1999). Inscription, description and deciphering chronic identities. In I. Parker (Ed.), *Deconstructing Psychotherapy*. London: Sage.

Mahoney, M. (2005). *Constructive Psychotherapy*. New York: Guilford Press.

Mahrer, A. R. (2007). If practitioners want new and better methods, shop in the public marketplace. *Journal of Psychotherapy Integration*, *17*(1), 10–32.

Makoul, G., & Marla, L. C. (2006). An integrative model of shared decision making in medical encounters. *Patient Education and Counseling*, *60*(3), 301–312.

Maluccio, A. N. (1979). *Learning from Clients: Interpersonal Helping as Viewed by Clients and Social Workers*. New York: Macmillan.

Markarian, Y., Larson, M. J., Aldea, M. A., et al. (2010). Multiple pathways to functional impairment in obsessive-compulsive disorder. *Clinical Psychology Review*, *30*(1), 78–88.

Markus, H., & Nurius, P. (1986). Possible selves. *American Psychologist*, *41*(9), 954–69.

Marley, E. (2009). Self-help strategies for psychological problems. Unpublished MSc Counselling dissertation, Tayside Institute for Health Studies, University of Abertay Dundee.

Martin, D. J., Garske, J. P., & Davis, M. K. (2000). Relation of the therapeutic alliance with outcome and other variables: A meta-analytic review. *Journal of Consulting and Clinical Psychology*, *68*(3), 438–450.

McBeath, A. (2007). *An investigation into the relationship between different types of goals and symptom change*. Unpublished dissertation University of Strathclyde/Glasgow Caledonian University, Glasgow.

McLellan, G. (1995). *Pluralism*. Buckingham: Open University Press.

McLeod, J. (2002). Research policy and practice in person-centered and experiential therapy: Restoring coherence. *Person-Centered and Experiential Psychotherapies*, *1*(1&2), 87–101.

McLeod, J. (2009a). Counselling: A radical vision for the future. *Therapy Today*, *20*(6), 10–15.

McLeod, J. (2009b). *An Introduction to Counselling* (4th edn). Maidenhead: Open University Press.

McLeod, J. (2010) *Case Study Research in Counselling and Psychotherapy*. London: Sage.

McMillan, M., & McLeod, J. (2006). Letting go: The client's experience of relational depth. *Person-Centered and Experiential Psychotherapies*, *5*(4), 277–292.

Mearns, D., & Cooper, M. (2005). *Working at Relational Depth in Counselling and Psychotherapy*. London: Sage.

Mearns, D., & Thorne, B. (2000). *Person-Centred Therapy Today: New Frontiers in Theory and Practice*. London: Sage.

Mearns, D., & Thorne, B. (2007). *Person-Centred Counselling in Action* (3rd edn). London: Sage.

Menchola, M., Arkowitz, H. S., & Burke, B. L. (2007). Efficacy of self-administered treatments for depression and anxiety. *Professional Psychology: Research and Practice*, *38*, 421–429.

Messer, S. B. (1992). A critical examination of belief structures in integrative and eclectic psychotherapy. In J. C. Norcross & M. R. Goldfried (Eds.), *Handbook of Psychotherapy Integration*. New York: Basic Books.

Michalak, J., & Holtforth, M.G. (2006). Where do we go from here? The goal perspective in psychotherapy. *Clinical Psychology: Science and Practice*, *13*, 346–365.

Miller, S. D., Duncan, B. L., Sorrell, R., & Brown, G. S. (2005). The partners for change outcome management system. *Journal of Clinical Psychology*, *61*(2), 199–208.

Moodley, R., & West, W. (Eds.). (2005). *Integrating Indigenous Healing Practices into Counselling and Psychotherapy*. London: Sage.

Moore, J. (2005). *Simple ideas, lightly held*. Available from: www.claritypartnership.co.uk/pdf/ms-5simpler2.pdf (retrieved 1 December 2009).

National Institute for Health and Clinical Excellence. (2009). *Depression: The Treatment and Management of Depression in Adults (Update)*. London: National Institute for Health and Clinical Excellence.

National Institute for Mental Health in England. (2005). *NIMHE Guiding Statement on Recovery*. London: Department of Health.

Neufeldt, S. A., Beutler, L. E., & Banchero, R. (1997). Research on supervisor variables in psychotherapy supervision. In C. E. Watkins (Ed.), *Handbook of Psychotherapy Supervision*. Chichester: Wiley.

Nilsson, T., Svensson, M., Sandell, R., & Clinton, D. (2007). Patients' experiences of change on cognitive-behavioral therapy and psychodynamic therapy: A qualitative comparative study. *Psychotherapy Research*, *17*, 553–566.

Norcross, J. C. (Ed.). (2002). *Psychotherapy Relationships that Work: Therapist Contributions and Responsiveness to Patients*. New York: Oxford University Press.

Norcross, J. C. (2005). A primer on psychotherapy integration. In J. C. Norcross & M. R. Goldfried (Eds.), *Handbook of Psychotherapy Integration*. New York: Oxford University Press.

Norcross, J. C. (2006). Integrating self-help into psychotherapy: 16 practical suggestions. *Professional Psychology: Research and Practice*, *37*(6), 683–693.

Norcross, J. C., & Goldfried, M. R. (Eds.). (2005). *Handbook of Psychology Integration*. New York: Oxford University Press.

Norcross, J. C., & Halgin, R. P. (2005). Training in psychotherapy integration. In J. C. Norcross & M. R. Goldfried (Eds.), *Handbook of Psychotherapy Integration*. New York: Oxford University Press.

Nuttall, J. (2008). The integrative attitude: A personal journey. *European Journal of Psychotherapy and Counselling*, *10*(1), 19–38.

O'Neill, P. (1998). *Negotiating Consent in Psychotherapy.* New York: New York Universities Press.

Omer, H. (1997). Narrative empathy. *Psychotherapy*, *25*, 171–184.

Orlinsky, D. E., & Rønnestad, M. H. (2005a). Clinical implications: Training, supervision and practice. In D. E. Orlinsky & M. H. Rønnestad (Eds.), *How Psychotherapists Develop: A Study of Therapeutic Work and Professional Growth.* Washington, DC: American Psychological Association.

Orlinsky, D. E., & Rønnestad, M. H. (2005b). Current development: Growth and depletion. In D. E. Orlinsky & M. H. Rønnestad (Eds.), *How Psychotherapists Develop: A Study of Therapeutic Work and Professional Growth.* Washington, DC: American Psychological Association.

Orlinsky, D. E., & Rønnestad, M. H. (2005c). Theoretical integration: Cycles of work and development. In D. E. Orlinsky & M. H. Rønnestad (Eds.), *How Psychotherapists Develop: A Study of Therapeutic Work and Professional Growth.* Washington, DC: American Psychological Association.

Orlinsky, D. E., & Rønnestad, M. H. (Eds.). (2005d). *How Psychotherapists Develop: A Study of Therapeutic Work and Professional Growth.* Washington, DC: American Psychological Association.

Orlinsky, D. E., Grawe, K., & Parks, B. K. (1994). Process and outcome in Psychotherapy – Noch einmal. In A. E. Bergin & S. L. Garfield (Eds.), *Handbook of Psychotherapy and Behavior Change* (4th edn). New York: Wiley.

Palmer, S. (2000). Multimodal therapy. In S. Palmer & R. Woolfe (Eds.), *Integrative and Eclectic Counselling and Psychotherapy*. London: Sage.

Paterson, C. (1996). Measuring outcomes in primary care: A patient-generated measure, MYMOP, compared with the SF–36 health survey. *British Medical Journal*, *312*, 1016–1020.

Paul, G. (1967). Strategy of outcome research in psychotherapy. *Journal of Consulting Psychology*, *31*(2), 109–118.

Pedersen, P. B. (1991). Multiculturalism as a generic approach to counseling. *Journal of Counseling and Development*, *70*, 6–12.

Pedersen, P. B., Crethar, H. C., & Carlson, J. (2008). *Inclusive Cultural Empathy: Making Relationships Central in Counseling and Psychotherapy*. Washington, DC: American Psychological Association.

Perren, S., Godfrey, M., & Rowland, N. (2009). The long-term effects of counselling: The process and mechanisms that contribute to ongoing change from a user perspective. *Counselling and Psychotherapy Research: Linking Research with Practice*, *9*(4), 241–249.

Pinsof, W. M. (2005). Integrative problem-centered therapy. In J. C. Norcross & M. R. Goldfried (Eds.), *Handbook of Psychotherapy Integration*. New York: Oxford University Press.

Piper, W. E., Azim, H. F. A., Joyce, A. S., & McCallum, M. (1991). Transference interpretations, therapeutic alliance, and outcome in short-term individual psychotherapy. *Archives of General Psychiatry*, *48*(10), 946–953.

Piper, W. E., Ogrodniczuk, J. S., Joyce, A. S., et al. (1999). Prediction of dropping out in time-limited, interpretive individual psychotherapy. *Psychotherapy: Theory, Research, Practice, Training*, *36*(2), 114–122.

Polkinghorne, D. E. (1992). Postmodern epistemology of practice. In S. Kvale (Ed.), *Psychology and Postmodernism*. London: Sage.

Powers, W. T. (1973). *Behaviour: The Control of Perception*. Chicago: Aldine.

Present, J., Crits-Christoph, P., Connolly Gibbons, M. B., Hearon, B., Ring-Kurtz, S., Worley, M., & Gallop, R. (2008). Sudden gains in the treatment of generalized anxiety disorder. *Journal of Clinical Psychology*, *64*, 119–126.

Rajkarnikar, K. (2009). *Assessment of Social Anxiety clients' symptoms: What do they really represent?* Unpublished dissertation University of Strathclyde/Glasgow Caledonian University, Glasgow.

Reeves, A. (2010). *Counselling Suicidal Clients*. London: Sage.

Reid, W. J. (1997). Evaluating the dodo's verdict: Do all interventions have equivalent outcomes? *Social Work Research*, *21*(1), 5–16.

Rennie, D. L. (1990). Toward a representation of the client's experience of the psychotherapy hour. In G. Lietaer, J. Rombauts, & R. Van Balen (Eds.), *Client-centered and Experiential Therapy in the Nineties*. Leuven: University of Leuven Press.

Rennie, D. L. (1994). Clients' deference in psychotherapy. *Journal of Counseling Psychology*, *41*(4), 427–437.

Rennie, D. L. (1998). *Person-Centred Counselling: An Experiential Approach*. London: Sage.

Rennie, D. L. (2000). Aspects of the client's conscious control of the psychotherapeutic process. *Journal of Psychotherapy Integration*, *10*, 151–167.

Rennie, D. L. (2001). Clients as self-aware agents. *Counselling and Psychotherapy Research*, *1*, 82–89.

Rennie, D. L. (2002). Experiencing psychotherapy: Grounded theory studies. In D. J. Cain, & J. Seeman (Eds.), *Humanistic Psychotherapies: Handbook of Research and Practice*. Washington, DC: American Psychological Association.

Rescher, N. (1993). *Pluralism: Against the Demand for Consensus*. Oxford: Oxford University Press.

Richards, B. M. (2000). Impact upon therapy and the therapist when working with suicidal patients: Some transference and countertransference aspects. *British Journal of Guidance & Counselling*, *28*(3), 325–337.

Rodgers, B. (2006). Life space mapping: Preliminary results from the development of a new method for investigating counselling outcomes. *Counselling and Psychotherapy Research*, *6*(4), 227–232.

Rodgers, B. (2010). *Life space mapping: Developing a new method for investigating counselling outcomes*. Unpublished PhD, University of Abertay, Dundee.

Rodgers, B., & Cooper, M. (2006). *Proposed Scoring Scheme for Qualitative Thematic Analysis*. Glasgow: University of Strathclyde. Available from: www.strath.ac.uk/counsunit/features/articles/.

Rogers, C. R. (1951). *Client-Centered Therapy*. Boston: Houghton & Mifflin.

Rogers, C. R. (1957). The necessary and sufficient conditions of therapeutic personality change. *Journal of Consulting Psychology*, *21*(2), 95–103.

Rogers, C. R. (1959). A theory of therapy, personality and interpersonal relationships as developed in the client-centered framework. In S. Koch (Ed.), *Psychology: A Study of Science*. New York: McGraw-Hill.

Rosenzweig, S. (1936). Some implicit common factors in diverse methods of psychotherapy: 'At last the Dodo said, "Everybody has won and all must have prizes"'. *American Journal of Orthopsychiatry*, *6*, 412–415.

Roth, A., & Fonagy, P. (2005). *What Works for Whom? A Critical Review of Psychotherapy Research*. New York: Guilford.

Rowan, J. (1990). *Subpersonalities: The People Inside Us*. London: Routledge.

Rowan, J. (2001). Counselling psychology and research. *Counselling Psychology Review*, *16*(1), 7–8.

Rowan, J. (2004). Three levels of therapy. *Counselling and Psychotherapy Journal*, *15*(9), 20–22.

Rowan, J., & Cooper, M. (Eds.). (1999). *The Plural Self: Multiplicity in Everyday Life*. London: Sage.

Rudd, M. D., Mandrusiak, M., & Joiner, T. E. Jr. (2006). The case against no-suicide contracts: The commitment to treatment statement as a practice alternative. *Journal of Clinical Psychology*, *62*, 243–251.

Rutter, M. (1987). *Developmental Psychiatry*. Washington, DC: American Psychological Association.

Ryle, A. (1990). *Cognitive Analytic Therapy: Active Participation in Change*. Chichester: Wiley.

Ryle, A. (2005). Cognitive analytic therapy. In J. C. Norcross & M. R. Goldfried (Eds.), *Handbook of Psychotherapy Integration*. New York: Oxford University Press.

Ryle, A., & Kerr, I. B. (2002). *Introducing Cognitive Analytic Therapy: Principles and Practice*. Chichester: Wiley.

Sabat, S. R. (2001). *The Experience of Alzheimer's Disease: Life through a Tangled Veil*. Oxford: Blackwell.

Safran, J. D., & Muran, J. C. (2000). *Negotiating the Therapeutic Alliance: A Relational Treatment Guide*. New York: Guilford Press.

Salkovskis, P. M. (1999). Understanding and treating obsessive-compulsive disorder. *Behaviour Research and Therapy*, *37*, S29–S52.

Samelo-Aro, K. (1992). Struggling with self: The personal projects of students seeking psychological counseling. *Scandinavian Journal of Psychology*, *33*: 330–338.

Sampson, E. E. (1988). The debate on individualism: Indigenous psychologies of the individual and their role in personal and social functioning. *American Psychologist*, *43*, 15–22.

Samuels, A. (1993). *The Plural Psyche: Personality, Morality and the Father*. London: Routledge.

Samuels, A. (1997). Pluralism and psychotherapy: What is good training? In R. House & N. Totton (Eds.), *Implausible Professions: Arguments for Pluralism and Autonomy in Counselling and Psychotherapy*. Ross-on-Wye: PCCS Books.

Sanders, P. (Ed.). (2004). *The Tribes of the Person-Centred Nation: An Introduction to the Schools of Therapy Related to the Person-Centred Approach*. Ross-on-Wye: PCCS Books.

Sanders, P., Frankland, A., & Wilkins, P. (2009). *Next Steps in Counselling Practice* (2nd rev. edn). Ross-on-Wye: PCCS Books.

Sartre, J.-P. (1996). Existentialism. In L. Cahoone (Ed.), *From Modernism to Postmodernism: An Anthology*. Cambridge, MA: Blackwells.

Schafer, R. (1976). *A New Language for Psychoanalysis*. New Haven, CT: Yale University Press.

Schmid, P. (2007). The anthropological and ethical foundations of person-centred therapy. In M. Cooper, P. Schmid, M. O'Hara, & G. Wyatt (Eds.), *The Handbook of Person-Centred Psychotherapy and Counselling*. Basingstoke: Palgrave.

Schmid, P. F. (2001). Comprehension: The art of not knowing. Dialogical and ethical perspectives in personal and person-centred relationships. In S. Haugh & T. Merry (Eds.), *Empathy*. Ross-on-Wye: PCCS Books.

Schottenbauer, M. A., Glass, C. R., & Arnkoff, D. B. (2005). Outcome research on psychotherapy integration. In J. C. Norcross & M. R. Goldfried (Eds.), *Handbook of Psychotherapy Integration*. New York: Oxford University Press.

Schulte, D. (1996). Tailor-made and standardized therapy: Complementary tasks in behavior therapy – a contrarian view. *Journal of Behavior Therapy and Experimental Psychiatry*, *27*(2), 119–126.

Schulte, D., Kunzel, R., Pepping, G., & Schulte-Bahrenberg, T. (1992). Tailor-made versus standardized therapy of phobic patients. *Advances in Behaviour Research and Therapy*, *14*(2), 67–92.

Schulte-Bahrenberg, T., & Schulte, D. (1993). Change of psychotherapy goals as a process of resignation. *Psychotherapy Research*, *3*(3), 153–165.

Scottish Intercollegiate Guidelines Network. (2010). *Non-pharmaceutical Management of Depression in Adults: A National Clinical Guideline*. Edinburgh: Scottish Intercollegiate Guidelines Network.

Seikkula, J., & Arnkil, T. E. (2006). *Dialogical Meetings in Social Networks*. London: Karnac.

Seikkula, J., & Trimble, D. (2005). Healing elements of therapeutic conversation: Dialogue as an embodiment of love. *Family Process*, *44*, 461–475.

Seikkula, J., Aaltonen, J., Alakare, B., Haarakangas, K., Keranen, J., & Lehtinen, K. (2006). Five-year experience of first-treatment nonaffective psychosis on open-dialogue approach: Treatment principles, follow-up outcomes, and two case studies. *Psychotherapy Research*, *16*, 214–228.

Seiser, L., & Wastell, C. (2002). *Interventions and Techniques*. Maidenhead: Open University Press.

Shafran, R., Clark, D. M., Fairburn, C. G., et al. (2009). Mind the gap: Improving the dissemination of CBT. *Behaviour Research and Therapy*, *47*(11), 902–909.

Shapiro, D. A., & Shapiro, D. (1982). Meta-analysis of comparative therapy outcome studies: A replication and refinement. *Psychological Bulletin*, *92*(3), 581–604.

Shaw, B. F., Elkin, I., Yamaguchi, J., et al. (1999). Therapist competence ratings in relation to clinical outcome in cognitive therapy of depression. *Journal of Consulting and Clinical Psychology*, *67*(6), 837–846.

Shlien, J. M. (1984) A counter-theory of countertransference. In R. F. Levant & J. M. Shlien (Eds.), *Client-Centered Therapy and the Person-Centered Approach: New Directions in Theory, Research and Practice*. New York: Praeger.

Shoham-Salomon, V., & Hannah, M. T. (1991). Client–treatment interaction in the study of differential change processes. *Journal of Consulting and Clinical Psychology*, *59*(2), 217–225.

Snyder, C. R., Michael, S. T., & Cheavens, J. S. (1999). Hope as a foundation of common factors, placebos, and expectancies. In M. Hubble, B. L. Duncan & S. D. Miller (Eds.), *The Heart and Soul of Change: What Works in Therapy*. Washington, DC: American Psychological Association.

Stanford Encyclopedia of Philosophy. (2006). Value pluralism. *Stanford Encyclopedia of Philosophy*. Available from: plato.stanford.edu/entries/value-pluralism/ (retrieved 1 December 2009).

Stellrecht, N. E., Gordon, K. H., Van Orden, K., Witte, T. K., Wingate, L. R., Cukrowicz, K. C., Butler, M., Schmidt, N. B., Fitzpatrick, K. K., & Joiner, T. Jr. (2006). Clinical applications of the interpersonal-psychological theory of attempted and completed suicide. *Journal of Clinical Psychology*, *62*, 211–222.

Stiles, W. B., Barkham, M., Twigg, E., Mellor-Clark, J., & Cooper, M. (2006). Effectiveness of cognitive-behavioural, person-centred and psychodynamic therapies as practised in UK National Health Service settings. *Psychological Medicine*, *36*(4), 555–566.

Stiles, W. B., Honos-Webb, L., & Surko, M. (1998). Responsiveness in psychotherapy. *Clinical Psychology: Science and Practice*, *5*(4), 439–458.

Stiles, W. B., Leach, C., Barkham, M., Lucock, M., Iveson, S., Shapiro, D., et al. (2003). Early sudden gains in psychotherapy under routine clinic conditions: Practice-based evidence. *Journal of Consulting and Clinical Psychology*, *71*, 14–21.

Strickler, G., & Gold, J. (Eds.). (2006). *A Casebook of Psychotherapy Integration*. Washington, DC: American Psychological Association.

Strike, C., Rhodes, A. E., Bergmans, Y., & Links, P. (2006). Fragmented pathways to care: The experiences of suicidal men. *Crisis*, *27*(1), 31–38.

Strong, T. (2009). Collaborative goal-setting: Counsellors and clients negotiating a counselling focus. *Counselling Psychology Review*, *24*(3&4), 24–37.

Suchman, A. (2006). A new theoretical foundation for relationship-centered care. *Journal of General Internal Medicine*, *21*(S1), S40–S44.

Sundet, R. (2009). Therapeutic collaboration and formalized feedback: Using perspectives from Vygotsky and Bakhtin to shed light on practices in a family therapy unit. *Clinical Child Psychology and Psychiatry*, *15*(1), 81–95.

Sundet, R. (in press). Collaboration: Family and therapist perspectives of helpful therapy. *Journal of Marital and Family Therapy*.

Swift, J. K., & Callahan, J. L. (2009). The impact of client treatment preferences on outcome: A meta-analysis. *Journal of Clinical Psychology*, *65*(4), 368–381.

Szasz, T. S. (1961). *The Myth of Mental Illness*. New York: Hoeber-Harper.

Tajfel, H., & Turner, J. C. (1979). An integrative theory of intergroup conflict. In S. Worchel & W. G. Austin (Eds.), *The Social Psychology of Intergroup Relations*. Monterey, CA: Brooks/Cole.

Thoma, N. C., & Cecero, J. J. (2009). Is integrative use of techniques in psychotherapy the exception or the rule? Results of a national survey of doctoral-level practitioners. *Psychotherapy*, *46*(4), 405–417.

Trimble, L., Jackson, K., & Harvey, D. (2000). Client suicidal behaviour: Impact, interventions, and implications for psychologists. *Australian Psychologist*, *35*, 227–232.

Tryon, G. S., & Winograd, G. (2002). Goal consensus and collaboration. In J. C. Norcross (Ed.), *Psychotherapy Relationships that Work: Therapist Contributions and Responsiveness to Patients*. New York: Oxford University Press.

Wampold, B. E. (2001). *The Great Psychotherapy Debate: Models, Methods and Findings*. Mahwah, NJ: Erlbaum.

Weaks, D. (2002). Unlocking the secrets of 'good supervision': A phenomenological exploration of experienced counsellors' perceptions of good supervision. *Counselling and Psychotherapy Research*, *2*(1), 33–39.

Weaks, D., McLeod, J., & Wilkinson, H. (2006). Dementia. *Therapy Today, 17*, 12–15.
Westbrook, D., Kennerley, H., & Kirk, J. (2007). *An Introduction to Cognitive Behaviour Therapy: Skills and Applications*. London: Sage.
Westen, D., Novotny, C. A., & Thompson-Brenner, H. (2004). The empirical status of empirically supported psychotherapies: Assumptions, findings, and reporting in controlled clinical trials. *Psychological Bulletin, 130*(4), 631–663.
Wheeler, S., & Richards, K. (2007). *The Impact of Clinical Supervision on Counsellors and Therapists, their Practice and their clients: A Systematic Review of the Literature*. Lutterworth: British Association for Counselling and Psychotherapy.
White, M., & Epston, D. (1990). *Narrative Means to Therapeutic Ends*. New York: W.W. Norton.
Wikipedia. (2009). *Goal*. www.en.wikipedia.org/wiki/Goal (retrieved 3 November, 2009).
Williams, E. N. (2002). Therapist techniques. In G. S. Tryon (Ed.), *Counselling Based on Process Research: Applying What We Know*. Boston: Allyn and Bacon.
Winter, D., Bradshaw, S., Bunn, F., & Wellsted, D. (2009). *Counselling and Psychotherapy for the Prevention of Suicide: A Systematic Review of the Evidence*. Lutterworth: British Association for Counselling and Psychotherapy.
Worden, W. (2001). *Grief Counselling and Grief Therapy: A Handbook for the Mental Health Practitioner*. London: Brunner/Routledge.
Worsley, R. (2004). Integrating with integrity. In P. Sanders (Ed.), *The Tribes of the Person-Centred Nation: An Introduction to the Schools of Therapy Related to the Person-Centred Approach*. Ross-on-Wye: PCCS Books.
Wosket, V. (2000). Integration and eclecticism in supervision. In S. Palmer & R. Woolfe (Eds.), *Integrative and Eclectic Counselling and Psychotherapy*. London: Sage.
Yalom, I. (2001). *The Gift of Therapy: Reflections on Being a Therapist*. London: Piatkus.

Making the Most of Your Therapy

An information sheet for clients

Thank you for your interest in our service.

Therapy is an opportunity to work on things in your life, and to find more satisfying and rewarding ways of living. Research shows that therapy can be very helpful for many people, and that most clients leave counselling or psychotherapy feeling much better than when they started. However, research also shows that the more clients know about therapy before they start, and the more they put into it, the more they are likely to get out of it. For this reason, we have provided an information sheet to tell you about the therapy we offer, and how you can make it as helpful as possible for you.

A therapy 'menu'

At our service, there are many different ways in which we can help you. We like to think of ourselves as providing you with a therapy 'menu', so that you can decide, with our support, what you would most like to work on. Some of the issues that clients often choose to focus on are:

- talking through an issue in order to make sense of what has happened, and to put things in perspective;
- making sense of a specific problematic event that sticks in your mind;
- problem-solving, planning and decision-making;
- changing behaviour;
- negotiating a life transition or developmental crisis;
- dealing with difficult feelings and emotions;
- finding, analysing and acting on information;
- undoing self-criticism and enhancing self-care;
- dealing with difficult or painful relationships.

Often, clients find it most helpful to work on these issues on a step-by-step basis. One of the ways that therapy may help is that your therapist can work with you to disentangle the various strands of the problem, and help you to decide what needs to be dealt with first.

A flexible, personalised approach to helping you

The therapy that we offer is based on the belief that people who come for therapy are experts on their own lives (even if they don't feel like they are), who have lots of potentially good ideas about how to deal with their problems. One of the main roles of a therapist, as we see it, is to help the person to make best use of their own experience and understanding.

This means that our approach to therapy (we call it a 'pluralistic approach') is to try to be as *flexible* as possible in responding to your needs. What we find (this is backed up by research) is that different people are helped in different ways. For instance, what some people find most helpful in their therapy is to express their feelings – sadness, anger, fearfulness. Other people find it more helpful to take a rational approach to their problems, and use the therapy to 'think things through'. People can shift, over the course of therapy, from finding one kind of activity helpful, to then preferring to work in a different way with their therapist.

We also try to be as flexible as possible around the practical arrangements for therapy. Most people attend for a one-hour session at the same time each week. For other people, this kind of arrangement may not fit with their lifestyle or their emotional needs. Please feel free to discuss with your therapist if you want to meet more often or less often, or for longer or shorter sessions. There may be constraints on what the therapist can offer, in terms of their schedule and the availability of therapy rooms, but they will do their best to accommodate your needs.

Flexibility can also involve the choice of therapist. Some people may only feel comfortable talking to a man, or a woman, or someone from the same ethnic group, etc. If you start with one therapist, and then start to feel – for whatever reason – that this is not the right person for you, then it is fine to mention this to your therapist. They will then do their best to find you another therapist who would be better for you.

Flexibility also applies to the *number* of therapy sessions that you receive. Some people come for one or two sessions, and find that this is enough to put them 'on the right track'. Other people attend therapy for many months. What is important is to do what is best for you personally. One of the options is what we call *intermittent therapy* – if you have some sessions and then want to stop, you can always come back at any time in the future, and pick up where you left off.

The following sections look at some ways you can prepare yourself to get the most benefit from the therapy you receive.

1. Thinking about what you want from therapy

It is important for your therapist to know what it is that you want to achieve in therapy – what your goals are. Your goals are a kind of 'contract' or agreement between you and the therapist, which specify what you want from him or her. If you go to a furniture store to buy a new sofa, then the visit will have failed if you come home with a new bed, or a carpet, no matter how attractive these objects might be. It is the same in therapy – a good outcome of therapy depends on getting what you came for.

At the start of therapy, most people find it hard to be clear about exactly what it is that they want to achieve. They have maybe only a vague sense of what they hope to get from therapy. This is perfectly normal – your therapist will encourage you to talk about your goals, and gradually they will become clearer. It is fine to have lots of goals, or just one goal. It is fine for your goals to change. What is important is to let your therapist know what it is that you want from therapy.

One of the ways that you can get the most out of therapy is to spend some time on your own thinking about your goals, before the first session, and between sessions. It can be useful to write your goals on a piece of paper, so you don't forget them. It is useful to keep your therapist updated if your goals change.

2. Thinking about what you think will be most helpful for you

As mentioned earlier, there are big differences between people in respect of what they find helpful in therapy. There is little point in the therapist trying to work with you to tackle a problem in a particular way if you think that the approach being taken is a waste of time! It is very useful, therefore, if you can think about what you believe might work best for you, and share these ideas with your therapist. You can do this by thinking back to times when you have had problems before, and identifying what was helpful or not helpful for you these times. You might also think about what you have heard from friends or family members, or seen on the TV, about how therapy can help. For instance, some people find it useful to be taught how to behave in different ways, others find it useful to 'blow off steam' and, for others, what is most useful is to try to solve problems in practical ways. Whatever you think is most helpful to you, your therapists will try to help you with this.

3. Identifying your own personal strengths and resources

The therapy you are being offered is not interested in diagnosing or labelling you. Instead, your therapist will assume that you possess a range of skills, experiences, relationships and abilities that can be used to overcome your present problems. Part of the job of the therapist is to help you to identify your existing strengths and resources, and work out how you can apply them in your current situation. For example:

- Jessica was depressed and isolated – she had always been a musical person, and with the support of her therapist joined a choir, where she met other people, and learned to feel better about herself;
- Jerry was a student who became very anxious before making a presentation in class – he had always been physically active, and realised that if he went and had a workout in the gym before making a presentation, he was able to cope much better.

It is useful if you can keep a list of your strengths and resources, and share this information with your therapist.

4. Being active between therapy sessions

Between therapy sessions, your therapist reviews what happened in the last sessions, and thinks about what they might do in the next sessions to take things forward. It is valuable if you do the same. Sometimes it can be helpful to work with your therapist to agree 'homework', or 'experiments', or 'projects' that you could complete between sessions. Even if this doesn't happen, it is still useful for you to think about what has come up in the therapy, whether you are getting what you need, how the therapy can be improved, and so on. It can be hard to remember these thoughts, and one option to consider is keeping a therapy diary, where you write about what the therapy has meant to you.

5. Giving feedback to your therapist

Effectively tailoring the therapy to your specific needs is only possible if you are willing to give honest *feedback* to your therapist. In our therapy, we use brief questionnaires every week, that you are asked to fill in, that provide information for your therapist about whether the therapy is being effective, and if any aspects of it need to be changed. These questionnaires can also be useful for you in terms of tracking your own progress. Your therapist will also ask you for feedback and comments during the therapy session, or may invite you to take some time to review overall progress after approximately every six sessions. When giving feedback, it is really important that you are as honest and detailed as you can be. It may be painful for your therapist to learn that you think that he asks too many questions (or not enough questions), or whatever. But ultimately, your therapist genuinely wants to help you, and does not want you to pretend that everything is OK when it isn't. You should regard the feedback that you give to your therapist as a *gift* – you are giving them an opportunity to learn how to be better at their job.

If you are worried about anything – please ask

Finally, there may be other questions that are not covered in this leaflet, that would make a difference to your ability to make effective use our therapy. If you have any further questions, please ask your therapist. If for any reason it is an issue that you do not want to mention to your therapist, you can contact the Centre Manager.

Therapy Personalisation Form

(Bowens, Johnston and Cooper, V1.1)

On each of the scales below, please indicate any changes that you would like to see in your therapy at this point in time. Please circle the appropriate number in each case along the scale.

I would like my therapist to:

1. Use more techniques and exercises					Just right for me					Use less techniques and exercises
5	4	3	2	1	0	1	2	3	4	5

2. Take more of a lead in the therapy					Just right for me					Allow me to take more of a lead in the therapy
5	4	3	2	1	0	1	2	3	4	5

3. Show their personality and humour more					Just right for me					Be more formal
5	4	3	2	1	0	1	2	3	4	5

4. Focus more on my past					Just right for me					Focus more on my future
5	4	3	2	1	0	1	2	3	4	5

5. Give me more advice					Just right for me					Give me less advice
5	4	3	2	1	0	1	2	3	4	5

7. Be more challenging					Just right for me					Be more gentle
5	4	3	2	1	0	1	2	3	4	5

8. Focus on specific goals					Just right for me					Just be with me in the therapeutic relationship
5	4	3	2	1	0	1	2	3	4	5

9. Tell me more of their thought processes about what's going on in therapy					Just right for me					Tell me less of their thought processes about what's going on in therapy
5	4	3	2	1	0	1	2	3	4	5

10. Give me more 'homework' to do					Just right for me					Give me less 'homework' to do
5	4	3	2	1	0	1	2	3	4	5

11. Focus more on my feelings					Just right for me					Focus more on my thoughts and cognitions
5	4	3	2	1	0	1	2	3	4	5

12. Focus more on my strengths and abilities					Just right for me					Focus more on my problems and difficulties
5	4	3	2	1	0	1	2	3	4	5

13. Focus more on my life in the past					Just right for me					Focus more on my life in the present
5	4	3	2	1	0	1	2	3	4	5

14. Interrupt me less					Just right for me					Interrupt me more and keep me more focused
5	4	3	2	1	0	1	2	3	4	5

15. Focus more on the relationship between us					Just right for me					Focus less on the relationship between us
5	4	3	2	1	0	1	2	3	4	5

16. Be more challenging of my own beliefs and views					Just right for me					Be less challenging of my own beliefs and views
5	4	3	2	1	0	1	2	3	4	5

17. Focus more on my current issues					Just right for me					Focus more on deeper, underlying issues
5	4	3	2	1	0	1	2	3	4	5

18. Focus more on what they think is best for me					Just right for me					Focus more on what I think is best for me
5	4	3	2	1	0	1	2	3	4	5

19. Tell me more about themselves as a person					Just right for me					Tell me less about themselves as a person
5	4	3	2	1	0	1	2	3	4	5

20. Allow more silence					Just right for me					Not allow so much silence
5	4	3	2	1	0	1	2	3	4	5

Goals Form

This page asks you to describe, in your own words, what you want to get from counselling:

- The two most important concerns, problems or goals for which you are seeking help.
- How much each of these areas is bothering you at the moment (during the last week).
- How important each goal or issue is for you, in the context of your life as a whole.
- How much progress you expect to make on each area over the course of counselling.

Goal or concern no. 1

Describe the goal or concern, as you see it:

....

....

....

....

How much has this issue **been bothering you** over the last week? (circle one number):

0 1 2 3 4 5 6 7 8 9

Not at all – I am close to achieving my goals in respect of this issue | Couldn't be worse – I am a long way from achieving my goals in respect of this issue

How **important** is this issue for you, in relation to your life as a whole? (circle one number):

0 1 2 3 4 5 6 7 8 9

Not at all important | Very important

How much **progress do you expect to make** on this issue over the course of counselling? (circle one number):

0 1 2 3 4 5 6 7 8 9

None at all | A great deal

Goal or concern no. 2

Describe the goal or concern, as you see it:

....

....

....

....

How much has this **issue been bothering you** over the last week?

0 1 2 3 4 5 6 7 8 9

Not at all – I am close to achieving my goals in respect of this issue | Couldn't be worse – I am a long way from achieving my goals in respect of this issue

How **important** is this issue for you, in relation to your life as a whole?

0 1 2 3 4 5 6 7 8 9

Not at all important | Very important

How much **progress do you expect to make** on this issue over the course of counselling?

0 1 2 3 4 5 6 7 8 9

None at all | A great deal

Index

Please note that page references to Boxes and Figures will be in *italic* print

FSC
www.fsc.org
MIX
Papier | Fördert
gute Waldnutzung
FSC® C083411

Kolibri 360 GmbH
Ferdinand-Jühlke-Straße 7
99095 Erfurt, Deutschland
produktsicherheit@kolibri360.de